Selected Scottish Poems Analysed

by

Maureen Brown

With
suggested study points,
revision checklists for each poem,
marking schemes for unseen textual analysis exercises
and outline plans for critical essays.

ISBN 0 7169 3236 9
© *M. Brown, 1999.*

ROBERT GIBSON · Publisher
17 Fitzroy Place, Glasgow, G3 7SF.

INTRODUCTORY NOTE

This book is designed to be used, in conjunction with its sister book *Selected Scottish Poems for Analysis and Discussion*, to cover **the compulsory Scottish element** in Unit 2: Literary Study, Outcome 2: **respond (critically) to seen imaginative texts**. I hope it will be useful to hard-pressed teachers in preparing poetry lessons, leading to the writing of critical essays for internal and external assessment. Every chapter ends with **Suggested Outline Plans for Critical Essays**.

Each chapter features a different poet and contains Suggested Study Points for two poems (three for Burns). I have chosen poets whose work is most commonly used in our schools and these Study Points are the product of more than twenty years' experience of teaching Higher English. I have no doubt, however, that you will disagree with some of my interpretations and find areas that I have not covered. Almost every time I teach a poem, I find something new, and during preparation of this book I have discovered, to my delight, many previously unnoticed details. This is, of course, what makes English teaching worthwhile.

As well as helping with the critical essay element of the course, and of equal importance, I hope this book will provide help in teaching the techniques of **Textual Analysis** in preparation for Paper 2 of the external examination. Each chapter features a third poem by the same poet, with textual analysis exercises at two levels to give practice in **Unseen Textual Analysis**, for which **Marking Schemes** are included in this book. Once the techniques have been grasped, the unseen poems in the chapters, which have not been studied, might be used for additional exam practice. Since most English Departments will want to introduce this new element of the course in earlier years rather than leave it to come as a nasty surprise in S5, the **exercises at the lower level might be used further down the school**.

The sister book contains, for each poem, a feature called **Using Your Notes for Revision**, at two levels. These are more broadly based, guided questions for which **Checklists** are included in this book. [Where the questions are similar, notes are provided for Higher and Intermediate 2 levels only, Intermediate 1 level being subsumed therein.] Individual questions might be useful as homework for reinforcement of a particular aspect of a poem.

The Suggested Study points in the sister book are in the form of points for discussion and will, I hope, be useful for **Talk Assessment** for Unit 3: Oral/Aural Communication, Outcome B: **Group Discussion**, especially those under Evaluation. Alternatively, they could be used for Outcome A: **Individual Presentation**, either done individually or as a group, with each member presenting a different part, according to individual strengths.

Lastly, to capitalise on the discussion and stimulus of the poems, I have included in the Pupils' Book some **Suggestions for Expressive / Creative / Report Writing** for Unit 1, Outcome 2: **Writing / Folio** practice. The questions, with some brief advice, are linked to the themes investigated in the poems. The Personal Reflective and Persuasive questions might also be used for Talk Assessment in Unit 3: Oral/Aural Communication, Outcome A: **Individual Presentation**.

Both books feature a glossary of **Some Useful Definitions**, to take account of the more technical requirements of the critical essay as well as the unseen textual analysis.

A Personal Note

The Higher English course is a particularly heavy burden, with so much to cover in such a short time. My aim in writing this book has been to help, in a small way, to lighten that load. I retired from the scene last year but continue to keep my hand in with occasional supply work. I would like to dedicate this book, firstly, to all of my former colleagues, scattered far and wide, with whom I have enjoyed exchanging ideas. Particular thanks are due to my friend and former Principal Teacher, Myra Young, now AHT in Biggar High School, for her help and forbearance, especially in the early stages of planning. I am grateful also to Alec Dunlop, Principal Teacher of English at Hutchesons' Grammar School, Glasgow, for his invaluable advice at the final draft stage. I owe a huge debt of gratitude to my husband, Roy, for his unwavering support and general dogsbody duties during the "creative process". When I was teaching, he and my two children were at times sadly neglected as I sat, night after night, preparing and marking work. I hope that this book might help other hard-working English teachers in my wake to spend a little more time with their families.

Maureen Brown

CONTENTS

CHAPTER 1 — Robert Burns

Suggested Study Points: *To a Mouse*

UNDERSTANDING

1.   The situation
The poet has accidentally destroyed a fieldmouse's nest with his plough. He talks to the mouse, apologising for the way most men treat small animals, commenting on the insecurity of such creatures, and ends by saying that for both mice and human beings, no matter how good their plans, Fate can step in and ruin them. This incident really happened to the poet in November, 1785, as he was ploughing.

2. The themes
- Accidental nature of Fate.
- Insecure nature of farming.
- Man's treatment of animals.
- Plight of the poor.

ANALYSIS

§1: Stanzas 1–3
- **Tone:** friendly, affectionate — uses diminutive "beastie / breastie"; assures the mouse he would not hurt it — "Thou needna start awa sae hasty", line 3;
- apologetic — regrets that mouse's instinct, born from experience, is to run from man — "man's dominion", against the laws of Nature — "Has broken Nature's social union", lines 7–8;
- talks to mouse as an equal — "earth-born companion, / An' fellow-mortal", lines 11–12 — they are both God's creatures;
- understanding, indulgent — realises mouse must steal to survive but the amount required by mouse is negligible and leaves plenty for him.

- **Imagery:** presents a vivid picture of mouse and its situation;
- string of adjectives in line 1 — show mouse's size, appearance, pose and feelings.
- **Lexical choice** shows the fragility and vulnerability of mouse:
- first word is "Wee";
- use of **diminutives**, "beastie", line 1; "breastie", line 2;
- addresses the mouse as "thou";
- indicates that mouse is "cowrin'", "tim'rous", line 1, heart is racing with fear — "what a panic's in thy breastie", line 2, and runs away from him.
- line 4, "bickering brattle", **alliteration** intensifies the sense of the phrase.
- **Onomatopoeia** gives precise representation of the sound made by the frightened mouse; interestingly, both words are noise words: "bickering" means running quickly and noisily, pattering (usually of running water) and "brattle" is a clattering noise, a quarrel. This admirable precision was a natural attribute of Burns.
- line 15, "a daimen icker in a thrave" — doesn't need much food because so small.

§2: Stanzas 4–6
- **Tone:** sympathetic — nest is ruined and no materials left to build another before the winter;
- admiring — mouse's foresight in building nest for coming cold season;
- remorseful — that he is the cause of the mouse's trouble — "cruel coulter", line 29;
- pitying — that mouse's hard effort was pointless — "monie a wearie nibble", line 32; "for a' thy trouble", line 33.

- Line 19, "wee-bit housie", adds to **image** of mouse — small, vulnerable;
- line 32, though nest is small, yet it was an effort for the mouse to make it — "monie a weary nibble" — adds to **image** of mouse as fragile, vulnerable.
- The **hypallage** in "weary nibble", line 32, gives a condensed image of the tired little mouse nibbling furiously to get materials into suitable condition for use in the nest, before winter comes. The effect is to link the weariness with the nibbling and so intensify it.

- Lines 20, 21, 25–26, 29, 34, 36: further examples of **alliteration** — intensify meaning.
- **Onomatopoeia**: "crash!", line 29; "sleety dribble", line 35; "cranreuch cauld", line 36 (hard c-sound).

§3: Stanzas 7–8
- **Tone:** empathic — "thou art no' thy lane", line 37, poor people suffer similar hardship.
- Philosophical — "The best-laid schemes o' mice an' men / Gang aft agley", lines 39–40.
- Envious — "thou art blest compar'd wi' me!", line 43, poet thinking of his own troubles.
- Pessimistic — "forward, tho' I canna see / I guess an' fear!", lines 47–48, poet's despair.

- line 37, "Mousie", continues **image** of mouse as small, harmless creature.

Looking over the whole poem
- Words / phrases which establish the **setting**:
- "fields laid bare an' waste", line 25, "leaves an' stibble", line 31;
- farming dialect: "pattle", line 6; "a daimen icker in a thrave", line 15; "foggage", line 22; "coulter", line 29.

- **Poetic Form — Burns Stanza:** Now called after Burns, though not original to him but one taken over and used to great effect by him. The form originated in the old folk songs, which were a great influence on the young Robert, who heard the songs from his mother and her old woman-servant. In the 17th century, the form was used by Robert Sempill of Beltrees in an elegy for the piper of Kilbarchan; it was called, at that time, the Habbie Simson stanza, later known as the Standard Habbie until Burns adopted it and made it famous.
- Rhyme scheme — *aaabab* — N.B. Rhyme needs Scottish pronunciation to work.
- Metre — the "*a*-rhyme" lines have 8 or 9 syllables;
                the "*b*-rhyme" lines have 4 or 5 syllables.
  The stanzas are often broken up into: lines 1–4 — description or statement,
                                          lines 5–6 — comment,
                       e.g., in stanza 1:   lines 1–4 — describe the mouse and what it is doing,
                                          lines 5–6 — the poet's attitude to the mouse,
- The rhyme in lines 1–3 holds together the ideas presented in those lines:
- line 4 provides a short, snappy conclusion to those ideas;
- line 5, through its rhyme, associates the comment it introduces with the ideas in lines 1–3;
- line 6 provides a short, snappy conclusion to the comment — the rhyme highlights the contrast with line 4, thus contrasting the ideas of the helpless mouse and cruel man.
- **Literary Form — Address:**
- The poet addresses his remarks to the mouse, which, according to line 4, has run only a short distance, presumably not wishing to expose itself further on the open field.
- Since the poet speaks to the mouse with nobody else present, the reader feels the sentiments expressed are genuinely held by the poet.
- The poet reveals his affection for animals, sorrow for the way most men would treat such a creature in those circumstances, sympathy for and understanding of the mouse's plight but ends on a pessimistic note as he compares the mouse's problems with his own.

- **Allegory:** Not just a sentimental poem about a little fieldmouse. Burns uses the mouse's trouble to illustrate the insecurity and vulnerability of the poor people dependent on the land and at the mercy of the factors who have the power to throw them out of "house or hald" if they fail to pay the rent. Those people, like Burns's father, and later himself and his brother Gilbert, were often struggling with poor land and few resources, at the mercy, too, of the weather which could ruin the year's crop. Like the mouse, they were subject to an outside force, be it factor or Fate, penury or plough, which controlled their lives.
  - In the poem, the mouse represents the poor farming people, the men and women who worked themselves into exhaustion, often with poor return for their efforts. The mouse is depicted as small and vulnerable — an appropriate symbol for the poor farming people of Burns's day. They lived in constant fear of losing their crops, their homes and even their lives (from diseases brought on by poverty — Burns's father died of consumption — now called TB — and the poet's tragically early death was due, not entirely to dissipated living as the myth goes, but to a rheumatic heart disease, the result of his early life of penury).
  - His expressions of sympathy and understanding for the mouse in the poem mirror his lifelong feelings for his fellow-men. He was taken up by the rich Edinburgh society but it is the ordinary people world-wide who have made him their own.
  - Equality amongst men is a plea made in many of Burns's poems, especially in *For a' that*, "That man to man the world o'er / Shall brithers be for a' that". In *To a Mouse*, the poet talks to the mouse as an equal, and he believed the rich should treat the poor as "fellow mortal(s)".
  - Responsibility for fellow-men — the poet is happy to share his food with the mouse, knowing he will have enough left to sustain him — so we should support charities or, even better, governments should ensure that their people have the means to support themselves without help from outside sources. Subsistence economies in 3rd World countries today are often headed by the richest of princes with fairy-tale lifestyles in the most extravagant of palaces.
  - The plough which crashed through the mouse's nest can also be seen as a metaphorical plough of change. At this time, industrialisation was growing but most ordinary people still scraped a living from the land. Industrialisation made fortunes for some, widening the already huge gaps between the classes, with the poor even more at the mercy of the rich.

- **Syntax:**
  - Exclamation marks strengthen the feelings expressed by the poet, both towards the mouse and about his own life — perhaps a trifle overdone for our modern taste!

- **Language:**
  - Scots appropriate to conversation with small animal; informal and less threatening.
  - Farming community dialect helps establish setting and shows Burns belongs here.
  - The poet's serious thoughts / ideas are largely in English and so stand out from the rest;
  - philosophical / Biblical words: "Man's dominion", line 7; "Nature's social union", line 8; "justifies . . . opinion", line 9; "proving foresight may be vain", line 38; "The best-laid schemes o' Mice an' Men", line 39; "the present only toucheth thee", line 44; "prospects drear", line 46.

EVALUATION

All of the following points are dealt with in more detail under Allegory.
- On surface a poem about a small mouse, but poet gives it universal significance — how effective is the allegory?
- Equality / poverty — deal with symbolic aspect of the poem.
- Relevance to our lives today — parallels between Burns's Scotland and 3rd World countries.
- Accidental nature of Fate — summed up in last two lines of poem, fitting conclusion to poem?
- Depicts way of life of country people among whom the poet lived — setting and allegory.

Using Your Notes for Revision: Checklist

UNDERSTANDING AND ANALYSIS *(Use these questions to revise important parts of the poem.)*

1.   **Themes:**
   (a)   **What theme is introduced in stanzas 1 and 2, lines 1–12?**
   -   Man's cruel treatment of animals.
   (b)   **How is this theme made clear to us?**
   -   Seen in the way the mouse behaves when poet ploughs through the nest;
   -   cowering, frightened, heart racing, runs off — stanza 1;
   -   poet apologises for his fellow-men who have gone against the laws of nature / community;
   -   poet addresses mouse as friend and equal: "earth-born companion", "fellow-mortal", making the point that the mouse (and, by inference, all animals) has as much right to exist as human beings have.
   (c)   **How does the poet develop this theme in the next four stanzas, lines 13–36?**
   -   Mouse regarded as pest by farmers because it eats corn; poet points out that it eats a very small amount, leaving plenty for the farmer — stanza 3.
   -   Mouse depends on foliage and stubble to build nest, to protect it from cold — stanza 4;
   -   mouse had foresight to build nest; farmer destroys it carelessly — "cruel coulter" —stanza 5;
   -   nest may not look much but mouse had to work hard to make it and now he must suffer the frost and sleet of winter — "sleety dribble / An' cranreuch cauld" — stanza 6.
   (d)   **What other theme comes out of the incident with the plough?**
   -   Accidental nature of Fate.

2.   **Tone:**
   (a)   **Trace the variations in tone used by the poet over the first six stanzas, lines 1–36.**
   (b)   **For each change, note how the poet's tone is conveyed.**
   -   Stanza 1   Friendly, affectionate — uses diminutive "beastie / breastie", assures the mouse he would not hurt it.
   -   Stanza 2   Apologetic — regrets that mouse's instinct, born from experience, is to run from man, against the laws of Nature — "Nature's social union";
talks to mouse as an equal — "earth-born companion, / An' fellow-mortal" — they are both God's creatures.
   -   Stanza 3   Understanding, indulgent — realises mouse must steal to survive but the amount required by mouse is negligible and leaves plenty for him.
   -   Stanza 4   Sympathetic — mouse's home ruined and no materials left to build another before the cold winter comes.
   -   Stanza 5   Admiring — mouse's foresight in building nest for coming cold season;
remorseful — that he is the cause of the mouse's trouble — "cruel coulter".
   -   Stanza 6   Sorry — that the mouse's hard effort has proved pointless — "monie a wearie nibble", "for a' thy trouble".
   (c)   **Note and account for the change of tone in stanzas 7 and 8, lines 37–48.**
   -   Stanza 7   Empathic — "thou art no' thy lane", compares mouse with poor peasants;
philosophical — "The best-laid schemes o' mice an' men / Gang aft agley".
   -   Stanza 8   Envious — "thou art blest compar'd wi' me!", now thinking of his own troubles;
pessimistic — "forward, tho' I canna see / I guess an' fear!"; poet's despair.
   (d)   **How does the language of those two stanzas help to convey the tone?**
   -   Stanzas 1–6 simple and Scots / dialect.
   -   Stanzas 7–8 more learned and some English words, e.g., "foresight", "prospects";
no longer talking to the mouse; thinking aloud, philosophising.

3. **Presentation of the mouse: note the effectiveness of the different techniques / devices used by the poet to create a vivid picture of the mouse.**
   - **String of adjectives** in line 1, covering: size — "wee"; appearance — "sleekit" = sleek-coated; also means sly, cunning, which describes the way the mouse is forced to go about because of Man's cruelty; position — "cowrin'"; feelings — indicates that mouse is "cowrin'", "tim'rous", line 1, heart is racing with fear — "what a panic's in thy breastie", line 2, and runs away.
   - **Lexical choice** shows fragility and vulnerability of mouse: first word is "Wee"; diminutives "beastie", line 1; "breastie", line 2; "wee-bit housie", line 19; "Mousie", line 37;
   - addresses the mouse as "thou";
   - doesn't need much food because so small — "a daimen icker in a thrave", line 15;
   - nest is small — "wee-bit housie", line 19; but a great effort — "monie a weary nibble", line 32.
   - **Alliteration** intensifies and **onomatopoeia** gives a precise representation of the sound made by the frightened mouse — "bickering brattle", line 4;
   - other examples of alliteration, intensify the meaning of the phrase — lines 20, 21, 25–26, 29, 34, 36;
   - other examples of onomatopoeia — "crash!", line 29; "sleety dribble", line 35; "cranreuch cauld", line 36.
   - The **hypallage** in "weary nibble", line 32, gives a condensed image of the tired little mouse nibbling furiously to get the materials into suitable condition for use in the nest, before winter comes. The effect is to link the weariness with the nibbling and so intensify it;
   - similarly with "weary winter" in line 26 — the season when life is hard and tiring for the mouse.
   - **Syntax:** exclamation marks intensify the panic in line 1, and so on.
   - **Poetic form:** see page 8.
   - **Literary Form — Address**
   - The poet talks directly to the mouse, enabling us to picture the contrast in size between the two, even though he tells us in stanza 1 that the mouse has run off.
   - The poet reveals his affection for animals, sorrow for the way most men would treat such a creature in those circumstances, sympathy for and understanding of the mouse's plight, thus enlisting our sympathy for the mouse.
   - Scots language is appropriate and reminds us that the poet is speaking to a small animal; informal and therefore less threatening.

EVALUATION *(Use this question for exam practice.)*

4. **Explain, with close reference to the poem as a whole, why stanza 7, lines 37–42, is central to the main ideas in the poem, making clear the extent to which the poet has succeeded in engaging your sympathy for those ideas. (10 marks)**
   - Answers should depend mainly on exposition of allegory and its effectiveness, discussed in detail in Suggested Study Points, Analysis, page 9;
   - must deal with accidental nature of Fate in relation to poor people;
   - references to mouse should be only in terms of allegory;
   + personal response to ideas — may deal with 3rd World, unemployed, homeless . . .

H — allegory well-explained, supported by good textual reference + intelligent comment / response.
Int. — allegory clearly understood, supported by some textual reference + appropriate comment / response.

Suggested Study Points: *Welcome to a Bastart Wean*

UNDERSTANDING

1. **The situation**
    The poet delights at the birth of his first child, despite the trouble her birth has caused him with the Church and community, and promises to share his meagre resources with her.

2. **The themes**
    - Love — physical and parental.
    - Attitudes of the community.
    - Repressive attitudes of the Calvinist Church.

ANALYSIS

§1, stanza 1, lines 1–6: sets the **tone** of tenderness, delight — a wholehearted welcome to the child runs through the whole poem. He vows that neither the child nor her mother will ever cause him to feel regret or shame, nor will he be embarrassed when the child calls him Daddy.

§2, stanza 2, lines 7–12: local gossips — **tone** of defiance — refuses to be upset by their "kintra clatter", line 8. He expresses the rather modern idea that there's no such thing as bad publicity!
- **Lexical choice** shows his attitude to the gossips; "kintra clatter," line 8 — dirty talk — cf. Hamlet's "country matters"? The **euphemism** is appropriate, as these people were too mealy-mouthed to speak openly of something as "sinful" as lovemaking.
- "An auld wife's tongue's a feckless matter", line 11 — **tone** is scathing — gossips are all classed as "auld wives" and nothing they might say is worth listening to.
- **Synecdoche** — using "tongue" instead of the person puts the emphasis on the tongue, suggesting that all an old wife does is gossip; helps us to picture the tongues "wagging".

§3, stanza 3, lines 13–18: shows his hatred of the Kirk's negative attitude to love, indeed to all earthly pleasures, lines 15–16. (Burns had to sit on the "cutty stool" for three consecutive Sundays from 9th July, 1785, as penance for his fornication and probably also had to pay a fine: a measure of the level of control the Kirk had over the community in those days.)
- Line 16 — He says he has fought "Baith Kirk and Queir" — the **metonymy** indicates that he has been attacked by people representing the church as a body, who think they have the right to judge and punish him, i.e., the minister and elders, as well as the congregation.

§4, stanzas 4 and 5, lines 19–30: shows his attitude to the child's mother and their lovemaking: ". . . my bonny Betty . . .", line 19, "my" indicates the possessiveness of love at the same time acknowledging her as his lover, as does the use of her name; "bonny" is affectionate;
- "ye're no unwrought for . . .", line 17 — tongue-in-cheek — he put a lot of effort into begetting her.
- **Tone** of affection for daughter — lines 20–21 — "As fatherly I kiss and daut thee, / As dear and near my heart I set thee"; "Sweet fruit . . . toil . . .", lines 25–26 — the child is the delightful result of many enjoyable occasions.
- **Metaphors**: line 25 — he calls her "Sweet fruit" — outcome of their love — the metaphor points up his pleasure at her birth, as well as the idea that lovemaking is natural;
- line 26 — "My funny toil" — emphasises the joy of the lovemaking, which produced the child; the tongue-in-cheek "toil" for the physical effort he expended in the process adds humour, which is set against the dour attitudes of Kirk and community;
- line 27 — ". . . ye come to the warld asklent" — i.e., illegitimate, outside marriage; the humour of the metaphor again shows the light-hearted way he disregards the criticism levelled at him.

- **Tone** of contempt for the ministers of the Kirk, suggesting they enjoyed visualising the poet's "sin", lines 22–24; ". . . a' the Priests . . . / That's out o' h___", lines 23–24, suggests that the priests are servants of Satan; not actually writing the word "hell" has a double impact: he is implying that he is a much more morally upright person than they are; poking fun, too, at the euphemistic (in his eyes, dishonest) way that they and their followers talk.
- "fools (may scoff)", line 28 — another reference to the gossips as being too stupid to appreciate the finer points of life, such as lovemaking.

§5, stanzas 6–8, lines 31–48:

- He makes an earnest promise — lines 29–30 — he will share his last penny with her;
- lines 31–36 — she will always have warm clothes and she will be well educated.
- Line 35 — "Wedlock's bed" — **metonymy** — he uses the institution of marriage to mean a married couple; **synecdoche** — focuses on "bed", to suggest that a child born to a loving couple is conceived in the same way whether the couple are married or not. He wants to show his child in as favourable a light as any born to a rich, married couple; he will provide for his child and take as much responsibility for her as he would if he and Betty were married.
- His hopes for her future — that she will look like her mother and have all her good points:
- "Thy mither's looks an' gracefu' merit", line 39 — commends her looks and shows his respect for her as being a good person; her "gracefu' merit" is balanced against his own "failins", line 40.
- **Humour** — that she will have her father's "spirit, Without his failins!" — shows that he does acknowledge his weaknesses as well as his strengths (of spirit, determination, defiance).
- **Tone** of final lines — pride — he will "brag" about being her father;
- but he builds up to it by imposing conditions — if she turns out as he would like and if she takes his advice — two ways in which he disappointed his own father!

Looking over the whole poem

- **The Title:** the short title was the poet's own choice; his publisher insisted on the longer one, which I have used underneath Burns's own. I think the shorter title expresses the poet's defiance and his honest refusal to be mealy-mouthed about the birth of his first child by using the euphemism "love-begotten", so typical of "polite society" of the time; the longer title provides us with more information. (The child, Elizabeth — a daughter born to Betty Paton, a servant girl of his mother's, on 22nd November, 1785 — married John Bishop, overseer at Polkemmet, near Whitburn, had a family and died in 1817.)
- Burns always acknowledged his children — he had 15 of whom only nine were legitimate — accepted responsibility and undertook to support them although, in practice, their upbringing often fell to his mother. According to his brother, Gilbert, he was led astray at the age of 22 by a sailor called Richard Brown, with whom he became friendly in Irvine and who "was of a freer manner of thinking and living than he had been used to . . . (and) had prepared him for overleaping the bounds of rigid virtue, which had hitherto restrained him." Burns, himself, admitted in his letter to Dr Moore that Brown "spoke of a certain fashionable failing with levity, which hitherto I had regarded with horror . . . the consequence was that, soon after I resumed the plough, I wrote the WELCOME enclosed." It is fashionable, nowadays, to deny that Burns was a libertine but with the best will in the world, 15 children to 7 different women in eleven years is pretty good going by anyone's book!

- **Poetic Form — Burns Stanza:** See *To a Mouse* SSP, page 8, for history and description. Rhyme and metre help to put across the defiant ranting of the poem: three rhyming lines — *aaa* — have the effect of piling up the ideas; short line 4 suggests the poet taking a breath, before launching into another dig at the object(s) of his wrath in line 5, rhyming *a*, and the stanza is neatly concluded with the short line 6 linked to line 4 with rhyme *b*.
- In the stanzas dealing with his love for the child, the rhyme and metre similarly emphasise the strength of his fatherly love, while those dealing with his love for her mother defiantly express his unrestrained joy in, and the liveliness of, their lovemaking.

- **Literary Form — Address:** Burns talks to the child — "Welcome! My bonny, sweet, wee dochter!", line 13; he appears to be holding the child — lines 19–21 — the effect is to make the sentiments expressed seem genuine.
- He reveals many aspects of his own personality in the poem, giving free rein to his feelings for the child and for her mother; his antipathy towards the oppressiveness of the Calvinist Church; and to the disgrace heaped on him by the parishioners.
- In the last stanza, he promises to "be a loving father . . . / And brag the name o't" — to refuse the shame which the parish gossips think he should feel. He believed physical and spiritual love between a man and a woman to be the most positive aspect of human life.
- The Scots **language** helps to create feeling of intimacy between father and child.
- Burns was most at home with Scots and sentiments expressed in his native tongue come across as genuinely felt by the poet.

- **Contrast:** Throughout the poem, the poet's honesty and openness in acknowledging his child is contrasted with the negative, "dirty-minded" attitudes of the Kirk and community;
- contrast is often achieved by **juxtaposition**, stanza by stanza or within stanzas — e.g., stanza 1, welcoming the child unreservedly, is followed by stanza 2, a scathing attack on the gossips; the last two lines of stanza 1 refer to the child's calling him Daddy while the first line of stanza 2 states that "they" call him "Fornicator", contrasting the affectionate "Daddy" with the scurrilous "Fornicator", emphasised by "What tho'", the first words in the line;
- the first line of stanza 3 repeats the loving welcome to the child and the word "tho" in line 15, within stanza 3, again points up the contrast between his attitude and that of the "Kirk and Queir", line 16; the same contrast between poet and priests appears in stanza 4, indicated by "**as** gude will . . . / **As** a' the Priests . . ." ;
- in stanza 5, he uses the **poetic form** to point up the contrast, with the first three *a*-rhyme lines referring to the child, the short *b*-rhyme line to the gossips, only to demolish them in the sixth line, connected with the fourth line by rhyme and metre.
- In the stanzas 6 and 7, the contrast is between rich and poor, a favourite topic of the poet's: again he uses both juxtaposition and poetic form — in stanza 6, he promises the child warm clothes and education, as good as any "brat" — the word contrasts with the earlier "nicely bred" of his daughter, the similarity of the words "bred" and "brat" helping the contrast between his child and a child conceived within marriage — not that he had anything against legitimate children — he had nine of his own! — but we can infer that illegitimate pregnancies among the rich could be, and were, easily concealed;
- in stanza 7, he says he would rather the child were poor and virtuous than well off, the dig at the rich coming in the last short line of the stanza as something of a sting in the tail.

EVALUATION

- Last stanza a fitting conclusion to the poem?
- Impression of the poet?
- Agree / disagree with his attitudes to love / illegitimacy / Church / community?
- Effectiveness of poet's depiction of society / influence / power of Church.

Using Your Notes for Revision: Checklist

UNDERSTANDING AND ANALYSIS *(Use these questions to revise important parts of the poem.)*

1. **Themes:**
   (a) **What theme is introduced in stanza 1?**
   - Love: parental love and physical love between a man and woman.

   (b) **How does the poet develop this theme?**
   - Stanza 1: poet welcomes his new-born daughter; hopes he may be cursed with bad luck if he ever regrets her arrival; or is embarrassed when she calls him daddy;
   - stanza 3 — acknowledges her as his daughter;
   - stanza 4 — kisses and cuddles her; will share his last penny with her, and she'll have the bigger part;
   - stanzas 5–6 — enjoyment of love-making; she will always have as fine, warm clothes and as good an education as any legitimate child of their class;
   - stanza 7 — hopes for her future;
   - stanza 8 — he will never regret the trouble he had, will love her and be proud of her.

   (c) **What theme is introduced in stanza 2, lines 7–12?**
   - Repressive attitudes of the Calvinist Church and resulting attitudes of the community.

   (d) **Note the poet's development of this theme.**
   - Stanza 2 — poet condemned as "Fornicator" by gossips.
   - Stanza 3 — required by Church to atone.
   - Stanza 4 — refers to hypocrisy of Church.
   - Stanza 8 — refers to the price he had to pay in terms of reputation, shame of the cutty stool.

2. **Tone:**
   (a) **Trace the changes in tone in the course of the poem.**
   (b) **For each change, note how the poet achieves that tone.**
   - Stanza 1 — sets the tone — **tenderness, delight** — a wholehearted welcome to the child runs through the whole poem.
   - Stanza 2 — **defiance** — refuses to be upset by the gossips' "kintra clatter", line 8.
   - Stanza 3 — **hatred** — of the Kirk's negative attitude to love / all earthly pleasures.
   - Stanza 4 — **affection** — lines 20–21 — he is holding and cuddling the child;
     - **contempt** — for the ministers of the Kirk, suggesting they would have enjoyed witnessing the poet's lovemaking, lines 22–24.
   - Stanza 5 — **humour** — lines 25–26 — lighthearted — "funny" is glossed as merry, full of fun — or reductive, tongue-in-cheek — acknowledging his rakish reputation?
     earnest promise — lines 29–30; he will share his last penny with her.
   - Stanza 6 — lines 31–36 — she will always have warm clothes and she will be well educated.
   - Stanza 7 — **hope** — for her future — that she will look like her mother and have all her good points; that she will have her father's "spirit, Without his failins!"
     — **humour** — reductive, tongue-in-cheek.
   - Stanza 8 — **pride** — he will "brag" about being her father.

3. **Contrast:**
   (a) **Note your ideas on the contrast between the two titles.**
   - The shorter title expresses the poet's defiance and honest refusal to be mealy-mouthed about the birth of his first child;
   - the longer title provides more information — that this is his first child;
   - but, more importantly, the longer title is couched in the typically euphemistic terms which would be used by the poet's enemies in the church and community;
   - the poet's choice is short and to the point; the publisher's choice is long-winded and tries to gloss over the truth with fine language — "love-begotten", "venerable appellation".

(b) **Note the various ideas and techniques / devices which carry on that contrast very effectively throughout the poem.**
  - Throughout the poem, the poet's honesty and openness in acknowledging his child is contrasted with the negative, "dirty-minded" attitudes of the Kirk and community.
  - Contrast is shown in **lexical choice**: examples showing his attitude to the child's mother and their lovemaking, contrasting with examples showing his attitude to the gossips, and
  - examples showing his attitude to the Church and its ministers;
  - Contrast is also achieved by **juxtaposition** of and within stanzas;
  - and **poetic form** used to point up the contrast – see page 14.

EVALUATION *(Use this question for exam practice.)*

4. (a) **What impression of the poet do you have from your reading of this poem? (7 marks)**
  - Head-strong — goes his own way, obstinately refusing to accept the rules of the Establishment and to be shamed by the criticism levelled at him by the community in which he lives — stanza 2 + quote / explain / comment.
  - Outspoken — "calls a spade a spade" — his choice of title — stanza 5 about lovemaking, stanza 4 about priests + quote / explain / comment.
  - Loving, affectionate father — evidence throughout poem + quote / explain / comment.
  - Responsible parent — promises to support and provide for the child though we know, in practice the upbringing of his illegitimate children was often left to his mother; also, his priorities are perhaps debatable — stanza 7, he would rather the child inherit his own "spirit" — which might be defined as waywardness! — than the means to live comfortably; rather a strange wish, considering the effects of penury which he has suffered throughout his own life.
  - Respects child's mother, refusing to condemn her — hopes the child will have her "gracefu' merit".
  - Delights in lovemaking — libertine — no mention of marriage.
  - Pokes fun at himself — stanza 5, lovemaking — stanza 7, "poor, worthless".
  H. and Int. — answers should show different views of the poet, good and bad, "rose-coloured-spectacle" answers gaining no more than half marks.

(b) **To what extent do you think he is justified in the attitudes he reveals? (3 marks)**
  - Personal response + justification.
  - Some answers may consider the poet in the light of his own time, others may deal with the more general aspects of love and refusal to conform or even relate the question to their own lives — all of these alternatives should be acceptable.
  H and Int. – Mark on merit.

Level — Intermediate 1 only

3. **You are told in the introductory note that this poem was written in 1785.**
  (a) **Without that note, how could you tell from the poem itself that it was not written in modern times?**
  (b) **Write down some evidence . . .**
  - The old Scots language (not irrefutable, but a reasonable answer at this level);
  - use of "thou" perhaps and other words / phrases like "kintra clatter", line 8; "clash", line 9; "daut", line 20; "tint", line 26; "Plack", line 29, etc.; not dialect words still in use like "fa", line 1; "mair", line 9; etc.
  - The interference in people's lives by the Church, lines 15–16 — society is more secular today.
  - The scandal attached to the birth of an illegitimate child — more acceptable nowadays.

Suggested Study Points: *Holy Willie's Prayer*

UNDERSTANDING

1. The situation
- Holy Willie (William Fisher, a middle-aged elder of the Kirk) is overheard at prayer.
- He starts by praising God and thanking Him for choosing to save him.
- He then confesses to sins of lust, with details of two young girls he has seduced.
- Then he gets to the point — asks God to wreak vengeance on his enemies, viz. Gavin Hamilton, the poet's landlord and friend, and his lawyer Robert Aiken, another of Burns's friends, who have recently won a case brought against them at the Presbytery of Ayr, by Willie and his minister, Mr Auld, who were humiliated in the process. Hamilton was accused of starting out on a journey on the Sabbath and of making a servant dig potatoes from the garden on another Sunday — hence the reference to his "kail and potatoes". Willie, by his own confession, was a drunkard and latterly misappropriated church funds. Returning drunk from Mauchline one night he fell into a ditch and died of exposure.

2. The themes
- Calvinism — Predestination, power and influence of the Kirk in lives of ordinary people.
- Hypocrisy of the "unco guid" — "the rigidly righteous" who have "a better art o' hidin." (From Burns's *Address to the Unco Guid*).

ANALYSIS

§1, Stanzas 1–6
- **Register:** language of prayer / Biblical: examples of words appropriate to prayer; "glory", line 4; "grace", line 10; "exaltation", line 14; "damnation", line 15; "creation", line 17; "temple", line 27.
- **Tone:**

stanza 1	—	**pious** — long vowel sounds in "Thou", "Wha", "A' " — resounding / lofty;
stanzas 2–3	—	**self-regarding / vain** — ". . . I am here . . . / . . . A burnin' and a shinin' light . . ."; asks God what is so special about him / his ancestry that he was "chosen";
stanza 4	—	**ranting** — exaggerated, graphic description of the Hell in which he might have expected to suffer, but for God's mercy;
stanza 5	—	**arrogant self-praise** — "I am . . . a chosen sample . . ." rising to a crescendo of self-aggrandizement in lines 29–30;
stanza 6	—	**priggishness** — compares others unfavourably to himself.

- The **absurdity of Willie's beliefs** revealed in this section:
- line 2 — ". . . as it pleases best Thysel" — very human way to refer to God's will — reduces God to level of Man; puts the idea of getting to Heaven on a par with winning the lottery!
- **Metaphors** — "a burnin' and a shinin' light", line 11 — symbol of superiority; ". . . a chosen sample", line 25 — best of type; ". . . a pillar in Thy temple . . .", line 27 — upholding God's teachings.
- **Simile** — "Strong as a rock", line 28 — reliable, perhaps comparing himself to St Peter;
- "A guide, a buckler, an example / To a' Thy flock" lines 29–30 — profusion of epithets — is there no end to this man's talents! — considers himself a role model, shepherd rather than sheep.
- If Willie is the type chosen by God for eternal salvation, it shows how absurd the whole idea of predestination is; he is bursting with pride — one of the Seven Deadly Sins.
- **Graphic visual image** of the Hell of the Calvinist teachings — lines 20–24:
- gnashing of gums (comic note — gums rather than teeth), weeping and wailing, burning lakes, devils roaring and yelling, chained to stakes — this is the gospel of hellfire which kept ignorant, uneducated people under the thumbs of Calvinist ministers, which Burns deplored.

- **Alliteration:** there are several examples in this section — lines 7, 10, 21, 23 — all intensifying the sense of the linked words and contributing to the general **hyperbole** of Willie's speech.
- **Alliteration** in line 32 intensifies his priggishness, introducing his hypocrisy: the behaviour, which he attacks in stanza 6 is less reprehensible than that to which he is about to confess!
- Throughout the poem, **ironic contrast** between prayer form and its content.
- One expects to find a Christian addressing God in a spirit of humility and repentance, demonstrating a genuine love for his fellow men.
- Lines 7–14: "I bless and praise Thy matchless might . . ." but he continually praises himself rather than God; ". . . That I am here . . ." (God's main claim to greatness seems to be his creation of one William Fisher!); ". . . That I should get sic exaltation" — not much humility!
- Stanza 6 performs a **linking function** between the first two sections:
- Willie introduces the subject of drinking, swearing and other vices, assuring God that he is "Free frae them a'", line 36.
- In the next section, he confesses to being drunk, using this as an excuse for even worse conduct with two young girls.
- The **juxtaposition** of those stanzas underlines Willie's barefaced hypocrisy.

§2, Stanzas 7–10

- **Tone:**

stanzas 7–8 — **confessional / whining / obsequious** — confesses to "fleshly lust", but not his fault — "Defil'd in sin"; promises not to touch her again.

stanza 9 — **boastful / whimpering / snobbish** — ". . . three times, I trow —" but if he hadn't been drunk he would not have touched her — presumably "Lizzie's lass" is a servant-girl, and so beneath him.

stanza 10 — **false piety, revealing his true vanity** — pretends to accept God's will but actually blames God for his failings!

- **Willie's hypocrisy** revealed: This "chosen sample" confesses his "fleshly lust" but excuses himself — it was his alter ego "Vile self", product of Adam's sin, which did wrong.
- He "sincerely" begs God's pardon and then proceeds to show his lack of contrition by bargaining with God over his future behaviour — with Meg.
- Even as he confesses, he reveals a nasty side, referring to a possible child born to Meg as "a livin' plague", line 45; and there is a coarseness in the phrase "lift a lawless leg", line 47, and "steer'd", line 54, showing, too, his inherent selfishness — he is more worried about his "dishonour", line 46, than about the welfare of Meg and the hypothetical child.
- **Metaphor**: "a livin' plague / To my dishonour" — reveals Willie's lack of charity and in particular the absence of love for his own hypothetical child and respect for the girl he seduced. We can see that Burns would have detested such sentiments, knowing the love he bore for his own children and the respect he showed for the women who bore his children. Also, the poet had suffered the full blast of Church and community in the process.
- **Hypallage** — line 47, "a lawless leg": clearly it is not the leg which is "lawless" but the whole man;
  effect is to emphasise that it meant nothing more to him than satisfying his animal urges, lifting his leg like a dog, with no thought for the girl he seduced. The **alliteration** adds to the disgusting picture of this middle-aged, "respectable " man behaving like an animal;
- line 38 — another example of **alliteration** (also middle '-sh-' sound) with same effect.
- The **contrast** between the prayer form and content is a bit stronger in this section.
- He confesses his sins but shows no sign of contrition and indeed blames other forces from drink to God Himself. He promises never to go near Meg again – IF God will ensure that she's not pregnant; and he makes no promises about other young women, giving himself carte blanche under the cloak of false piety — lines 59–60 — one can almost hear him licking his lips as he accepts this cross he has to bear.
- **Register:** Biblical language — "Vile self", line 40; "Defil'd in sin", line 42.

§3, Stanzas 11–16
- **Tone:**

  stanzas 11–16 — **vicious / spiteful / vengeful** — asks God to damn his enemies, rising crescendo of hatred, asking God to destroy them.

  stanza 15   — **whingeing** — we see the true, cowardly Willie, lines 86–88.
- Further evidence of **Willie's hypocrisy**: he excuses himself as he was "fou", line 51, yet in lines 67–68, he asks God to punish Gavin Hamilton for drinking.
- His **vicious spite** revealed: he asks God to "confound their stubborn face / And blast their name", lines 63–64; "Curse . . . his basket and his store" (his means of survival), line 77; to bring down His "strong right hand . . . / Upo' their heads", lines 81–82; "destroy 'em", line 95.
- **Contrast** between prayer form and content: we discover Willie's real reason for prayer — i.e., asking God to destroy his enemies — yet he expects God to forgive him for his sins.
- **Register:** Biblical language — "Thy han' maun e'en be borne", line 59; "Lord, visit them", line 92.

§4, Stanza 17
- **Tone: mealy-mouthed / wheedling** — asks God to look after him, materially and spiritually;
- intensified by **alliteration** in lines 97 and 99.
- Further evidence of **Willie's hypocrisy** — asks God for personal favours for God's own sake! — "a' the glory shall be Thine", line 101.
- His **material greed** is revealed: he asks for material and spiritual "mercies", line 98; spiritual and worldly wealth, line 99; and to be "Excelled by nane", better and richer than all others, line 100.
- **Contrast:** he is back to his wheedling, asking God to give him material wealth — clearly he is choosing to ignore the teachings of St Matthew, xix, 24, about camels and eyes of needles!
- The elements of prayer are there — see Prayer Form — but the spirit of prayer is absent, providing us with some wonderful **comic satire.**

Looking over the whole poem
- **Structure:** poem divides neatly into four sections, the **juxtaposition** adding to the satire:
- stanzas 1–6   Willie praises and thanks God for making him so perfect;
- stanzas 7–10   Willie confesses to fornication / possible seduction and drunkenness;
- stanzas 11–16   Willie asks God to destroy his enemies — no Christian charity!
- stanza 17   Willie asks God to look after him, materially and spiritually.
- **Satire:** Burns detested the repressive influence of the Calvinist Church, with good reason, having been brought to book more than once on fornication charges. (See *Welcome to a Bastart Wean.*) Here, he shows the Church elder committing the same sin with impunity.
- He ridicules the Calvinist God and the "auld licht" views held by the extreme Calvinists; not that Burns was an atheist but he held the more enlightened views which came with the widespread Enlightenment of the 18th century, with belief in a loving, forgiving God.
- In his attempt to curry favour with his God, Willie unwittingly reveals for us a selfish deity, who selects people at a whim (lines 2–4).
- In stanza 3, he refers to the doctrine of Original Sin, held by the Calvinists — that Man is born bearing the sin committed by Adam and Eve in the Garden of Eden, and can be shriven of that sin only by God's grace. [Some religions still believe that Original Sin is removed only by the sacrament of Baptism.]
- By ridiculing Willie, he makes the whole idea of predestination — or, at least, Willie's interpretation of that doctrine — appear absurd. One can see Willie as simply mistaken about his "chosen" status but the doctrine of the elect seems almost to encourage him to sin, as he seems to think that, no matter what he does, he has been chosen for eternal salvation (line 25); he can always regard his weaknesses as God's way of reminding him that he is not actually divine — yet! (stanza 10)!

- **Literary Form: Prayer:** addressing God — Biblical language;
- contains the elements of prayer: praising God, confession of sins, asking for God's pardon and for His help in one's daily life; ends with "Amen";
- much of the **humour** comes from the contrast between the expectations set up by the prayer form and the actual contents and tone of Willie's prayer. (See **Tone and Contrast**)
- **Dramatic Monologue:** Willie talks to his God. He believes that he is one of the chosen few whom God will save from eternal damnation; the Calvinist doctrine of Predestination held that God randomly preselected a few of His creatures for eternal salvation.
- In this poem Burns uses a **persona** to put across his ideas. He wouldn't have dared to express those ideas as himself — these were real people, after all — and it is perhaps no coincidence that Hamilton was Burns's landlord and friend; Aiken, Hamilton's lawyer, was another friend of the poet. Even using the persona, he did not include this poem in the Kilmarnock edition but circulated it by hand, unacknowledged, as he did with many of his more controversial poems, a practice which, incidentally, makes more feasible the recent discoveries by Burns scholars of "new" poems attributed to Burns.
- Willie **reveals much of his own character** to us:
- **hypocrisy** — presents himself as role model whilst confessing to fornication, seduction of young women and drunkenness;
- **pride / vanity** — thinks he stands out above all others — line 11, "A burnin' and a shinin' light";
- **smugness** — asks God what is so wonderful about him that he has been exalted — line 14;
- **false humility** — line 15 — "I wha deserv'd sic just damnation";
- **priggishness** — stanza 6 — compares others unfavourably with himself;
- **lack of contrition** — while confessing his sins, continues to blame outside forces — "Vile self", line 40 (i.e., the legacy of evil "Through Adam's cause", line 18); drink — line 51, and even God — lines 56–57 — who may be making him sin "Lest he owre high and proud should turn", in which case he will have to put up with it — and go on sinning till God sees fit to stop him!
- **vicious spite** — asks God to curse his enemies whose worst crime seems to have been to humiliate Willie and his ally, Auld, lines 75–76;
- **greed** — asks God to look after him and his with material as well as spiritual wealth.
- Effect of using persona and prayer form: Willie condemns himself, and all the rest of the "Unco guid", out of his own mouth. One would expect a man to speak truthfully in a prayer, so the attack on the Calvinist Church and its doctrines is more convincing.
- **Poetic Form — Burns Stanza:** See *To a Mouse* SSP, page 8, for history and description.
- Rhyme and metre help to put across the prayer's theatricality — and resulting hypocrisy.
- In stanzas 1–4, three rhyming lines — *aaa* — pile on the praise, create a vivid picture of Willie's merciless God and the horrors of the hell to which He sends the unlucky majority who are not chosen.
- The effect is similar in stanzas 5–10, with the addition of some imperfect rhymes (e.g., line 27, "temple") which echo the behaviour of this "example" to good Christians!
- In stanzas 11–16, the effect is of a rising crescendo of hatred and rage.
- The short line 4 has the effect of taking a breath before launching into a further exaggeration, or sometimes a contrast, in lines 5–6, with the rhymes linking line 5 to lines 1–3, and the final short line finishing off the stanza with a final thrust.

EVALUATION

- Effectiveness of the satire.
- Effectiveness of persona.
- Relevance of ideas to modern day;
- there are still religious fanatics with extreme beliefs — may cite Middle East, N. Ireland.

Using Your Notes for Revision: Checklist

UNDERSTANDING AND ANALYSIS *(Use these questions to revise important parts of the poem.)*

1. **Calvinist Religion**
   (a) **Doctrine of Predestination**
   - Evidence from stanzas 1 and 2 + lines 25 and 61–62, "chosen".
   (b) **Original Sin**
   - Evidence from stanzas 3 and 4 + line 42, "Defil'd in sin".
   (c) **Hellfire and damnation**
   - Evidence from stanza 4 + lines 63–64, "confound . . . blast . . ."; lines 77–78, "Curse Thou . . ."; lines 81–84 "Thy strong right hand, Lord, make it bare . . . and dinna spare . . ."; and stanza 16.
   (d) **Calvinists' idea of what God is like**
   - Selfish; selects people, His creations, for salvation at a whim, to demonstrate his power.
   - No suggestion of a loving, forgiving God.
   - It should be stressed that these were the extreme "Auld Licht" Calvinists.

2. **Satire:**
   (a) **What was the poet's purpose in writing this poem?**
   - Burns detested the repressive influence of the Calvinist Church and the hypocrisy of the "unco guid".
   - He ridicules the Calvinist God and the "auld licht" views held by the extreme Calvinists like Willie.
   (b) **How does he use poetic and literary form and structure to achieve his purpose?**
   - **Poetic Form** — see page 20 for details.
   - **Literary Form** — Dramatic monologue, see page 20.
   - Use of **persona**;
   - Willie reveals much of his own character to us — see page 20 for details.
   - Effect of using persona:
   - Willie condemns himself, and all the rest of the "Unco guid", out of his own mouth;
   - one would expect a man to speak truthfully in a prayer, so the attack on the Calvinist Church is more convincing.
   - **Structure** — juxtaposition;
   - poem divides naturally into four sections, the juxtaposition of which adds to the satire; for details of how each section is undermined by the next, see page 19.
   - Reminds us of Willie's hypocrisy and his lack of Christian principles.

3. **Techniques / devices used by the poet to convey his satire.**
   - **Lexical choice, imagery, other devices** — help to put across the satire by ridiculing Willie and his beliefs.
   - Revealing the absurdity of Willie's beliefs:
   - Stanzas 1–4: hyperbole, intensified by alliteration; graphic imagery (Hell).
   - Revealing Willie's hypocrisy and lasciviousness:
   - Stanzas 1–6: Willie puts himself forward as being perfect, a role model, lines 29–30; metaphors, line 11, line 25, line 27; simile, line 28; hyperbole, intensified by alliteration, line 10;
   - Stanzas 7–10: confesses to "fleshly lust", line 38; "Vile Self", line 40; drunkenness, line 51; metaphor, lines 45 – 46; hypallage, intensified by alliteration, line 47;

- Stanza 12 — excused himself as he was "fou", yet asks God to punish Hamilton for drinking.
- Revealing his vicious spite:
- Stanzas 11–16: extreme language — "confound . . . blast . . . curse . . . dinna spare . . . destroy".
- Showing his material greed:
- Stanza 17: "mercies temp'ral . . . gear".
- **Contrast** — throughout the poem, **ironic** contrast between prayer form and its content:
- one expects to find a Christian addressing God in a spirit of humility and repentance, demonstrating a genuine love for his fellow men; but he is full of self-praise, lines 7–14;
- confesses sins but refuses to accept responsibility for his actions, shows no contrition, nor any intention to change, stanzas 7–10;
- real reason for prayer is to ask God to destroy his enemies; not appropriate to prayer, stanzas 11–16;
- contrast also between sections — see juxtaposition, 2*(b)*.

EVALUATION *(Use this question for exam practice.)*

4.   *(a)*   **How does your impression of the persona differ from his own idea of himself?**   **(6 marks)**

- He thinks he is a good Christian and one of the elect + quote / explain / comment.

- We see him as vain, smug, hypocritical, selfish, seducing young girls, getting drunk, vicious, spiteful towards his enemies, jealous, cowardly — certainly not worthy of eternal salvation + quote / explain / comment.

H — well-developed portrait of Willie, supported by good textual reference + intelligent comment;
Int. — clear understanding of Willie's character, supported by some textual reference + some comment.

(b)   **To what extent do you agree with the poet's attitude to the persona and to the ideas expressed in the poem?**   **(4 marks)**

- Personal response — unlikely to disagree! — *Mark on merit.*

- Should deal with Willie — lacking any Christian virtues, not entitled to eternal salvation — and his beliefs.

*Both levels should elaborate on at least one specific trait, not already covered in (a), e.g. seducing young girls, **and / or** one element of his beliefs, e.g. Predestination. Mark on merit.*

Unseen Textual Analysis: Marking Schemes
Such a Parcel of Rogues in a Nation

Levels: Higher and Intermediate 2

1. (a) **Show how the syntax of lines 1–4 has helped you to understand the speaker's mood and why he feels this way.** **(2) AU**
    - Repetition of "Fareweel" (anaphora), piling up the things that he feels have been lost (½) + exclamation mark, line 4 (½) +
    - intensify his feeling of regret / sadness / yearning for loss of nationhood (1).

    (b) **Comment on the poet's use of contrast in this stanza.** **(1) A**
    - Lines 1–4 deal with past glories (½) + "Now", line 5, indicates move to present situation (½);
    - or, reference to poetic form — rhyme scheme *ababcdcd* + / alternating metrical pattern (½) + explanation (½).

    (c) **Comment on the tone of "England's province", line 7, and explain the importance of this phrase in the context of the poem.** **(2) AU**
    - Tone is bitter (1) +
    - phrase sums up the prevailing situation: Scotland has become a part of England. (1).

2. (a) **Explain the additional idea that is introduced in line 8.** **(1) U**
    - That the situation is result of treachery.

    (b) **How is that idea developed in stanza 2?** **(2) U**
    - Scotland could not be defeated by the English in battle. (1) +
    - But had now been betrayed by a few people for financial gain. (1)

    (c) **Comment on the effectiveness of two examples of lexical choice in lines 9–12, which reinforce the idea introduced in line 8.** **(4) A**
    - "Coward few", line 11 — both words merit discussion:
    - "coward" is a noun used here as an adjective — effect is to draw attention to the word, thus intensifying the contrast with the brave Scots who fought and died for their country "Thro' many warlike ages", line 10, making the word even more derogatory. (1) +
    - "few" used as a noun emphasises that it was a minority of Scots who betrayed their country, contrasts with the many who were loyal; more effective than "a few cowards". (1)
      Award full mark only if reversal of functions is recognised, at least implicitly.
    - "hireling traitors' (wages)", line 12:
    - combination of two derogatory words: "hireling" employed by someone; here suggests doing someone else's dirty work, (1) +
    - "traitor": betraying a cause, and therefore despicable; again contrasts with loyal countrymen, (1).
      Award ½ mark each if phrases are identified only, no comment.

3. **"English steel", line 13; English gold", line 15.**
    (a) **Explain how these two phrases encapsulate the speaker's argument.** **(2) U**
    - "English steel" refers to the English armies which had been unable to defeat Scotland in the past; (1) +
    - "English gold" refers to the bribes, which induced the MSPs to betray their country and vote for union with the English parliament. (1)

    (b) **By referring closely to the rest of the poem, show how effectively the poet uses military / monetary metaphors to reinforce his argument.** **(4) A**
    - **Military language** used — a reminder of Scotland's former strength and glory, now lost:
    - line 4, "martial story" — exploits of old heroes like Bruce and Wallace, named in stanza 3, who fought bravely for the country now given away by a "coward few", line 11;

- line 9, "force . . . subdue" — the English had tried to conquer by force but had failed;
- line 10, "warlike ages" — our history of fighting bravely;
- line 11, "coward" set against "valour" of brave fighters;
- line 13, "English steel" — a reminder that he is talking about hand-to-hand fighting with swords and knives, but still they could not overcome the Scottish nation;
- line 20, "Bruce and loyal Wallace" — refers to old heroes who fought for their country, now given away by politicians.
- Set against **monetary language** — contrasts attitude of speaker to brave heroes and to "traitors" who sold their country for financial rewards;
- line 12, "hireling traitors' wages" — in the pay of the English to betray their country;
- line 15, "English gold" — literal but also suggests the attraction of the money for the "traitors", that they were dazzled by it, could not resist;
- line 18, "Treason thus could sell us" — again links MSPs' actions with money;
- line 23, "We're bought and sold for English gold" — intensifies the bitterness felt by the speaker at his nation's being traded like a commodity for personal profit; internal rhyme and direct speech intensify the scathing tone.
- **Metonymy:**
- Line 13, "The English steel we could disdain" — we could treat the English attack with contempt:
- steel, meaning swords, knives, etc is used to mean the whole attack, which the brave soldiers did not fear, being sure of the courage of every man called upon to fight.
- Set against line 15 — "English gold" — similarly, used to mean the discussions and agreement to vote for the union — underlining the fact that the votes were traded for personal gain by the "gentry" who sold out their own country.
- In these two examples, the metonymy focuses our attention on "steel" and "gold", respectively, "steel" emphasising what the Scots withstood to secure their country, in contrast with "gold", which emphasises the ease with which a few "traitors" gave it away.

Both levels might be expected to recognise the way the two are set against each other, H – also perhaps the metonymy.
H — four references for each, fully explained + intelligent comment;
Int. — at least three references from each, clearly understood + some comment.

4. (a) **How does the stance of the persona change in the last stanza?**   (2) A
- Stanzas 1 and 2 — first person plural; stanza 3 — first person singular.
- Stanzas 1 and 2 rhetorical, speaking for whole nation;
  Stanza 3 — more personal; more Scots words used. (1) +

  [It is noticeable that the only Scots words, which require to be glossed, are in the last stanza — appropriate as poem is about loss of nationhood. Scots had become discredited as a language of any standing with the earlier Union of the Crowns in 1603, when James VI of Scotland acceded to the English throne, to become James I of the united countries. James moved south and the Court went with him, leaving Scotland as something of a backwater. Writers and poets followed the Court and thereafter began to write in English rather than their native Scots. After the second Union — of Parliaments — there was something of a Scottish backlash and people started to collect Scottish works, fearing that they might be lost forever.]

- Stanzas 1 and 2 deal with whole nation's lament for the past and sorrow at what has happened; stanza 3 deals with speaker's personal lament and intentions for the future. (1)

(b) **Identify and account for the change of tone in lines 21–23.**
  (2) A
  - Tone is defiant. (1) +
  - The speaker refuses to bow down to authority; wishes he had died in battle rather than live to see his country betrayed; will go on proclaiming the treachery until he dies — presumably Burns's own sentiments — direct speech strengthens his declaration and determination to speak out. (1)

H — two marks for full explanation of tone, supported by good textual evidence, well-explained + intelligent comment;
Int. — two marks for clear understanding of tone, supported by some textual evidence, explained + some comment.

5. (a) **How effective do you find the poet's use of a persona?**
  (4) E
  - Stanzas 1 and 2 — 1st person plural, "we", "our" — as if speaking on behalf of the whole nation, gives stature to the persona.
  - Stanza 3 — becomes more personal to speaker — uses 1st person singular, "I", "my", allows him to express deep, personal feelings.
  - Speaker is an old man — "My auld grey head", line 19 — not hot-headed, sword-happy youth but a mature, experienced man.
  - Perhaps an old soldier? — use of martial language — stanza 2 — knows what he is talking about.
  - Loves his country — prepared to speak out against the government — shows depth of feeling, prepared to take risk.
  - Old man is speaking at the time of the Union — use of present tense; "Now", line 5 — has experienced the situation at first hand, not hearsay.

H — two points, supported by textual evidence, well-explained, or 4 points dealt with less fully, + intelligent comment;
Int. — at least two points, supported by textual evidence, clearly understood + some comment.

(b) **To what extent has the speaker engaged your sympathy for his cause?**
  (4) E
  - Personal response: may take objective view—what else could the government do — may have seemed like a good deal / right thing to do at the time;
  - or may take nationalistic view—love of country, independence, etc.;
  - or may consider that, while the union seemed to be a practical solution to Scotland's problems, the price was too high; or any other reasonable stance.

H and Int. — Mark on merit. [Note on Darien Scheme should help better students to take objective view of situation.]

Level: Intermediate 1

1. **The first 3 lines of the poem begin with the word "Fareweel". Explain, in your own words as far as possible, to whom or what the speaker is saying goodbye.**
  (1) U
  - To the days when Scotland was an independent country;
  - famous for her success in battle;
  - the name, now people were even calling the country North Britain.
  (Any two for ½ mark each).

2. *(a)* **According to the speaker, in lines 5–7, what has happened?** (2) U
- Scotland has become part of England, (1) + attempt to elaborate, e.g., a county like Kent or Yorkshire. (1)

(b) **Write down the phrase from stanza 1, which refers to Scotland.** (1) U
- "England's province".

3. *(a)* **Who are the rogues referred to in the title?** (1) U
- Members of the Scottish Parliament.

(b) **What did those people do?** (2) U
- Accepted bribes (1) + to vote for union with the English parliament. (1)

(c) **Write down one phrase from lines 9–12, which helps you understand what those people did.** (1) A
- "hireling traitors' wages".

(d) **How does the speaker feel about those "rogues"?** (2) A
- Despises them (1) + for betraying their country for financial gain (1) / hates them. (1)

(e) **Write down a different phrase from lines 9–12, which tells you how the speaker feels about those people.** (1) A
- "coward few" (1); "traitors" (½).

4. *(a)* **What is meant by "English steel" in line 13?** (2) U
- The English army / attack (2); (English) swords (1).

(b) **What does the speaker say about "English steel" in lines 13–14?** (2) U
- English could not defeat Scots in battle (1) + Scots were too brave for them (1).

(c) **Write down another phrase from the same stanza, which contrasts with "English steel".** (1) A
- "English gold".

(d) **Explain why the poet makes this contrast.** (2) U
- Saying the English could not defeat us in battle (1) + but they could get round us with money. (1)

5. *(a)* **What physical details do we find about the speaker from stanza 3?** (2) U
- Old (1) + grey-haired (1).

(b) **What is the tone of his words lines 17–20?** (1) A
- Bitter (1); wishes he were dead (½); angry (½).

(c) **What is the tone of his words in lines 21–22?** (1) A
- Defiant (1); determined (½); forceful (½).

(d) **Write down some evidence from this stanza to support each of your answers at *(b)* and *(c)*.** (2) A
- Bitter — wishes he had died rather than witness this disgraceful treachery (1).
- Defiant — he refuses to stay quiet about it; he will keep complaining till he dies (1).

6. *(a)* **How do you feel about the speaker in the poem?** (1) E
- Feel sorry for him; think he is brave to speak out; *any reasonable response.*

(b) **Referring to the poem, explain why you feel this way.** (3) E
- Because he is an old man; obviously very sad; must feel strongly if he wishes he had died; he was alive at the time, so knows what he is talking about; possibly an old soldier, who fought for his country . . . *Mark on merit.*

(c) **Has the speaker convinced you that Scotland was betrayed by some members of the Scottish Parliament or can you suggest a good reason for their actions? Remember to justify your answer.** (2) E
- *Mark on merit, but full credit should be given if answer agrees or disagrees, with at least one reason + at least acknowledges the dire financial situation caused by failure of the Darien Scheme; or more than one reason without that acknowledgement.*

Suggested Outline Plans for Critical Essays

1. **Select one poem dealing with the world of nature — plants / animals — and, by close examination of the poet's techniques / devices, show to what extent he is commenting, not merely on the world of nature but on some aspect of human emotion or behaviour.**
   (To a Mouse)
   §1   Title, poet, **brief** statement of situation + brief reference to aspect of human life dealt with.
   §2   Deal with imagery, lexical choice and tone, showing mouse's fragility and poet's feelings + quote / explain / comment.
   §3   Mouse as symbol for poor peasant farmers — explain all areas of symbolism + quote, etc.
   §4   Personal response to poet's ideas + final statement on poem.

2. **Explain what you believe to be the essential "message" contained in any poem you know well Show how the skill of the poet, in constructing the poem and in choosing words and language features, has given power to the message and contributed to your enjoyment of the poem.**
   (*Welcome to a Bastart Wean*)
   §1   Title, poet, **brief** statements of situation presented in poem and "message".
   §2   More detail on criticism heaped on poet by Church and community + quote, etc.
   §3   Poet's skill: use relevant notes on tone, lexical choice, figurative language, to show how he makes attitudes clear.
   §4   Personal response to the poet's message + how poet's skill contributed to enjoyment.

3. **A dramatic monologue can reveal a character clearly, merely by the words he / she speaks. By close examination of the poetic techniques / devices used, show the skill with which the poet does this in a monologue you have read, and discuss how the poet's attitude is also revealed.**
   (*Holy Willie's Prayer*)
   §1   Title, poet, **brief** statements of situation presented in poem and character speaking.
   §2   Poet's skill in making Willie reveal his true character: tone, hyperbole, hypallage + quote.
   §3   Elements of prayer present in poem + ironic contrast between prayer form and content.
   §4   Poet's attitude — how revealed — satire + personal response.

4. **Choose a poem in which satire is used to ridicule the Establishment of the day. By referring to one poem, show how effective you consider this device to be in putting across the poet's personal feelings and / or beliefs.**   (*Holy Willie's Prayer*)
   §1   Title, poet, **brief** statements of situation, character speaking and target(s) of satire.
   §2   How satire put across: by exaggerated picture of God, Hell, rules of the Established Church.
   §3   By ridiculing Willie, who condemns himself out of his own mouth — humour — quote, etc.
   §4   Personal response to poet's attitude to the Church and in particular Willie and Auld + to his enlightened religious beliefs.

5. **Compare and contrast two poems by the same writer and, by close reference to the techniques / devices used in both poems, explain which, in your opinion, has put across the stronger message.**   (*Welcome to a Bastart Wean* and *Holy Willie's Prayer*)
   §1   Titles, **brief** statement of situation presented in each poem.
   §2   Points of comparison: **both** dramatic monologues, deal with Calvinism + quote / explain.
   §3   Points of contrast: WBW — personal repression suffered by poet at hands of Church on birth of illegitimate child + quote and explain.
            HWP — satire — use of persona to reveal absurdity of Calvinist doctrines + quote and explain.
   §4   Personal response — opinion on which puts across stronger message + reasons: e.g. in WBW, poet's personality, sympathy for his situation / that of child; in HWP, persona, comic satire . . .

CHAPTER 2 — Hugh MacDiarmid

Suggested Study Points: *The Watergaw*

UNDERSTANDING

1. The situation
- The poet talks to his father, who has been dead for some time (in fact, his father died when MacDiarmid was 18 years old).
- Seeing a rainbow, he has been reminded of the last look in father's eyes before he died.

2. The themes
- The mystery of human existence.
- Question of life after death.

ANALYSIS

Note on Language:
- Artificial — "dictionary dredging" — synthetic Scots.
- This was the first of the Scottish language poems to appear under the name of Hugh MacDiarmid, "friend of Christopher Grieve", who just happened to be the editor of the *Scottish Chapbook*, in which it was published. Grieve heaped praise on his "friend's" work, particularly its "Doric economy of expressiveness" — typically mischievous of MacDiarmid.
- Many of the abstruse words he used in his early lyrical poems came from Jamieson's *Etymological Dictionary* and yet, he had such a native feeling for the language that the poems do not sound artificial and should pose no more difficulty for students than reading Burns or Shakespeare. Indeed, MacDiarmid was trying to effect a Scottish Literary Renaissance but came up against considerable opposition. He abhorred and rebelled against the "Kailyard" Scots being used by Scottish writers of the late 19th / early 20th centuries, to write sentimental stories, e.g. Ian Maclaren's *Beside the Bonnie Briar Bush,* published in 1894; the title came from a Jacobite song "There grows a bonnie briar bush in our Kailyard" — hence the "Kailyard School". MacDiarmid, of course, had to go to the other extreme!
  > *"I'll hae nae hauf-way hoose, but aye be whaur*
  > *Extremes meet . . ."*   (From *A Drunk Man Looks at the Thistle*)
- Positive advantages of this language, mixed with colloquial Border Scots:
- economical precision / compression of ideas — e.g. "yow-trummle," line 1 — consider the lack of poetry and long-windedness of English equivalent; "watergaw" — particular kind of rainbow.
- Unfamiliarity makes us look and think more deeply about those words.
- The vernacular lends immediacy and strength to poet's beliefs — they appear to be heartfelt. (In my opinion, his poetry in Scots, whether synthetic or colloquial, is his best work and is among the most accessible to non-specialist students.)

Stanza 1, lines 1–6:
- Obviously rural **setting** — "yow-trummle", line 1 (+ "laverock's hoose", line 7).
- Conversational **tone** — helped by metrical pattern and enjambment:
- metrical / stress pattern — alternating long / short lines — strong stresses: 4/3/4/2/4/2;
- along with enjambment, helps conversational tone / intimacy of son talking to dead father.

- **Mood** is dreary, intensified by rain ("weet", line 1) and time of day ("forenicht").
- Extended cold **imagery** begins in line 1 — as with mood, appropriate to death:
- "yow-trummle", line 1 — sheep trembling because they have been shorn (usually in June) and it has turned unexpectedly cold — very vivid, precise image;
- "chitterin'" — trembling / shaking — rainbow's unsteady form.
- Lines 5–6: **tone** > reflective / wistful — rainbow reminded him of father's death-bed.
- Whole poem is an **extended comparison** of rainbow and dying look;
- incongruous comparison — the two are unconnected in reality, only connected in poet's mind — linked in poem by word "licht", lines 3 and 9; typical of MacDiarmid to juxtapose the symbolic and the ordinary, the latter being the more significant.
- Also linked by **puns**;
- "chitterin", line 3 — literally of the indistinct, unsteady rainbow + trembling fear of dying man;
- "the on-ding", line 4 — literally of the rain / storm + dying man is beyond life's struggle / storm.
- Only in line 5 that it becomes clear that this is an **Address**;
- poet addresses his dead father "ye", line 5 (+ "your", line 12).

Stanza 2, lines 7–12:
- **Tone** becomes heavier — remembers feeling of cold emptiness when father died.
- **Metaphor** — "nae reek i' the laverock's hoose / That nicht — and nane i' mine", lines 7–8: proverbial expression meaning it was cold and stormy: "the laverock's hoose" = the sky; "nae reek" > no fire > no warmth in poet's house because father has died > no life.
- **Cosmic image** — links father's death to the elements in the proverbial expression, line 7, "and nane i' mine", line 8 — as if the heavens were in mourning for his father, just as he was.
- In his early lyric poetry, MacDiarmid frequently moves from the human in stanza 1 to the cosmic in stanza 2. Perhaps the most beautiful example, and a good demonstration of this technique, is *Empty Vessel* about a young woman, wandering high in the hills, "Ayont the cairney", singing to her dead child, whom she believes she is cradling in her arms. The second stanza moves into the cosmic with "Wunds wi' warlds to swing / Dinna sing sae sweet".
- He says he has puzzled over the last look in father's eyes ever since the night he died — line 9;
- "foolish licht" here, I think, refers mainly to the look but links back to the watergaw through the delayed rhyme / echo — see below in Poetic Form.
- MacDiarmid also refers to that look of his father's in *Kinsfolk*, where he writes:

> "I wonder then what he
> Foresaw or hoped and hoo — or gin it squares   (how — or if)
> Wi' subsequent affairs."

- Lines 11–12: **tone** is tentative — he has been puzzling over something and now thinks perhaps he knows the answer;
- but with an undercurrent which is almost sarcastic / gloating — we are alerted to this aspect by "foolish", line 9 — in the case of the watergaw, similar to Burns's use of "silly" (of the mouse's nest) in *To a Mouse*, line 20, i.e. feeble, in this case, hazy / indistinct / watery — of the rainbow, and of the last look, watery-eyed; but also, of the look, the more mischievous idea of foolish in its ordinary sense, i.e. stupid — for expecting life after death? Ties in with "wild", line 5 — idea that the dying man is terrified to find himself looking into an empty abyss. MacDiarmid was a declared atheist; his father was deeply religious.
- In the end he is almost wickedly mysterious / almost sinister — he thinks he may know the answer but he doesn't tell us, leaves us wondering — we have to work it out for ourselves.

Looking over the whole poem
- **Irony** of the comparison central to poem:
- the rainbow is a romantic symbol, associated with hope, God's sign that he was giving mankind another chance after the Flood;
- a watergaw is a hazy, indistinct, watery type of rainbow, which, to country people, is a sign of worse weather to come, therefore it is an imperfect symbol.
- It is a watergaw which reminds the poet of his father's dying look > a bleak outlook > no hope of eternal salvation.

- **Poetic Form:**
- regular — two stanzas;
  rhyme scheme – *abcbdd*;
- *abcb* lines deal with the natural world; *dd* lines deal with the reflective / philosophical;
- in stanza 2, *dd* lines provide sting-in-tail.
- The two stanzas are linked by the delayed rhyme / echo — "licht", lines 3 and 9.

- **Literary Form:**
  Monologue / Address: one can imagine the poet, standing at his father's grave or looking at a photograph; he has obviously been greatly moved by his father's last look;
- because he is speaking to dead father and no one else is present, gains reader's sympathy in stanza 1 but we begin to doubt his sincerity at the end of stanza 2, where he seems almost to gloat over his father's foolishness at expecting life after death.
- **Lyric:** fulfils the requirements — fairly short, expressing the feelings and thoughts of a single speaker in a personal and subjective fashion.

EVALUATION

- How does MacDiarmid raise the poem from the particular to the universal?
- Title — poem is not about watergaw but about father's last look.
- Incongruous juxtaposition of watergaw and dying look;
- by linking the two — human and elemental — and note, it is the watergaw which reminds him of his father's last look, not the other way round;
- as always with MacDiarmid, it is the human being in the picture who is the more important [see also *The Bonnie Broukit Bairn*, (i.e. Earth) in which he praises Mars, Venus and the moon but ends by telling Earth: "But greet, an' in your tears ye'll droun / The haill clanjamfrie" — there is so much human suffering on Earth that mankind's tears would drown all of the other planets];
- also link in proverbial expression, lines 7–8, see under cosmic image above.
- In the end, we realise the poem is not about the poet's father either but about the mystery of death and the question of life thereafter. Although MacDiarmid declared himself an atheist, he was brought up in a religious home and studied the Bible industriously as a young man. Kenneth Buthlay, late of the Scottish Literature Department, Glasgow University, an expert on the poet and his work, has said that MacDiarmid "was forever talking about God, whom he could not forgive for failing to exist." In Mr Buthlay's opinion, the poet felt the need to fill the void left by the destruction of his faith.
- Mystery of death:
- poet has been moved by the experience of his father's death — "and nane i' mine", line 8;
- has held the image of his father's dying look in his mind since his death;
- was reminded of it by a hazy, indistinct watergaw — not a beautiful rainbow which we view with awe, but a watergaw — indicates poet troubled by father's last look;
- does not share his father's deep religious feelings — interprets that look in the light of his own beliefs, i.e. that his father could only have been disappointed at the moment of his death;
- but he is not sure — line 11: "I think . . . mebbe . . . at last" — he leaves us hanging at the end, does not tell us what he thinks he knows — is he acknowledging that he could be wrong?
- The mystery of death is intensified by inconclusive ending of poem.

Using Your Notes for Revision: Checklist

UNDERSTANDING AND ANALYSIS *(Use these questions to revise important parts of the poem.)*

1. **Language:**
   See note on language, page 28, and glossary.

2. **Situation:**
   Summarise the situation dealt with in the poem and note the extent to which the title conveys the sense of the poem.
   - The poet talks to his father, who has been dead for some time.
   - Seeing a rainbow, he has been reminded of the last look in father's eyes before he died.
   - Title — suggests poem will be about the watergaw.
   - In stanza 1, the poem appears to be not about watergaw but about father's last look;
   - note: it is the watergaw which reminds him of his father's last look, not the other way round.
   - In the end, we realise the poem is not about the poet's father either but about the mystery of human existence and the question of life after death.

3. **Tone:**
   Identify and account for each change in tone throughout the poem.
   - Stanza 1 — **reflective / anecdotal** — remembers the watergaw;
   - **reminiscing / wistful** — rainbow reminded him of death-bed scene, lines 5–6.
   - Stanza 2 — remembers **feeling of cold emptiness** when father died;
   - **tentative** — he has been puzzling over something and now thinks perhaps he knows the answer, lines 11–12;
   - **almost sarcastic / gloating** — we are alerted to this aspect by "foolish", line 9.
   - Ending — **mysterious / almost sinister** — he may know the answer but he doesn't tell us.

4. **Poetic and Literary Forms:**
   Note how the poetic and literary forms used have contributed to your understanding of the poet's mood.

   Poetic Form:
   - rhyme scheme — *abcbdd* — *abcb* lines deal with the natural world; *dd* lines deal with the reflective / philosophical;
   - in stanza 2, *dd* lines provide sting-in-tail — when tone changes.
   - Metrical / stress pattern — alternating long / short lines — strong stresses: 4/3/4/2/4/2;
   - along with **enjambment**, helps general, conversational tone / intimacy of son talking to dead father.

   Literary Form — Monologue.
   - Poet addresses his dead father "ye", line 5; "your," line 12;
   - says he has puzzled over the last look in father's eyes ever since the night he died — lines 9–10.
   - He has obviously been greatly moved by his father's last look.
   - Vernacular lends immediacy and strength to poet's beliefs — they appear to be heartfelt;
   - because he is speaking to dead father and no one else is present, gains reader's sympathy in stanza 1, but we begin to doubt his sincerity at the end of stanza 2, where he seems almost to gloat over his father's foolishness at expecting life after death.

5. **Devices / techniques:**
    Revise the effectiveness of the devices / techniques used to create a vivid picture of the scene at the poet's father's death-bed.
    Imagery:
    - extended cold imagery — appropriate to death;
    - see page 29 — "yow-trummle". line 1, linked to "chitterin", line 3;
    - see page 29 – metaphor: "nae reek i' the laverock's hoose / That nicht — and nane i' mine", lines 7–8.
    - Dreariness intensified by rain ("weet", line 1) and time of day ("forenicht").

    - Whole poem is an extended comparison of rainbow and dying look: see page 29.
    - Also linked by **puns**: "chitterin", line 3 ; "the on-ding", line 4; "foolish", line 9.

6. **Irony:**
    - See page 29, Looking over the whole poem.

EVALUATION *(Use this question for exam practice.)*

7. **Explain how MacDiarmid moves from the particular to the universal in this poem,**
    - Title suggests watergaw is subject of poem.
    - Stanza 1 seems to contradict expectations set up by title: rainbow simply reminded him of his father's dying look;
    - incongruous juxtaposition of watergaw and dying look;
    - by linking the two — human and elemental — raises look in father's eyes to cosmic level.
    - Further cosmic image in stanza 2 — links father's death to the elements in the proverbial expression, line 7, "and nane i' mine", line 8 — as if the heavens were in mourning for his father, just as he was.
    - Inconclusive ending evokes the mystery of human existence / death, which is the real subject of the poem: see under Evaluation, page 30.

    Both levels should deal with three steps: watergaw > look in father's eyes > mystery of life / death.
    H – well-developed discussion, with good textual support + intelligent comment;
    Int. — three steps clearly understood, with some textual support + some comment — 7 marks

    making clear the extent to which you find yourself approving of the attitudes he reveals.
    - Personal response but should be linked to attitudes found in the poem.
                                                                                — Mark on merit — 3 marks

Level: Intermediate 1 only

4. **Setting:**
    (a) **Note some words / phrases which tell you that the poem is set in the country.**
    - Obviously rural — "yow-trummle", line 1, "laverock's hoose", line 7 + *(b)* explanation.

5. **Weather:**
    (a) **When the poet saw the watergaw:** cold imagery, line 1 + mood revealed.
    (b) **On the night of his father's death:** storm metaphor, line 7 + mood revealed.

6. (a) **What is it the poet thinks he now knows? (2)**
    - That there is nothing after death — *no mark for "what look meant"; must specify.*
    (b) **How sure is he? (1)**
    - Not at all sure.
    (c) **Quote from the poem to support answer. (1)**
    - "I think" or "mebbe".

7. **What is your response to the poet in this poem? (6)**
    - *Any reasonable response, with attempt to justify and some textual reference — mark on merit.*

Suggested Study Points — *Lo! a Child is Born*

UNDERSTANDING

1. The situation
- The poet reflects on the atmosphere of love surrounding the birth of a child.
- He compares it with the indifference of God towards His creation.

2. The themes
- Humanism.
- Warmth of human love.
- God's indifference towards the world and His creatures.

ANALYSIS

Note on Structure:
- The poem divides clearly into sections: lines 1–7, 8–12, 12–17 and 18–19.
- The sections alternate: human > cosmic > human > cosmic.

§1: lines 1–7: The **tone** of the first section (lines 1–7) is reflective:- "I thought of a house . . .", line 1;
- gradually becoming warm / caring: — "warm", line 3, "warmth . . . tenderness . . . longing . . . smiling anxiety", line 4.
- This section creates a vivid **image** of the household awaiting the birth of a child:
- line 1 is slowed by the **alliteration** and the three different vowels, each with a strong stress, in ". . . stones seemed suddenly . . .": the effect is to create the hush of the waiting family.
- In line 2, **personification** of the stones — the very building was on tenterhooks — suggests the security of the home awaiting the child; the strength of the loving care with which the child will be enveloped, an unwavering love, "as solid as (the stones) themselves".
- In line 2, the **repetition** of ". . . hope, hope . . ." , separated by a comma, creating a **caesura** between them, making the reader pause as if to consider, intensifies the feelings of love / family.
- In lines 3–4, he creates an atmosphere of warmth and love through the **lexical choice**:
- "warm", "lovely heat" in line 3, echoed in line 4 with "warmth", "longing" + "tenderness" and
- "smiling anxiety", the **oxymoron** in the last phrase neatly capturing the contradictory feelings of fear for the survival of the mother — in those days of home confinements without the medical expertise of today, a very real fear — coupled with the joy of the occasion.
- In line 5, the word "rules" shows the way the household is totally taken over by these feelings.
- Line 6 — he reworks a **cliché** — "The walls were full of ears" — again showing how alert the whole family was, waiting for the child's first cry — rephrasing the idiom draws attention to it, giving it more impact than the straight cliché and reinforces the idea of the "stones" in lines 1–2.
- In its usual form, "Walls have ears", it generally refers to children / servants / outsiders, who may hear something they should not know about — in this case it includes the youngest and lowliest members of the household who also care about the arrival of a new baby.
- The two short simple sentences in line 6 capture the tension of the situation.
- The **caesura** created by the mid-line full stop reminds us of the hush — everyone listening — followed by another short statement: "All voices were lowered" — any talk was in whispers.
- In line 7, the longer sentence coming after the two short sentences in line 6 emphasises, strengthens the sense of that statement: "Only the mother had the right to groan or complain." The woman in labour was to be cherished, respected, all action centring on her, doing whatever possible to help her, acknowledging the pain of her labour to produce for them the family's future.

§2: lines 8–12: The **tone** in this second section is pitying: ". . . the whole world. Who cares . . .?"
- In line 8, **alliteration** and **long vowels**, all sound variations of "o" in ". . . the whole world. Who . . .", coupled with the **caesura** created by the mid-line full stop, slow the line; the effect in this case is to support the tone of pity for this creature, the world, shown no love by its Creator.

- The whole poem is a reasoned argument for the superiority of human love over that shown by The Creator for the world; the argument is presented in terms of **comparison** and **contrast**.
- The **juxtaposition** of the wonderful picture of human love (lines 1–7) with the cosmic imagery (lines 8–12), so typical of MacDiarmid: "Then I thought of the whole world", introduces the contrast, stressed by "Then" and the **repetition** of "I thought of" from line 1.
- He presents an **image** of The Creator overseeing the birth of the world — a sibling for the other planets — with the future as midwife. This God's-eye-view of the world, familiar enough to modern Space Age readers, must have had a tremendous impact in the 1920s.
- Throughout this section, we find words which link back to the "human love" section before it, pointing up the comparisons and stressing the contrast: "travail", line 8 — the word used in the Bible of a woman in childbirth — initiates the link, specifically with line 5: ". . . a child is about to be born" — the Biblical word is appropriate to this "God" section;
- "encompass" line 9, links back to the "house" and "stones" in line 1, enclosing the mother-to-be; in the case of the world, the poet finds no such security; "like lovingkindness", line 9 — the phrase is intensified by the **alliteration** and the **compound** word "lovingkindness", which brings together the feelings of love and the practical application of that love in acts of kindness, enjoyed by the human mother but not replicated in the cosmic birth.
- The "monstrous din", line 10, which holds an implied contrast with the music of the spheres, is set against "peace", line 9, the hush evoked in line 6.
- The **tone** here becomes angry, scathing: ". . . monstrous din of the sterile who contribute nothing . . ." — referring to ministers and adherents of religion; "sterile" is used metaphorically to mean they contribute nothing useful or important to the realities of this life, their minds firmly fixed on the "Life Hereafter"; appropriate to this poem about birth and contrasts with the fertility (of ideas and feelings, especially love) of ordinary, secular, human beings.

§3: lines 12–17

- In the third section, the **contrast** is introduced by "not like", line 12, which echoes "like", line 9.
- In this section we hear a **tone** of quiet pride in the superiority of human love over God's "love" — pride in / admiration for the qualities of human beings: the child in the womb is "a strategic mind already . . ." — intelligence; "seeking the best way . . ." — power of reasoning; "Springing into history . . ." — action. The last phrase provides a strong contrast with the cosmic birth, at which ". . . the future fumbles, / A bad birth . . .", lines 11–12: the sense of each phrase intensified by the **alliteration** and **personification**;
- "quietness", line 13, links back to "monstrous din" in line 10.
- The human birth is **ironically** presented in the imagery of Nature: the child comes "Springing into history, quivering like a fish". The **simile**, as well as proclaiming the superiority of the human being in Nature, suggests the great leap into the current of life taken by the human child, overcoming the odds, just as the salmon extraordinarily leaps upstream; "quivering" — with the life force;
- "Dropping into the world like a ripe fruit in due time", line 17 — this simile reiterates the idea of Man as part of Nature.

§4: lines 18–19: Last two lines — **tone** is disparaging / provocative: "But where is the Past . . .". There's no comparison!

- The **contrast** in those final two lines of the poem is introduced by "But where is . . ."
- We come back to the cosmic with the **anthropomorphism** of the cosmic couple, presenting Time as the mother and the Past / God as the father. "smiling through her tears", line 18, links back to "smiling anxiety" (line 4) — in this case noted by its absence.
- The final **question mark** emphasises his inability to find a similar cosmic element.

Looking over the whole poem

- Though a professed atheist, MacDiarmid was brought up in a strictly religious home and was a keen student of the Bible in his youth. (See notes on *The Watergaw*)
- In this poem, he uses **irony** to put across his Humanist ideas in the title and by centring his whole argument around one of the most important aspects of Christianity — the birth of a child.
- He uses the Biblical **symbol** — the sacred significance of stones, associated with the Resurrection, another fundamental element of Christian faith — to present Man as the truly sacred being, at the same time reminding us of the stable in the story of the birth of Christ.
- In line 12, the human home is described as "gracious", literally full of grace, an epithet generally reserved for the Holy Virgin, compare the *Ave Maria*: "Hail, Mary, full of grace . . ."
- The human child, still in the womb, is presented as "A strategic mind, seeking the best way / To present himself to life, and at last, resolved . . ." — a thinking, rational, intelligent being, superior to the apparently random nature of God.
- The similes describing the human child being born, in lines 16 — 17, use elements of the story of the Creation — fish and fruit: see Genesis I, v. 11: "God created the fruit tree yielding fruit", and v. 20: "God said, Let the waters bring forth abundantly the moving creature that hath life."
- In the last two lines, he uses the **image** of the Holy Family, the Christian symbol of family love, with Time as mother, the Past as father, and the cosmic child is a new-born son.
- In these lines he is saying there is no cosmic mother, nor is there a father to whom she can turn crying: "I love you" — love is a human attribute. (The use of **direct speech** emphasises the human aspect.)

Poetic Form

- Free verse: No regular metre or line length; depends on natural speech rhythms.
- MacDiarmid wrote of his own poetry in *The Caledonian Antisyzygy*:
    "sometimes .... the true lyric cry
    Next but chopped-up prose."
- We saw the "true lyric cry" in *The Watergaw*; here we have "chopped-up prose".
- If it were written as prose, however, we would call it poetic.
- Effect is to make the sentiments appear natural, the true result of the poet's thought processes — he has reasoned it out:
- "I thought . . .", line 1, echoed by prosaic "Then I thought . . .", line 8 — language of argument.

Literary Form — Monologue

- The poet expresses his ideas directly, setting out the case of Mankind v. God.
- He reports on the atmosphere of love present when a human child is born, and
- compares that human love to God's apparent indifference towards his creation, the world.
- No particular audience — the poet merely reveals his thoughts, without trying to impress anyone. The ideas thereby acquire credibility; this is serious thought, not poetic posturing.

EVALUATION

- Irony of the title and of the Christian imagery used to put across Humanist ideas.
- Poet's attitude to ideas in poem.
- Human v. cosmic — isn't it possible to believe in both?

Using Your Notes for Revision: Checklist

UNDERSTANDING AND ANALYSIS *(Use these questions to revise important parts of the poem.)*

1. **Situation / argument: Summarise the situation in the poem;**
   - The poet reflects on the atmosphere of love surrounding the birth of a child.

   and outline the argument put forward by the poet.
   - Compares warmth of human love with the indifference of God towards His creation.
   - Uses occasion of the imminent birth of a child:
   - describes the expectant hush as the family awaits the moment of delivery with great joy;
   - but also with trepidation — in those days childbirth much more dangerous than today.
   - Poet can find no evidence of such love coming from God to his creation, the world.
   - Refers to ministers and adherents of Christian religion as "sterile" and their preachings as a "monstrous din" — no real love behind it, simply empty ranting. In the early part of this century, preachers were still inclined to preach of Hellfire and damnation rather than of the love of a benevolent, forgiving God.
   - The poet concludes that human love is superior to the love of God; it therefore follows that Mankind is more important than God.

2. **Structure: Note the structure of the poem and the linking words which signal each change of view.**
   - Lines 1–7, "I thought of . . ." / "child is about to be born."
   - Lines 8–12, "Then (I thought of) . . ." / ". . . bad birth".
   - Lines 12–17; "not like (the child) . . .".
   - Lines 18–19; "But (where is) . . .".

3. **Tone: Note textual references which show how the tone varies in accordance with the structure of the poem.**
   - §1 (lines 1–7) describes the scene in a house where a child is about to be born: tone is **reflective** at the start: "I thought of . . .".
   - Gradually becoming **warm / caring**: lexical choice, lines 3–4.
   - §2 (line 8 — ". . . bad birth", line 12) considers the world as a new-born child with the future as midwife;
   - tone is **sad / pitying**: "Who cares . . .?";
   - becoming **angry, scathing**: reference to religion, lines 10–11.
   - §3 (line 12, ". . . not like . . ." — line 17) comes back to the human household — direct comparison;
   - tone of **quiet pride** in the superiority of human love over God's "love", lexical choice, lines 12–13;
   - **pride in / admiration for** the qualities of human beings, lexical choice, lines 14–16.
   - §4 returns to the cosmic image;
   - tone is **disparaging / provocative**: "But where is . . .?".
   - He concludes that there is no comparison.

4. **Devices / techniques: Revise the effectiveness of the devices / techniques used to underline the contrast between the two sides of the poet's argument.**
   - The argument is presented in terms of **comparison** and **contrast**:
   - Lines 1–7: creates a vivid **image** of the household awaiting the birth of a child.
   - Line 1 is slowed by the **alliteration**; creates the hush of the waiting family.

- line 2, **personification**: stones; + **repetition, caesura**;
- lines 3–4, atmosphere of warmth and love through the **lexical choice**; + "smiling anxiety" — **oxymoron**;
- line 5, **lexical choice**: "rules;
- line 6 — reworks **cliché**; + two short simple sentences and **caesura** capture the tension;
- line 7, longer sentence coming after the two short sentences in line 6 — strengthens sense.
- **Juxtaposition** of this human love with the cosmic imagery (lines 8–12);
- line 8, **alliteration** and long vowels, this time all sound variations of "o", coupled with the **caesura** slow the line, support the tone of pity for the world; contrasts with tone of wonder at love surrounding human child.
- Words which link back or forward to the "human love" sections before and after it, pointing up the comparisons and stressing the contrast: "travail . . . encompass . . . like loving kindness (**alliteration, compound**) . . . monstrous din".
- In the third section (lines 12–17), the contrast is introduced by "not like", line 12, which echoes "like", line 9; human birth **ironically** presented in the imagery of Nature.
- The final two lines of the poem are contrasted with the previous section in "But where is . . .";
- back to the cosmic with the **anthropomorphism** of the cosmic parents — no love there.

EVALUATION *(Use this question for exam practice.)*

5. *(a)* **How successful do you think MacDiarmid is in his use of Christian imagery to put across his humanist beliefs? (7 marks)**
   See page 35, Looking over the whole poem.

   H — well-developed and clear discussion of Christian imagery and irony, with good textual support + intelligent comment. Int. — Christian imagery and irony clearly understood, with some textual support + some comment.

   (b) **To what extent does this imagery help you to understand the poet's message? (3 marks)**
   - Personal response to imagery.
   - Perhaps along the lines of familiarity of Christian story, especially birth of Christ, which every child loves and knows well as part of Christmas celebrations in primary schools.
   - Appeal of the irony — reveals something of the mischievous nature of MacDiarmid.
   - Appeal of the provocative — meat and drink to young people!

   Mark on merit.

Level: Intermediate 1 only

5. **Similes:**
   See page 34, lines 12–17, for details.

6. *(a) Some understanding of poet's Humanist beliefs, even implicitly that he is on the side of human beings.*

   (b) Any reasonable attempt to comment on at least one part of poem. Mark on merit.

Levels: Higher and Intermediate 2

Unseen Textual Analysis: Marking Schemes
With the Herring Fishers

1. (a) **Drawing your information from stanzas 1 and 2, show how the poet conveys the impression that the herring fishers are fairly "rough and ready" men.**   **(2) U**
    - They are unshaven — "ilka blue jowl", line 2;
    - they speak in broad dialect: "Soom", line 5, "auld", line 7, "braw", line 8;
    - their work is physically heavy: "haul on the nets", line 3.

    (b) **In those same lines, how does he convey a quite different impression of those men?**   **(2) U**
    - He makes them appear romantic, as we see them "'gainst the moon", line 2.
    - They enjoy their work: "the glad cry", line 1, when the fish are spotted.
    - They talk to the fish, trying to coax them into the nets; call them "bonnie herrin' . . . ", line 5.

    For parts (a) and (b):
    H — at least 2 points with textual support, well-explained + intelligent comment;
    Int. — at least 2 points with textual support, clearly understood + some comment.

2. **"For this is the way that God sees life", line 13.**
    (a) **Show the importance of this line to the structure of the poem,**
    - Introduces new idea / marks a shift in poet's line of thought, (1) +

    making clear how the words link back to the first three stanzas.   **(2) A**
    - "this" refers to the way the fishermen catch the herring, described in stanzas 1–3.

    (b) **Explain the relationship between the two parts of the poem.**   **(2) A**
    - Poet uses the story told in stanzas 1–3, describing the fishermen at work, from the moment they sight the herring till they haul in their catch, as a parable to illustrate how God operates: "For this is the way that God sees life", line 13.
    - Stanzas 4–6 describe God's view of the human race on the Day of Judgment.
    - Says God is like the fishermen and we are like the fish, moving through Life as the fish swim in the sea.
    - When we appear before Him on Judgment Day, He will haul our souls up into Heaven.
    - Just as the fishermen haul in their catch indiscriminately, so God will make no distinction between "Reid and yellow and black and white", line 18 — everyone will be accepted.

    H — a clear understanding of the parallels, well-explained + intelligent comment;
    Int. – clear understanding of parallels + some comment; both sides must be dealt with for full mark.

    (c) **Demonstrate, with detailed reference to the text, how the poet uses repetition or echoing words / phrases to make this relationship clear.**   **(4) A**
    - Line 13 — ". . . God sees life" echoes line 1 — "I see herrin' . . .";
    - line 16 — "It's his happy cries I'm hearin' . . ." echoes line 1 — "I hear the glad cry";
    - line 17 — "— O come in and see me," repeats the fishermen's invitation to the herring in line 6.
    - Stanza 6 is almost the same as stanza 1: "the" > "his"; "ilka" > "his muckle", line 3 is worded differently but the sense is the same; "And sing" > "Singin' . . .".

    H — should explain the principle + at least 2 examples + intelligent comment;
    Int. — at least two examples in which principle is at least implicit + some comment.

3.   (a)   **Comment on the effectiveness of the image in stanza 3 (lines 9 – 12) of the
             herring being brought on board in the nets.**   **(2) A**
             -      The herring are described as "walkin' on board . . . As if o' their ain accord."
             -      We picture the herring upright, strolling onto the boat, all happy and smiling;
             -      the effect is humorous.

      Both levels should deal with image + effect.

      (b)   **Explain, briefly, how he offsets this picture against another extended image later
             in the poem.**   **(1) A**
             •   The later image is of the human race, "The haill jing bang o's . . ." appearing
                    before God on the Day of Judgment, "Toddlin' up into Heaven . . .".

      (c)   **Referring closely to the two extended images, explain what this technique
             contributes to the impact of the whole poem.**   **(5) A**
             •   There is a two-way link between the herring and the human race;
                    line 10 — "To watch the herrin' come walkin' on board" — **set against**
                    lines 12–13 — "The haill jing-bang o's appearin' / Up owre frae the edge o'
                    naethingness";
             -      as the nets are hauled in, the fish appear to be upright, walking on their tails, like
                    their human counterparts in the second section of the poem: a comic image;
             -      the image of the whole human race ("the haill jing-bang o's") peeping up over the
                    parapet between earth and Heaven, like timid children or animals is equally
                    comical;
             -      and made even funnier by the analogy with the fish.

             •   Line 11 — "In the wee sma' 'oors o' a simmer's mornin' . . ." is **set against**
             -      line 20 — : "At peep o' day frae the endless night";
             -      fish are caught at first light;
             -      mankind will be judged at the dawn of Eternity;
             -      the implication of the analogy is that mankind is walking into a snare, just as the
                    fish are.

      The "wee sma' oors" is the time when dastardly deeds are done and spirits are abroad
      — sinister!

             •   Line 12 — "As if o' their ain accord" is **set against**
             -      line 19 — "Toddlin' up into Heaven thegither" :
             -      "Toddlin'" is normally used of young children, with no cares, walking unsteadily but
                    happily, without knowing where they are going.
             -      The implication is that human beings, with blind faith in God and Heaven, have no
                    more idea of what is in store for them than the herring swimming into the
                    fishermen's nets.

      H — at least two examples, fully explained + intelligent comment on impact.
      Int. — at least two examples, clearly understood + some comment on impact.

4.   **This is "a poem of two halves" (to paraphrase the football reporters' cliché). In which
      "half" do you think you detect the genuine voice of the poet? (Refer closely to the
      poem to justify your decision.)**   **(10) E**
      •   First half is genuine celebration of hard-working fishermen, who brave the elements to
             supply us with fish.
      -      He portrays them as "rough diamonds", unshaven but big softies underneath.
      -      Direct speech in stanzas 1 and 2 — broad dialect makes them sound more real,
             genuine — he presents them as they are.
      •   He delights in the incongruity of these hardy men chanting / talking to the fish, coaxing
             them into the nets as if they were talking to children or domestic pets.
      •   Poet makes clear his admiration for them and the job they do;
      -      he writes the poem in the first person — "I hear the glad cry", line 1, and
      -      narrative stanza 3 is written in same broad dialect, thus aligning himself with the men.
      -      Use of ballad form — 4-line stanzas, rhyming *abcb* — sets these men in tradition of all
             fishermen, lends them stature — quintessential fishermen.

- Second half introduces the "parable", deployed here **ironically** since he clearly uses it to demote God to the level of the rough fishermen — but with much more sinister intentions.
  - ". . . the auld man . . .", line 7, referring to the fisherman by analogy becomes an irreverent reference to God.
  - The use of the fishing analogy strengthens the irony: In St. Luke, chapter 5, v. 1–10, Jesus filled the nets of his disciples with "a great multitude of fishes" and told Simon, "From henceforth thou shalt catch men".
- On the surface, God is seen as the supreme fisherman, hauling souls up into Heaven, and treating all men alike regardless of race or colour;
  - looking more closely into the analogy, however, we consider why the fishermen are catching fish — to kill and eat;
  - line 21 "I see herrin'," I hear his glad cry — is this how God sees us — so much fodder?
- The balancing of the herring against mankind (which can be dealt with in detail here if not fully explored in question 3; otherwise passing reference only) puts Man in the same position as the herring — i.e. trapped.
- God seems less indulgent than the fishermen, coaxing the herring into their nets;
  - line 17, "Left, right . . ." has connotations of the army sergeant major, barking out orders which must be obeyed.
- In the last stanza, MacDiarmid becomes quite irreverent;
  - no capital at "his" / "he" referring to God in lines 21–23;
  - refers to his "muckle blue jowl";
  - God speaks in the same broad dialect as the fishermen — a tactic normally reserved for the Devil — trying to trick them into feeling that He is one of them and they are safe.
  - Last line has connotations of gas ovens — suicide — clearly demonstrates MacDiarmid's irony in his portrayal of God and Christians who follow His teachings blindly.

Both levels should state clearly which half reveals the genuine voice of the poet, supporting that statement with at least two textual references for each side, fully developed and explained + intelligent comment for H; clearly understood with fair attempt to demonstrate + some comment for Int.

Level — Intermediate 1

1. **Look closely at stanzas 1 and 2 (lines 1 – 8). What is your impression of the herring fishers from those lines? (You should consider and give some examples from those stanzas of:)**
   (a) **their appearance;**
      - unshaven, "blue jowl", line 2; (1) +
   (b) **how they talk;**
      - broad dialect: "Soom", line 5; "auld", line 7; "braw", line 8 (1) +
   (c) **the kind of job they do;**
      - work at night, "gainst the moon", line 2; "the wee sma' 'oors", line 11; or heavy work: "haul on the nets", line 3 (1) +
   (d) **how they feel about their work;**
      - enjoy their work, "glad cry", line 1; "sing", line 4; talk to fish.　　　　　　**(4) UA**

2. **The poem divides neatly into two halves:**
   Explain, in your own words:
   (a) **what stanzas 1 to 3, lines 1–12, are about.**　　　　　　　　　　　　　　**(2) U**
      - The fishermen at work, from the moment they sight the herring till they haul in their catch;
   (b) **what stanzas 4 to 6, lines 13–24, are about.**　　　　　　　　　　　　　**(2) U**
      - Describe God's view of the human race on the Day of Judgment.
   (c) **Explain how the two halves are connected to each other.**　　　　　　　**(2) A**
      - *Some attempt to explain the parallels between fishermen and God on Judgment Day. (See H. and Int 2. Levels, question 2(b).)*

(d) **Give two examples from each half which show this connection.** (2) A
- Some attempt to deal with the repetition or echoing of words / phrases:
- line 13 — ". . . God sees life," echoes line 1 — "I see herrin' . . .";
- line 16, — "It's his happy cries I'm hearin' . . ." echoes line 1 — "I hear the glad cry";
- line 17, — " — O come in and see me," repeats the fishermen's invitation to the herring in line 6.
- Stanza 6 is almost the same as stanza 1: the > his, ilka > his muckle, line 3 is worded differently but the sense is the same, And sing > Singin'.

3. (a) **In stanza 3, lines 9 — 12, how does the poet describe the herring?** (2) A
- The image is of the fishermen cajoling the herring into the nets;
- the herring are described as "walkin' on board . . . As if o' their ain accord."

(b) **Which one of the following words best conveys what you think of this description?** (1) E
- Funny.

(c) **Give a reason for your answer at (b).** (2) E
- We picture the herring upright, strolling onto the boat, all happy and smiling.

4. (a) **In stanzas 4 and 5, lines 13–20, what is the poet describing?** (2) A
- The human race (1) + appearing before God on Judgment Day (1) or God hurrying us on into Heaven. (1)

(b) **What do you think of this description?** (1) E
- Funny is perhaps the most likely response — or stupid / ridiculous; or
- frightening / sinister.

(c) **Give a reason for your answer at (b).** (2) E
- Funny — comparison with fish; God speaking in dialect; "Toddlin' up into Heaven".
- Frightening / sinister — don't like to think of death and afterwards.
Accept anything reasonable.

5. **Think about this question: Why do fishermen catch fish?**
- *Anticipate: to kill and eat.*
(a) **With your answer to that question in mind, what might the poet be saying about God, when he compares Him to the fishermen?** (3) E
- That God may not love us; may want us for his own purposes + explanation.
Any reasonable answer along those lines, but not that God may want to eat us!

(b) **What do you think the poet's attitude to God is?** (2) E
- Does not believe in a loving God; he is an atheist, sceptic, humanist.

6. **Write a paragraph explaining what you like and / or dislike about the poem, giving reasons for your opinions.** (3) E

Anything goes here, if justified; mark on merit.

Suggested Outline Plans for Critical Essays

1. **Poetry is often written as a result of an intense emotional experience. Examine the techniques used by one poet to convey the significance of an experience, which gave rise to a poem. (*The Watergaw*)**
    §1.   Title, poet, brief description of the event which gave rise to the poem.
    §2.   Details of the intensity of the poet's experience — effects of literary form used.
          Techniques which help us to appreciate the poet's feelings at the time — imagery.
    §3.   Poet's later reflections on the incident — extended comparison, irony.
    §4.   Personal response to the poet's reflections + final statement on poem.

2. **Choose a poem which was initially difficult for you because of such things as its subject, language, theme, word choice . . . Briefly outline the difficulty and in greater detail explain in what ways closer study of the poet's techniques made the experience of reading it worthwhile. (*The Watergaw*)**
    §1.   Title, poet, brief statement of the initial difficulty(-ies).
    §2.   Outline main difficulty — e.g. language — what further study revealed / advantages realised.
    §3.   Outline second difficulty — e.g. incongruity of the comparison — how resolved.
    §4.   Any other minor difficulty — e.g. inconclusive ending — reaffirm value of close study.

3. **Choose a poem in which the poet uses an everyday event to convey his own strongly-held ideas and show how the devices and techniques which he uses have helped you to understand his ideas. (*Lo! a Child is Born*)**
    §1.   Title, poet, brief description of the event + statement of poet's ideas.
    §2.   Discuss use of poetic and literary form and structure to convey ideas.
    §3.   Work through linguistic devices used to convey ideas.
    §4.   Personal response to the poet's ideas + final statement on poem.

4. **It is often thought that poetry is solely about serious and sad subjects. Select a poem which is about a happy event, a joyful experience, a fulfilling emotion . . . Closely examine the techniques / devices, which make you both enjoy and understand what is being communicated to you. (*Lo! a Child is Born*)**
    §1.   Title, poet, brief description of the event described in the poem.
    §2.   Image of loving anxiety created in first and third sections.
    §3.   Structure / techniques used to provide contrast and how contrast intensifies human sections.
    §4.   What was learned + personal response / enjoyment.

5. **Compare and contrast two poems by the same writer which deal with the same or similar themes and, by close reference to the techniques / devices used in each poem, explain which one, in your opinion, has put across the message more strongly. (Any two** of the three poems in the chapter, if the unseen poem has also been discussed. In sections 2 and 3, it is generally better to deal with less-favoured poem first.)
    §1.   Titles, poet, brief descriptions of the event / situation described in each poem + brief statement of the common theme + which conveys theme better.
    §2.   Points of comparison, other than theme — e.g. poetic and literary form, structure, tone.
    §3.   Points of contrast: poems 1 and 3 deal with what happens after death; poem 2 deals with human love v. God's love + quote and explain for each.
    §4.   Restate which poem conveys the theme better + further justification for opinion + why student personally responds more strongly to chosen poem.

CHAPTER 3 — Edwin Muir

Suggested Study Points: *Childhood*

UNDERSTANDING

1. The situation
- Child lies on a hillside near his home during a long afternoon, viewing the familiar landscape;
- imagines what the outside world will be like. A ship passes in the bay, from that world.
- Evening comes and his mother calls him in.
- Opposing impressions: "sunny", line 1 / "gloom", line 14; "below", line 2 / "far off", line 3; "saw", line 5 / "unseen", line 8 . . .

2. The themes
- Childhood — main theme, introduced in title and stanza 1.
- Sense of unity with the earth / landscape / Nature, introduced in stanza 1.
- Sense of belonging to our past.

ANALYSIS

Stanza 1.
- Poet creates an almost tangible **sense of place** — tiny island of Wyre, off Orkney, island of his own childhood, here remembered, perhaps partly imagined: "hill", line 1; ". . . his father's house below", line 2; "Far off the . . . sound", line 3; ". . . black islands lying thick around", line 4.
- Initial **mood / atmosphere** is one of timelessness, peace, security:
- "Long time he lay . . .", line 1 — long summer day in far north, relaxed attitude of the people; "sunny", line 1; "securely bound", line 2; ". . . islands lying thick around", line 4 — as if protecting him;
- line 3 — "the silent, changing sound was still": here we have the underlying contrast between "silent" and "sound" (in the sense of noise) and between "changing" and "still", giving effect of balance / harmony in landscape = harmony in child's life and in childhood in general
- **Sound:**
  l-sounds throughout the stanza have a lulling effect;
  s-sounds throughout the stanza create a whispering effect;
  used to same effect in **alliteration** in line 3, line 13;
  both sounds appropriate to child lying on grassy slope on calm day; create feeling of harmony, all is well; carefree, protected aspects of childhood.
- **Imagery:** "To his father's house below securely bound", line 2 — **metaphor** — the image is one of a child in safety reins or the kind of wrist strap we use nowadays; the metaphor emphasises the safe haven provided by the child's parents; safety of childhood in general.
- A further image of security can be seen in line 4: ". . . the black islands lying thick around" — "thick" suggests a security blanket, appropriate to child, protecting the tiny island where the child is.

Stanza 2.
- **Setting:** ". . . each separate height . . .", line 5 — Orkney being quite bare, each hill stands out; the **repetition** of "each" stresses the way hills stand out individually; and yet, the total effect is of a protective barrier . . . or obstacle to his future development, knowledge of the world?
  ". . . massed islands", line 6 — the islands appear to be gathered together, giving sense of unity:
  ". . . all ran together in his view", line 7 — sense of whole; Wyre such a tiny island that child could assimilate his entire world as an entity;
  ". . . unseen straits between them . . .", line 8 — he is aware of their separate unities, but sees the landscape as a whole, the harmony / balance emphasised by contrasting words: "separate / massed / ran together" and "view / unseen".

- **Mood:** the child's view pans out to the surrounding hills and islands: here the underlying menace of the outside world / adulthood is introduced — ". . . unseen straits . . .", line 8; contrary view indicated by "though", line 7.
- **Pun** on "straits" in line 8: — literally — the narrow strips of water between the islands, based on his experience of his own island; underlying meaning — difficulties. The child's innocence is here imbued with the poet's adult experience of the world beyond the island, life beyond childhood; a hint from the poet that the childhood idyll will not last.

Stanza 3.

- The child knows intuitively that a different world lies ahead of him and, in his innocence, imagines it to be a reflection of his present life, peaceful and calm:
  ". . . new shores . . .", line 9 — he can imagine the outside world only as more islands like his own — reflects the narrow experience of childhood; ". . . sand . . .", line 10; "shallow water . . .", line 11; ". . .strand to strand . . .", line 12. Poignant — harsh reality of life.
- The **mood / atmosphere** is dream-like — child's innocent day-dreams almost surreal:
- in his mind he sees "the still light on the sand, / The shallow water clear in tranquil air", lines 10–11, and looks forward to walking "through it in joy . . .", line 12.
- The s- and l-sounds, which echo throughout the poem, are supplemented here by a sh-sound, e.g., in "shores", line 9; "shallow", line 11 — to give a feeling of hush, comforting.

Stanza 4.

- **Setting:** "Over the sound a ship . . . would pass", line 13; ". . . black hill . . .", line 14, "The evening sound was smooth", line 15.
- We come back to the menacing **mood / atmosphere** with the ship passing:
- **pathetic fallacy**, line 14, "the black hill's **gloom**", reflects the menace of the passing ship, symbol of the outside world, not quite impinging on his idyll, but adulthood is out there and the suggestion from the word "gloom" is that it will not be pleasant.
  (Muir regarded childhood as a kind of Eden: the innocence of childhood before adulthood is like Man before the Fall. The child's innocent dream of the future is made more poignant by the contrast, in our minds, with the reality of adulthood, and intensifies the whole unworldly, dream-like nature of childhood.)
- The **mood** of peace and timeless atmosphere of stanza 1 returns midway through stanza 4, to emphasise that the child's security is still intact:
  ". . . time seemed finished ere the ship passed by.", line 16 — time stands still: the passing of time is not important to, nor even noticed by, a child.
  (Time and eternity are key themes in Muir's poetry.)
- In line 15, we have both a simile and a pun on the word "sound": the **simile**, in which the water in the bay is compared to "sunken glass", takes the cliché — a glassy calm — and adds a further layer of meaning with "sunken", suggesting the almost solid aspect of still water. The reworking of the cliché gives the comparison a freshness and originality, appropriate to child's view.
- The **pun** on the word "sound" spreads the comparison to take in both senses, sight and hearing — the water in the bay is perfectly calm and silent — an image of perfect peace.
- We had a hint that the menace was still far off in line 13 — The long vowels in "so slow" emphasising the ship's inability to affect the boy; even time seems to stand still as it passes — as if it belongs to another time zone than his own.

Stanza 5.

- **Setting** — "Grey tiny rocks . . .", line 17; ". . . grasses threw straight shadows . . .", line 19.
- the landscape appears to provide further protection for the boy, e.g., in line 17, **personification**: the "rocks **slept** round him".
- The threat has passed with the ship and once more the **mood** is totally serene:
- ". . . tiny rocks slept", line 17; "Moveless . . .", line 18.
- Mentioning the child's father in line 2 and his mother in line 20 — as if they enclose the whole poem, which is concerned with the child, embracing him, giving a sense of unity in the family, echoed by the unity and harmony of the landscape.
- In the final line of the poem, the **repetition** of "his" in "his house, his mother . . . his name", stresses that he belongs to this place, with these people; calling his **name** clinches it.

Looking over the whole poem:
- **Setting**
  - General feeling of harmony of the landscape, of timelessness, eternity;
  - suggests the pureness of the child's view, uncontaminated by experience, memory, associations.
- We have a sense of child's unity with the landscape:
  - ". . . he lay upon the hill", line 1 — at one with the earth beneath him;
  - "In thought he saw . . . strand", lines 10–12 — fills his imagination with joy;
  - "Grey tiny rocks slept round him where he lay", line 17 — the rocks are tiny and sleeping, not threatening but surrounding, protecting him, like siblings or a litter of puppies — image of security. "Moveless as they . . .", line 18 — he is as one of the rocks.
- Attention to detail in the landscape suggests the fresh view of the child, regarding his surroundings with the interest of childhood, seeing things for the first time.
- The **structure** of the poem emphasises the mixing of the **moods**, with the menacing lines from lines 7–14 firmly enclosed by the serenity of the first stanza and the section from line 15 to the end; the surreal passage, lines 10–12, is bang in the middle. So we have alternating peace / menace / dream / menace / peace.
  - The underlying mood of menace serves to make the child's innocent feelings of peace and security the more poignant. It can't touch him yet but the future is out there waiting for him.
  - Reminds us that the poem is written by an adult looking back to his childhood, with the experience of adulthood and the world beyond the tiny, idyllic island of Wyre.

- **Poetic Form**
  - Regular: four-line stanzas — supports ideas of harmony between man and Nature and security of the state of childhood;
  - iambic pentameter occasionally slowed down with two strong stresses at start of line, e.g., line 1 — "Long time . . . ";
- rhyme pattern *abab*; note variation — "view" at end of line 17, echoed at start of line 18 — "He knew" — supports sense of unity in family and in landscape.

- **Literary Form**
  - Ballad influence — in word order, e.g., "Long time he lay . . .", line 1; ". . . rolled in mist away", line 6;
    — in lexical choice, e.g., "ere", line 16; "strand", line 12.
  - Language spoken in Orkney a bit archaic, like 17th century;
  - gives sense of ancestry, generations stretching back from this small boy — increases sense of his belonging.
  - Simple form fits theme of uncomplicated, secure childhood, and bare landscape.

EVALUATION

- Childhood — not just about Muir's childhood, but the state of childhood:
  - time of innocence — Eden, before the Fall;
  - perhaps the fundamental goodness of Man?
- Only possible if child is allowed to be close to Nature — in his autobiography, he wrote: "A child could not grow up in a better place than a farm; for at the heart of human civilisation is the byre, the barn and the midden." He believed that a farm provided a secure world for a child, the cyclical nature of farming activities providing continuity in the child's life.
- He saw such traditions and ritual as part of what he called the Fable, the underlying pattern of Man, our past which each individual re-enacts — the individual life, he called the Story.
- Implied criticism of modern society, which has lost touch with Nature — life today is mostly in towns and cities.

Using Your Notes for Revision: Checklist

UNDERSTANDING AND ANALYSIS *(Use these questions to revise important parts of the poem.)*

1. **Situation: summarise the situation presented in the poem**
    - Child lies on a hillside near his home during a long afternoon.
    - He is viewing the familiar landscape and imagining other shores.
    - A ship passes.
    - Evening comes and his mother calls him in.

2. **Setting: How does the setting contribute to the poet's presentation of his ideas about childhood?**
    - Poet creates an almost tangible sense of place — tiny island of Wyre, off Orkney, island of his own childhood, here remembered, perhaps partly imagined.
    - Orkney being quite bare, each hill stands out, protective barrier.
    - The islands appear to be gathered together, giving sense of unity.
    - Sense of whole; Wyre such a tiny island that child could see all of it, his entire world, as an entity.
    - He is aware of their separate unities but sees the landscape as a whole, the harmony / balance emphasised by contrasting words.
    - He can imagine the outside world only as more islands like his own — narrow experience of childhood.
    - General feeling is one of harmony of the landscape, of timelessness, eternity.
    - We have a sense of child's unity with the landscape.
    - Attention to detail in landscape suggests fresh view of child, regarding his surroundings with interest of childhood, seeing things for the first time.
    - Also suggests the pureness of the child's view, uncontaminated by experience, memory, associations.

3. **Mood / Atmosphere:**
    (a) **How the poet creates mood / atmosphere.**
    (b) **The effectiveness of the devices / techniques used by the poet to create a particular atmosphere.**
    (c) **How that mood / atmosphere contributes to the overall impact of the poem.**
    - Initial mood is one of timelessness, peace, security: metaphor, line 2; Imagery, line 4.
    - In stanza 2, the child's view pans out to the surrounding hills and islands: here the under-lying menace of the outside world / adulthood is introduced: lexical choice, line 8; pun, line 8.
    - In stanza 3, the mood is dream-like — daydreams almost surreal: Imagery, lines 10–12; -s, -l, -sh sounds.
    - In stanza 4, we come back to the menacing feel with the ship passing + pathetic fallacy, lexical choice, line 14;
    - but it is fused with the calm and timeless atmosphere of stanza 1: long vowels, line 13; simile, pun, line 15; time stands still, line 16.
    - In stanza 5, the threat has passed with the ship, mood is totally serene: personification, line 17; lexical choice, line 18.
    - Contrast: the underlying mood of menace serves to make the child's innocent feelings of peace and security the more poignant.
    - Structure: emphasises this poignancy, with the menacing lines firmly enclosed by the serenity of the first and last stanzas. It can't touch him yet but the future is out there waiting for him.
    - Reminds us that the poem is written by an adult looking back to his childhood, with the experience of adulthood and the world beyond the tiny, idyllic island of Wyre.

EVALUATION *(Use this question for exam practice.)*

4.   **Referring closely to the poem, consider the effectiveness of Muir's portrayal of childhood.**
- Childhood — main theme, introduced in title and stanza 1:
- shows child belonging in home surroundings, emphasises feelings of peace, calm;
- child's innocence and inexperience shown by the way he imagines other places as being just like his own small island;
- ship, passing in the distance, represents outside world; does not impinge on him yet but is there in his future — slightly menacing;
- when ship has gone past, back to childhood idyll.
- Muir regarded childhood as a kind of Eden, the innocence before the Fall / adulthood. Work through devices, which help to put across his idea of childhood.
- **Sound:** l-sounds throughout stanza 1 have a lulling effect;
- s-sounds throughout stanza 1 create a whispering effect;
- used to same effect in alliteration in line 3, line 13;
- both sounds appropriate to child lying on grassy slope on calm day, create feeling of harmony, all is well in child's world. These two sounds echo throughout the poem, supplemented by a sh-sound, e.g., in "shores", line 9; "shallow", line 11 — to give a feeling of hush.
- **Imagery:**
- **security** of childhood seen in imagery;
- "To his father's house below securely bound", line 2 — metaphor + quote / explain / comment;
- line 4, ". . . the black islands lying thick around" + quote / explain / comment;
- sense of **unity in the family** — mention of father in line 2 and mother in line 20 + quote, etc.;
- echoed by the **unity and harmony of the landscape** +quote / explain / comment;
- personification, line 17, + quote / explain / comment.
- In line 15, simile and a pun on the word "sound" + quote / explain / comment.
- In the final line of the poem, the repetition of "his" in "his house, his mother . . . his name", stresses that he belongs to this place, with these people; calling his **name** clinches it.
- **Contrast** — the child's innocent dream of the future intensifies the whole unworldly, dream-like nature of childhood, made more poignant by the underlying note of menace from the outside world + quote / explain / comment (**pun** on "straits" in line 8 — explain).
- The child's innocence is here imbued with the poet's adult experience of the world beyond the island, life beyond childhood.
- The child knows intuitively that a different world lies ahead of him and in his innocence, imagines it to be a reflection of his present life, peaceful and calm + quote / explain / comment;
- "straits" carries an underlying hint from the poet that the childhood idyll will not last into adulthood.
- Pathetic fallacy in line 14, "the black hill's **gloom**" + quote / explain / comment.
- The long vowels in "so slow" emphasise the ship's inability to affect the boy; even time seems to stand still as it passes — as if it belongs to another time zone than his own.
- **Poetic Form** — regular: four-line stanzas — supports ideas of harmony between man and Nature and the security of the state of childhood.
- **Literary Form** — Ballad influence — in word order and lexical choice + quote / explain / comment; gives sense of ancestry, generations stretching back from this small boy — increases sense of his belonging;
- simple form fits in with theme of uncomplicated, secure childhood, and bare island landscape.

making clear the extent to which you agree with him. (10 marks)
- Personal response but should refer to ideas in poem, e.g., narrow world of child, child's view of future, etc.

H — well developed and clear exposition of Muir's ideas of childhood, with good textual support and comment; Int. — clear understanding of ideas, with some textual support and comment.

Suggested Study Points — *The Horses*

UNDERSTANDING

1.   The situation
- Nuclear war has destroyed most of the world.
- No communications; machines rust; oxen pull ploughs, as in olden days.
- About a year later, strange horses appear, no-one knows from where.
- The horses pull the ploughs but people have different attitude towards them — no longer treat them as beasts lower than mankind.

2.   The themes
- Nuclear war.
- Destruction of civilisation by technology.
- Mystery and importance of animals / Nature.
- Modern society has lost its way.
- Fundamental goodness of humanity.
- Muir's Story and Fable.

ANALYSIS

1.   Structure
- narrative with flashback:
- line 1–4   prologue: introduction of horses;
- lines 5–30   flashback — immediate aftermath of nuclear attack;
- lines 31–50   narrative — arrival of horses;
- lines 51–53   epilogue: brings story up to time of telling.

§1: lines 1–4, Prologue:
- establishes **register**: **Saga** (story told, orally until 12th century, about great event(s) of the past, mainly Norwegian, Icelandic, but there are some sagas about earls of Orkney, called the Orkneyinga saga) — appropriate to sense of poem, going back to old ways.
- Archaic language: ". . . a twelvemonth after", line 1 — sets **tone** of saga;
- ". . . the strange horses came.": told in matter-of-fact way; Orkney people believed readily in legend, the supernatural or the fabulous;
- line 3, "Late in the evening . . .": supports the saga feel; detail suggests storyteller was there.
- line 4, by the time the horses arrived, they had come to terms with the situation:
- "covenant", line 4: **archaic / Biblical** word, usually used of an agreement made between God and a person or a people;
- line 2, "The seven days war . . .": according to the Bible, the world was created — and now apparently destroyed — in seven days;
- line 2, ". . . that put the world to sleep,":
- **Euphemism** — sounds pleasant but we know the effects of nuclear attack are far from that.
- **Irony** — It's what we do to our domestic animals when they are suffering.
- **Litotes** or **understatement** — Intensifies the enormity of wiping out almost the entire human race.

§2: lines 5–30, Flashback:
- *(a)*   Lines 5–12 continue the **Biblical analogy** with echoes of Genesis:
- "The seven days war" mentioned in line 2; the stages are now enumerated as in Genesis: line 7, "On the second day.."; line 9, "On the third day . . ."; line 10, "On the sixth day . . ."; nuclear war is a reversal of the Creation; suggests that nuclear war might have been God's way of destroying a civilisation that had gone wrong.

- **Mood / atmosphere** — lines 5–6, shocked silence: "We listened to our breathing and were afraid." — idea of the world being plunged into sudden silence, so quiet they could hear themselves breathing.

- In this section, **line layout** and **syntax** indicate halting narration in keeping with the mood:
    - line 7 — short line suggests gulp before narrator can go on;
    - line 8 — semicolons and end-stopped line suggest pauses, hesitation;
    - line 10 and line 11 — **caesurae**, all give idea of narrator's inability to believe this could happen;
    - lines 11–12 — "Thereafter / Nothing.": non-sentence, enjambment followed by full stop;
    - all emphasise the finality of the words.
- Matter-of-fact **tone**: relating events with no emotion — loss of communication, ship piled with dead bodies, plane plunges into sea, "Thereafter / Nothing." — combines with the syntax to give impression of people still in shock.
- Warship and plane are symbols of war, destruction; ship with dead bodies reminiscent of the curse of The Ancient Mariner?
- line 12 "The radios **dumb**": the word normally used of living creatures, especially human beings; **personification** makes the radios into a **symbol** of the technological age of Man.

(b) **lines 12–15** — vivid **image** of world's silence: radios turned on but no sound; **pun** on "still", line 13.
- **Repetition** of "stand", commas, "perhaps" and "million" in line 14 combine to give idea of the silence "All over the world.", line 15; caesura emphasises the completeness of the silence.

(c) **lines 15–20**, **tone** of resolution, determination to start afresh, strengthened by short, monosyllabic "But now", line 15 — both words individually introduce something new, different;
- **Repetition** in lines 15–17, which are identical in meaning, with each line adding something to build up to a climax in line 20 with "We would not have it again."
- "if", lines 15, 16 and 17, and at the **beginnings** of lines 16 and 17 gives added emphasis;
- the conditional "should speak", lines 15, 16 and 17, as well as the repetition of conditional "would not" in line 18, twice, each followed by word beginning with letter 'l', and line 20, "We would not have it again." following a **caesura** gains further intensity, and the end-stopped line gives it finality.
- Lines 19–20, "That old bad world that swallowed its children quick / At one great gulp.":
- **Personification** — intensifies the horror of nuclear war, like a monster from a horror movie;
- **pun** on "quick": suggests the suddenness of the disaster and also "quick" in the sense of living — people's lives were snuffed out. (Note no internal punctuation — ties in with sense of words.)

(d) **lines 20–23**, **tone** becomes reflective, sad:
- vivid **image** of whole nations lying dead, unburied, "Curled blindly in impenetrable sorrow,";
- "Curled" suggests the foetal position, a natural position to assume in time of fear or sorrow; also returning to the oblivion from which they came, appropriate to idea of "decreation";
- "blindly" has an element of irony: Man's moral blindness led to his destruction and radiation causes blindness, so blindness was both cause and result.
- Mystery of human existence: line 23, ". . . the thought confounds us with its strangeness."

(e) **lines 24–30**: vivid **image** of the devastation and aftermath of attack:
- rusting tractors lying about fields ". . . like dank sea-monsters couched and waiting", line 25: the **simile** highlights the destruction caused to the earth by such machinery as well as the uselessness of the tractors now, like dinosaurs from another age.
- **Direct speech**, line 27: suggests decision made by the whole community; the sense of it continues the idea in the simile of the tractors as once-living creatures, which will return to dust (the archaic feel of "loam" fits in with saga register).
- Lines 28–30 show their acceptance of the situation: oxen used to pull ploughs; the survivors have gone back generations, in terms of work methods.

§3: lines 31–50, The arrival of the horses
(a) **lines 31–32** — return to saga register with details, ". . . that evening / Late in the summer";
- **juxtaposition** suggests that the horses would come only when people had seen the error of their ways and were willing to make a fresh start. Confirmed by **line layout**, suggesting passage of time necessary for lessons to be learned.
- Note also the title: *The* Horses, particular horses, not just any horses — symbolic.

   (b)   **lines 33−37**: vivid, precise **image** of the horses' gradual approach, first sound then sight:
- **lexical choice**: "distant **tapping**", line 33 > "deepening **drumming**", line 34 > "hollow **thunder**", line 35 — a crescendo of noise, stopping as if seeking the way and then coming on with confidence.
- Then the horses are sighted, their heads ". . . like a wild wave charging", line 37: the simile reinforces the inexorability of their approach, their combined manes like waves crashing in on the shore, and justifies the reaction. ". . . and were afraid.", line 37.
- Man had exploited and then discarded horses in the past; now perhaps they were seeking revenge.

   (c)   **lines 38−50** take us back into the idea of myth, legend, fable — **saga**.
- Lines 40−41, "As fabulous steeds set on an ancient shield. / Or illustrations in a book of knights.":
- these **similes** emphasise the strangeness of the horses to the modern community;
- they also set up the horses as a **symbol** of the old ways of our ancestors, as if the horses have come to give mankind a second chance by taking them back in time, before civilisation took a wrong turning into the age of technology;
- line 42, "We did not dare go near them.": as if the people knew those were no ordinary beasts;
- line 43, **personification** — horses behave like human beings, "stubborn and shy";
- lines 43−44, idea that horses sent by ancestors of the survivors, to help them back on right path.
- line 45, ". . . that long-lost archaic companionship" i.e., between Man and Nature (Muir believed that our gravitation away from the countryside into "unnatural" habitats in towns and cities was the reason for our fall from grace; the horses had come to show the survivors the way back.)
- lines 46−47 carry on the idea of "companionship" in line 45 — they immediately recognised that those creatures were not "to be owned and used"; compare line 38, "sold";
- lines 48−50: **tone** of wonder: colts = new life, new generation; they will go on breeding;
- line 49, "Dropped in some wilderness of the broken world,": mystery of their origins = mystery of human life, rising like some phoenix from the ashes of civilisation to start afresh;
- line 50, ". . . new . . . from their own Eden": world of innocence, purity.

§4: Epilogue: lines 51−53, brings story up to time of telling: "Since then . . .";
- line 52, ". . . free servitude": **oxymoron** — the horses serve by pulling ploughs and carrying loads but remain free in spirit, unexploited; compare line 28, "We make our oxen . . .";
- people feel humbled by the horses' attitude to life, seek to follow their example;
- line 53, "Our life is changed;" — note singular "life" = the whole community, which, as presumably the sole survivors of the nuclear attack, represents the whole of mankind;
- "their coming our beginning": balanced phrase gives feeling of new balance in their lives.

Poetic Form
- Free verse form with speech rhythms appropriate to narrative, especially to oral transmission; lends reality, immediacy, naturalness, credibility.
- Long verse paragraphs and prose syntax used to great effect in creating atmosphere of devastation after nuclear attack and tension of the horses' approach.

EVALUATION

- Poem reflects fear of our society in 1950s that nuclear war would destroy civilised world;
- era of cold war, when western missiles were poised to meet a nuclear attack from the east, with mutual destruction the only outcome.

- Poem about destruction of civilisation as we know it, yet it is not a depressing poem:
- Muir has faith in human beings to regain the innocence of childhood — Eden.
- He believes human beings are fundamentally good;
- solution is to get back to Nature: small communities work together, in cities people are strangers; this loss of fellowship with neighbours has led us astray.
- Muir believes in a loving, forgiving God, Who will show us the way.
- In the poem, Man learns his lesson and gets back on the right path;
- but, is he saying the destruction of civilisation, as we know it, would be no bad thing?

Using Your Notes for Revision: Checklist

UNDERSTANDING AND ANALYSIS *(Use these questions to revise important parts of the poem.)*

1. **Situation: summarise the situation presented in the poem**
   - Nuclear war has destroyed most of the world.
   - No communications; machines rust; oxen pull ploughs, as in olden days.

   and explain the significance of the horses referred to in the title.
   - About a year later, strange horses appear, no-one knows from where.
   - It seems as if the horses would come only when people had seen the error of their ways and made a fresh start.
   - Title: *The* Horses, particular horses, not just any horses — symbolic;
   - they are compared to heraldic or fabulous horses, emphasising their strangeness;
   - the horses are presented as a **symbol** of the old ways of our ancestors, as if the horses have come to give mankind a second chance by taking them back in time, before civilisation took a wrong turning into the age of technology, which has now destroyed it.

2. **Tone: Trace and account for the variations in tone in the course of the poem.**
   - First few lines establish **register / tone of saga** — appropriate to sense of poem, going back to old ways.
   - Archaic language: sets tone of saga, line 1;
   - told in matter-of-fact way, line 3;
   - line 3, "Late in the evening . . .": supports the saga tone; detail suggests storyteller was there.
   - "covenant", line 4: archaic / Biblical word, appropriate to saga tone.
   - lines 5–6: tone of **shocked silence** as speaker recalls the first reactions of the survivors to the attack;
   - matter-of-fact tone : relating events with no emotion — loss of communication, ship piled with dead bodies, plane plunges into sea; "Thereafter / Nothing." — gives impression of people still in shock.
   - lines 15–20: tone of **resolution, determination to start afresh**, strengthened by short, monosyllabic "But now", line 15 — both words individually introduce something new, different;
   - repetition in lines 15–16, building up to a climax in line 20;
   - lines 20–23: tone becomes **reflective, sad**;
   - mystery of human existence, line 23.
   - We come back to **saga tone** in line 31 with details, continuing narrative.
   - In line 37, speaker recalls the **fear** they felt at the arrival of the horses, conveyed to us in lines 33–37 as we listen with the survivors to the gradual, inexorable approach of the horses.
   - Lines 48–50: tone of **wonder**: colts = new life, new generation; they will go on breeding;
   - line 49, "Dropped in some wilderness of the broken world,": mystery of their origins = mystery of human life, rising like some phoenix from the ashes of civilisation to start afresh;
   - line 50, ". . . new . . . from their own Eden": world of innocence, purity.
   - Final tone is one of **humility**: people feel humbled by the horses' attitude to life, seek to follow their example, lines 52–53.

3. **Evil of nuclear war:**
    Revise the effectiveness of the devices / techniques used by the poet in lines 1–30, to convey the evil of nuclear war.
    - Line 2, "that put the world to sleep" — **euphemism**, **irony**, **litotes**.
    - Lines 5–12 continue the **Biblical analogy** — echoes of Genesis: nuclear war is reversal of Creation; God's way of destroying civilisation that had gone wrong?
    - **Line layout** and **syntax** indicate hesitant, halting narration, indicating narrator still finds it hard to talk.
    - Lines 9–10, **image** of warship piled up with dead bodies and plane plunging into the sea are vivid symbols of war, destruction.
    - Lines 12–15, vivid **image** of world's silence: radios turned on but no sound;
    - **pun** on "still", line 13.
    - **Repetition** of "stand", commas, "perhaps" and "million" in line 14 combine to give idea of the unnatural silence "All over the world.", line 15; caesura emphasises the completeness of the silence.
    - Lines 20–23, vivid image of whole nations lying dead, unburied; foetal position suggests reversal of birth process; **irony** in "blindly".
    - Lines 24–30, vivid image of the devastation and aftermath of attack: rusting tractors — **simile**.
    - Line 27, continues the image of the tractors as once-living creatures which will return to dust ties in with "decreation" idea.

EVALUATION *(Use this question for exam practice.)*

4. **To what extent would you agree that, although it deals with the aftermath of the destruction of civilisation as we know it, this is not a depressing, pessimistic poem?**

    (10 marks)

    - Agree — poem ends in tone of humility and hope for the future;
    - Muir has faith in human beings to regain the innocence of childhood — Eden;
    - he believes human beings are fundamentally good.
    - The solution is to get back to Nature: small communities work together, in cities people are strangers; this loss of fellowship with neighbours has led us astray.
    - His portrayal of the horses makes this clear.
    - Lines 33–37, vivid, precise **image** of the horses' gradual approach emphasises their power and the inexorability of their approach, as if sent by some supernatural force + explanation.
    - Lines 40–41, **similes** — horses as **symbol** of the old ways of our ancestors + explanation.
    - People's immediate reaction to horses: knew those were no ordinary beasts.
    - Lines 43–44, idea that horses sent by ancestors of the survivors, to help them back on right path.
    - Line 45, ". . . that long-lost archaic companionship" + explanation, continued in lines 46–47.
    - Lines 48–50, **tone** of wonder: colts = new life, new generation; they will go on breeding.
    - Line 49, "Dropped in some wilderness of the broken world,": mystery of their origins = mystery of human life, rising like some phoenix from the ashes of civilisation to start afresh.
    - Line 50, ". . . new . . . from their own Eden": world of innocence, purity;
    - line 52, ". . . free servitude": **oxymoron** + quote / explain / comment.
    - Longer term effect of horses on survivors.
    - **Biblical analogy** – see page 48:
    - Muir believes in a loving, forgiving God, Who will show us the way.
    - In the poem, Man learns his lesson and gets back on the right path.
    - *Note:* *Students may, of course, **disagree** with the question but should not go into evils of nuclear war in any great detail, certainly not to the extent of taking them away from the text. Answers that do not agree with the question should at least acknowledge and deal with the optimistic aspect, which is certainly Muir's attitude. Disagreement may be on the grounds of Muir's apparently naive belief that technology can be wiped out; the student may suggest that it is not possible to "disinvent" nuclear power, for example, but should see that the uses to which technology has been put might be redirected.*
    - *H — well developed argument for or against question, with good textual support and thoughtful comment; Int. — clear response to the question with some textual support and thoughtful comment.*

Unseen Textual Analysis: Marking Schemes — *Horses*

Levels: Higher and Intermediate 2

All answers should be supported by close reference to the text.

(Based on an authentic incident — in his wartime diary, he writes of seeing horses in a field from a train in a station: "They looked wild and legendary, as if they had just risen full-grown from the mould . . . necks arching and leaping, like four waves overtopping each other . . . I felt that these creatures had been fed in fields of inalienable strangeness, in quite another world from the world we knew . . .")

1. **Referring to stanza 1 (lines 1–4), describe the effect that the horses have on the poet.** (2) U
   - They frighten him ½ + "They seemed terrible" ½ +
   - Momentarily ½ + "just now" ½.

2. **Explain the relationship between line 5 and stanza 1.** (2) A
   - Stanza 1, wonders why ½ + the horses frightened him ½ +
   - Line 5 suggests reason ½: + they bring back memories of his childhood ½.

3. **Basing your answer on information drawn from stanzas 2–6, lines 5–24, what kind of childhood would you say the poet had?** (2) U
   - Brought up on a farm which had working horses — ½ +
   - "stony grange", line 4 (farm steading); "trod the stubble down", line 9; "field" line, 10; "furrows", line 16 — ½ +.
   - Seemed to have a lot of freedom as a child — ½ +
   - allowed to roam around the fields; still out at dusk: stanzas 3, 4 and 5 — ½.

   H — should get both points, supported by textual reference, well-explained + intelligent comment;
   Int. — first point, supported by textual reference, explained + brief comment.

4. **Referring to the first three stanzas of the poem, lines 1–12, show how the poet suggests:**
   (a) **the size of the horses;** (2) A
   - line 1, "lumbering" — size, heaviness of horses;
   - line 4, their heavy horseshoes strike sparks of fire on cobbled yard;
   - line 5, "fearful" — cf. "terrible", line 3 — wonder of childhood, smallness of child cf. to size of horse;
   - line 11, "great hulks";
   - line 9, "trod the stubble down" — **weight** of horses.

   H — any two, well explained + intelligent comment; Int. – any two, clearly understood + some comment.

   (b) **the power / strength of the horses;** (2) A
   - line 3, "wild and strange" — power, stature of the horses;
   - line 6, "through the blackening rain" — power of elements linked to power of horses; both beyond the control of Man; (Muir wrote: "horses have a power of their own, cars do not.");
   - line 7, simile — hooves move up and down, cf. to mechanical pistons — power, never-tiring;
   - line 8, alliteration — intensifies the sense of effortless strength of horses.
   - line 9, "conquering hooves . . ."

   H — any two, well explained + intelligent comment; Int. – any two, clearly understood + some comment.

   (c)   **the fabulous / legendary aspect of the horses;**   **(2) A**
- Line 10, "ritual" — horses are part of the comforting, cyclical nature of life on farm;
- . . . seraphim of gold' — (singular form "seraph": angel of the highest of the nine orders) — glory of horses, sacred beasts to be revered — horses part of myth, legend — Muir's "Fable"; (Orkney retains its past heritage; nearer to the Middle Ages than to the present. Muir said he was born before the Industrial Revolution, and caught up with present only when he moved to Glasgow.)
- Line 12, metaphor, alliteration: heraldic image, cf. *The Horses*, ". . . fabulous steeds . . ." — horses are part of the past; "ecstatic" here, I think, is meant literally in the sense of standing, rearing up, rampant in the heraldic sense, but also connotations of "larger than life"; (Modern students will understand the latter meaning only too well!) used here suggests horse as symbol, like lion rampant on Royal standard;
- "monsters" — strangeness, not to be controlled by men, cf. "terrible", line 3; "fearful", line 5.

H — any two, well explained + intelligent comment; Int. – any two, clearly understood + some comment.

5.   **Show how the poet uses light imagery in stanzas 4 to 6, lines 13–24, to convey:**
    (a)   **the beauty of the horses;**   **(3) A**
- lines 13–14, intense appreciation of the beauty of the horses, felt by child as "They marched . . . . to the sinking sun" — horses linked to beauty of sunset;
- line 15, "The light flowed . . . flakes": combines light with beauty of movement;
- line 17, ". . . at dusk . . . gloom" = gloaming, twilight, dusk, continues idea of setting sun, line 14; links horses with life-giving force of the sun, starting and stopping work as the sun rises and sets;
- line 19, "glowing" echoes "gloam", line 18; manifestation of "mysterious fire";
- lines 21–22, simile — "brilliant . . . wide as night / Gleamed . . ." — starry image.

    (b)   **the mystical / magical aspect of the horses;**   **(3) A**
- line 19, "mysterious fire"; they give off a strange, unworldly glow;
- line 20, "smouldering" — as if light comes from within, some mystical power illuminating their bodies, cf. "magic power", line 4;
- lines 21–22, simile — "brilliant . . . wide as night / Gleamed . . ." — link to Nature, starry image, as fathomless as the night sky;
- line 22, "cruel apocalyptic light" — suggests they can see into the future (when Man will reject them, and they know this wrong turning on Man's part will lead to the end of civilisation as suggested in *The Horses*?)

For each part, (a) and (b), H — at least three examples, effects fully explained + intelligent comment;
Int. — at least two examples, effects clearly understood + some comment.

6.   **How appropriate is the poetic form used in this poem?**
- Ballad form appropriate to recording an incident / telling a story;   **(2) A**
- Appropriate to theme — the old ways, the past, nostalgia; Muir's idea of the Fable: "mute ecstatic monsters on the mould", line 12;
- simple / regular form appropriate to uncomplicated childhood.

Any two, justified, for both levels.

7.   **To what extent do you consider the final stanza of the poem to be an effective and fitting conclusion to the poem, in terms of**

    (a)   **structure;**
- comes **back to present time** in last stanza: **(1) AE**
- stanza 1 — present time: "just now", line 2; stanzas 2–6 — flashback to childhood.

(b)   **tone;**   **(3) AE**
- • Tone of last stanza an appropriate follow-up to the flashback section;
- - encapsulates the effect on him of seeing the horses in the field.

- • Line 25, "Ah" + ! — tone of regret, longing as the picture of his childhood fades from his mind and he is back in the present — as if trying desperately to hold on to it.
- • The last line, "Were bright and fearful presences to me" — past tense — tone of sorrow and longing.

H — should make the connection between tone and effect on him of incident more explicit than Int.

(c)   **theme?**   **(6) UE**
- • Title refers to all horses, not just the ones poet sees — symbol of the old ways, the past, ancient civilisation, when Man was closer to Nature;
- - technology has impoverished Man's spirituality, his sensitivity, his soul;
- - now retained only in childhood, a time of innocence and wonder, a kind of Eden.

- • Line 26, metaphor — "that dread country crystalline " — Eden of his childhood — quote / explain / comment — — "dread" = to be regarded with awe, wonder, respect, to be worshipped? — "crystalline" — pure, clear, uncomplicated, beautiful nature of childhood.

- • Line 27, metaphor — "the blank field"= Garden of Eden before the sin of Adam, cf. "bare field", line 2;
- - links childhood directly to horses, which sparked off the memory presented in poem up to this point;
- • "the still-standing tree" — alliteration, compound-word gives phrase stature, reference to tree, which would be cut down to be used as The Cross — images of purity, sinlessness which Muir connects to childhood.

- • Line 28, "presences" — such pictures of Eden, etc., were real to him as a child;
- - "bright and fearful" — echoes line 6, linking his feelings about those images of faith directly to his childish feelings towards the horses; he loved and dreaded them, with a passion he could neither understand nor articulate, but, with a child's intuition, knew he should worship them.

- • He longs for the purity of spirit and the simplicity of the life he knew as a child.
- - The horses symbolise not only his own childhood, but a past age, when Man was closer to Nature, before he took a wrong turning along the path of technology, losing his purity, his spirituality, his soul, like the Fall from the Garden of Eden.

H — fully developed discussion on Muir's Eden might be expected, if other poems in the chapter have been studied; may refer to "Childhood". Difference between grades will be seen in grasp of Muir's ideas of childhood. Mark on merit.

Level: Intermediate 1

1.   **Explain, in your own words, what the poet is watching, at the beginning of the poem.**   **(1) U**
- • Horses ½ + ploughing a field ½.

2.   (a)   **Why do the horses make such an impression on the poet?**   **(1) U**
- • They bring back memories of his childhood.
     (b)   **Quote from the poem to support your answer at** *(a)*.   **(1) A**
- • "Perhaps some childish hour has come again", line 5.

3.   *"Those lumbering horses . . ."* (line 1)
     (a)   **What does that phrase tell you about the horses?**   **(2) A**
- • They are big (1) + heavy (1).
     (b)   **Write down and explain a phrase from stanza 3, lines 9–12, which gives the same idea as "lumbering".**   **(2) A**
- • "conquering hooves", line 9 (1) / "trod the stubble down", line 9 (1) / "great hulks", line 11 (1) / "monsters" line 12 (½) + simple explanation (1).

4. (a) **Write down the simile from stanza 2, lines 5–8.**   **(1) A**
    • "(Their hooves) like pistons in an ancient mill".
    (b) **Explain, in your own words, what is being compared to what.**   **(1) A**
    • Horses' feet compared to metal cylinders / heavy machinery.
    (c). **What does this comparison tell us about the horses?**   **(1) A**
    • Powerful; tireless.

5. **Basing your answer on information drawn from stanzas 2–6, lines 5–24, what kind of childhood would you say the poet had?**   **(2) U**
    • Brought up on a farm which had working horses: (1) +
    - "stony grange", line 4 (farm steading); "trod the stubble down", line 9; "field", line 10; "furrows", line 16. (Any two — ½ + ½)

6. (a) **How did the poet feel about horses when he was a child?** *Any two of:*   **(2) U**
    • frightened of them; thought they were huge; thought they had some mysterious power; thought they were beautiful.
    (b) **Quote from the poem to support your answer at (a).** *As appropriate:*   **(1) A**
    • "terrible", line 1; or "fearful", line 6; "gigantic", line 18; "like magic power", line 4; "rapture", line 13.

7. (a) **Which farming process is referred to in lines 9–10?**   **(1) U**
    • Ploughing up stubble field.
    (b) **Why does the poet refer to this process as "ritual"?**   **(1) A**
    • Happened every year; cyclical.

8. *"And their great hulks were seraphim of gold"*, line 11.
    (a) **Seraphim are angels. What do you find surprising about this description of the horses?** — *Must get the contrast:*   **(2) A**
    • Horses are great hulking brutes (1) + angels are dainty, flimsy creatures (1),
    (b) **How is the idea in "seraphim of gold" continued in lines 13–16?**   **(2) A**
    • "sinking sun", line 14 (1) + "light flowed off their bossy sides", line 15 (1).
    (c) **Write down another image, from stanza 5, lines 17–20, which uses the idea of light.**   **(1) A**
    • "glowing with mysterious fire". line 19 (1) or "lit their smouldering bodies", line 20
    (d) **Describe, in your own words, the picture this image brings into your mind.**   **(2) A**
    • Own words essential — *Mark on merit.*

9. (a) **Which phrase in the poem do you think best presents the horses as exciting or strange or beautiful?**   **(1) E**
    (b) **Explain why you chose that phrase.**   **(1) AE**
    • Any reasonable phrase (1) + explanation which demonstrates appreciation of quality.

10. *"Ah, now it fades! it fades! and I must pine"*, line 25.
    (a) **What has the poet been picturing in his mind?**   **(1) U**
    • His childhood days (1); the horses of his childhood (½); horses (0).
    (b) **Explain why you think it was a happy or a sad picture.**   **(2) E**
    • Time of happiness, no worries; could roam around the fields, carefree; simple life, close to Nature then; peace (poem based on incident during war); Muir a child at end of last century.
    - No tractors then, not many cars.
    (c) **How does he feel when the picture fades?**   **(1) A**
    • Sad (1) / longs to be back in those days (1).

Suggested Outline Plans for Critical Essays

1. **Choose a poem in which the poet puts across his views on some aspect of human life. Discuss the techniques / devices he has used to convey his ideas to you and the extent to which you consider those ideas to be reasonable.** (*Childhood*)
   §1. Title, poet, brief statement of aspect of life (childhood) and poet's view of it — idyllic.
   §2. Child in poem — mood of peace, security; how created in first and last stanzas + quote.
   §3. Contrast in stanzas 2–4, child's dream of future v. poet's adult reflections + quote.
   §4. Personal response — reasonableness of poet's views.

2. **Choose a poem in which the poet's skill in the use of linguistic devices makes a significant contribution to the poem's impact and show how this skill has helped you to understand the poet's ideas and / or beliefs. (You may wish to deal with such aspects as imagery, lexical choice, syntax . . .)** [(*a*) *Childhood*; (b) *The Horses*].
   (*a*) §1. Title, brief summary of ideas / beliefs dealt with in poem — childhood innocence, idyll.
   §2. Sound effects — l / s / sh-sounds; imagery of peace, security; anthropomorphism + quote.
   §3. Contrast between surface and underlying moods: pun on "straits"; ship as symbol + quote.
   §4. Personal response to poet's ideas.

   (b) §1. Title, brief summary of ideas / beliefs dealt with in poem — destructive power of technology.
   §2. Evils of nuclear war — analogy with Creation; vivid images of silence / devastation + quote.
   §3. Horses as symbol of old ways, sent by ancestors — imagery: mystery/ power of horses.
   §4. Personal response to idea modern society has gone wrong, lost contact with Nature.

3. **Choose a poem which tells a story and show how the poet uses the particular techniques / devices of the narrative form to put across his ideas and beliefs.** (*The Horses*)
   §1. Title, brief summary of ideas / beliefs dealt with in poem — destructive power of technology.
   §2. Structure: flashback adds immediacy; narrator lends credibility esp. to description and feelings.
   §3. Saga tone — how achieved — appropriate to thesis of returning to old ways; free verse.
   §4. Personal response to optimistic conclusion — how feasible?

4. **Choose a poem, which has an important message to convey. Explain the significance of the subject and show how the poetic devices used in the poem help to convey the importance of its theme. (You may wish to deal with such aspects as poetic / literary form, analogy, symbolism, imagery . . .).** (*The Horses*)
   §1. Title, brief summary of message and its importance — must get back to Nature to survive.
   §2. Narrative form; saga tone; verse form — see question 3 above.
   §3. Analogy and imagery convey evils of advanced technology / nuclear war — see question 2.
   §4. Personal response to symbolism /imagery conveying power/ mystery of horses — convincing?

5. **Compare and contrast two poems by the same writer which touch on the relationship between Man and Nature, making clear in your evaluation of the techniques / devices used in the poems which, in your opinion, puts the poet's ideas across more strongly.** (*Childhood* and *The Horses*)
   §1. Titles and brief summaries of how each poem touches on Man / Nature relationship.
   §2. *Childhood* — child as part of Nature, very close, childhood as time of innocence, idyll + quote.
   §3. *The Horses* – society/ adult has lost closeness; advanced technology destructive + quote.
   §4. Personal response — which poem puts over ideas more strongly; e.g., might take view that in *Childhood*, poet is looking back, through rose-coloured spectacles — or in *The Horses* that he is looking ahead and overreacting to cold war situation of 1950s.

CHAPTER 4 — George Mackay Brown

Suggested Study Points: *Hamnavoe*

UNDERSTANDING

1. **The situation**
   The poet's father, a postman, is delivering letters round the streets of Hamnavoe (Stromness). He uses this framework to present the community / way of life through the eyes of his father.

2. **The theme(s)**
   - Tribute to father.
   - Dignity / importance of simple people.
   - Celebration of a community / way of life.

ANALYSIS

§1: lines 1–12 — morning in Hamnavoe (Norse-haven bay).

- Line 1, "penny letters" — introduces father as postman; "penny" dates it back to the poet's childhood; also suggests frugality — postman would not be paid much;
- line 2, "opening and shutting like legends" — sense of the **past** within the present ("opening and shutting" suggests glimpses); father following generations of postmen, becomes the essence of the messenger, bringer of news, an important Christian symbol;
- line 3: **metaphor** links with "legends", before civilisation; **sound effect: synecdoche**, focuses on the raucous cries of gulls; **contrast** with quiet man going about his work, intensified by two shorter lines; line 4, with three strong stresses, all suggest the town awakening to a new day.
- Line 5, **enjambment** — suggests movement of the postman's journey; **caesura** — pause to introduce the next **image**, "Herring boats", suggests close community, all pulling together. These two techniques recur throughout the poem, with same effect.
- Line 6, "puffing red sails"; line 7, "leaned" — visual image of fishing boats; "tillers" — **pun** — cultivators of the sea, as crofters work the land; many islanders did both; line 7, "of cold horizons" — **metaphor** — hard life of the fishermen, braving the elements, to bring in fish;
- line 8, "gull-gaunt" — **compound word**, connects the two words, intensified by **alliteration**; freshness / surprise as well as compression of meaning — fewer gulls suggests the distance from the shore but gulls link fishermen to the land; "gaunt" also suggests the grim situation;
- line 9, "dark nets" — under the water, but also bringing death; "sudden" — movement of fish; "silver" — accurate picture of herring but also suggests their value for the community, cf. Neil Gunn's "silver darlings"; "harvests" — suggests large number of fish caught; also link to **crofters**, cf. "tillers", line 6 — whole image intensified by **alliteration**; note also **enjambment**.
- Line 10, **alliteration** continued into next **image** — stallion at the town fountain — adds to idea of interdependent community. **Contrast** between powerful stallion and "sweet" water; **contrast** continues in **lexical choice**, line 11 — "dredged" suggests huge amount of water needed to assuage a huge thirst; implies power of horse; also suggests noise of drinking;
- line 12, "steel-kissed" — **compound word** emphasises the contrast between hardness of steel and softness of "kissed", referring to the horseshoes striking sparks on the cobbled street; reminiscent of Muir's *Horses* — "magic power on the stony grange".
- **sense of place:** closes (not tenement closes but narrow passages leading off the street); gulls place it by the sea; harbour steps, line 5; fishing boats on horizon and stallion — two most important livelihoods.
- **sense of time:** early morning; time for postman but also for fishermen, crofters . . .

§2: lines 13–24 — afternoon.

- Line 13, "noon" indicates passage of time; "Hard" suggests sense of **merchants**' purpose, but also an appropriate epithet for those men; bearded, mature, well practised in their wiles.

- Line 14, image intensified by **alliteration**; *p* and *t* sounds are **onomatopoeic**; **hypallage** — pipe-spitting pier-head" — also **synecdoche**, intensified by the **compound word**, focuses on the pipes and the spitting rather than on the **old men** — who are not impressed by the merchants; "strolled" suggests ease, **contrasting** with hard life of fishermen;
- line 15, "Holy with greed" — **metaphor** — profit / money is their religion, pursued as rigorously as religious fanatics live their faith; continued in "chanting" and line 16, "slow grave . . ."; "jargon" — sets them apart from the rest; GMB's father a great egalitarian: disapproval unmistakeable.
- Line 17: **juxtaposition** of tinker and merchants emphasises **contrast** between the two types;
- "keened" — **tinker** advertising his services — suggests the unhappy lot of the tinker, scraping a living mending kettles and pans; contrasts with the "chanting" of the successful merchants. **Simile** links tinker with gulls through sound; the tinker is a recurrent figure in GMB's works. Imbued with the freedom of the gulls, he wanders, not rooted to one place, his life a constant journey; he is to be welcomed and treated with respect when he comes into the community; "tartan" — tinker wearing a plaid? line 18: "cuithe-hung" — "cuithe" is an Orkney word, describing a coalfish before fully grown, hung up to dry — the perfect snack for a gull; similarly, knocking on doors, crying out his services is the tinker's means of feeding himself.
- Line 19, "trudged" suggests **crofter lass** has difficulty in walking through the mud; also weary from hard work, early start; "lavish dung" — **oxymoron** — lavish, literally abundant quantity; "dung" — unpleasant, noisome. Line 20, "in a dream" — **contrast** with what she is walking through! "cornstalks and milk" —**symbols** of new life (corn), femininity (milk) . . . thinking of her young man perhaps, or just a simple country girl's dream of being a wife and mother.
- Line 21: pub; number 3 — trinity — Wise Men — signals that these are good men, who have earned their leisure in their old age, not to be confused with the four bearded merchants; "blue elbows" indicates **old fishermen**, wearing fishermen's jerseys; **synecdoche** — focuses on elbows, lifting and lowering the glasses, "bending the elbow" in common parlance — they drink all day — perhaps slight disapproval, but tempered with understanding, here.
- Line 22, **sea imagery** links the old men with the sea — **simile**; **lexical choice**: "spumy": froth of beer = sea foam; line 23, "amber" — colour of beer and sunset glow; "ebbed" = tides;
- line 24, "black dregs" — darkness of night = last of beer — also indicates passage of time / life.

§3: lines 25–36 — evening.

- The next two **images** are vigorous in contrast to the old men in the bar: line 25: the long o sound suggests the **fishermen's** determined progress; "furrows" anticipates the **simile** — link with crofters; plough a **symbol** of life-giving fertility: fishermen and crofters provide food. Line 26, **metaphor** — "blizzards" reflects colour of gulls and their profusion.
- **Caesura** — pause before the next stage in the process: the **fisher girls** gut and clean fish;
- line 27: **zeugma** — flash of knives, speed / dexterity in their use; "dirge" as object of "flashed" suggests the bursts of song in Gaelic tradition; **lexical choice**: "dirge" — dead herring, also mournful sound of many Gaelic airs; zeugma links the two, gutting and singing, the singing helping the work along; line 28: "drifts" connects with "blizzards" in line 26.
- Line 29: "penny wands" — as in line 1, "penny" suggests frugality: the **boys** have no fancy fishing rods; "wands" suggests the magic of fishing to a young boy (GMB possibly writing from experience); "lured" suggests a natural skill of the boys who will grow up to be the next generation of fishermen, reminding us of the innate bond between fishermen and the sea;
- "gleams" — **synecdoche**, focusing on the silver sheen of the fish, adds to idea of magic;
- line 30: "tangled veins of the flood": **personification** — seaweed / tangle; "veins" suggests that the sea, like the land, is part of the community; "flood" — poetic word with Biblical connotations.
- **Caesura** — pause before next **image** of grief emphasises the interconnections; **pun** on "blind" — blinds pulled down at windows; people engrossed by their grief; line 31: all houses in close grieving — community like one big family; line 32: "shrouded nets" — **pun** on "shrouded" — the death at sea of fisherman, or a boat lost; we sense the grief shared by the postman.

- The solution to the grief is in the next **image**, indicated through the **juxtaposition** and **contrast** between the silent grief behind shrouded windows and the loud, public worship:
- line 33: **metonymy**: "The Kirk" = the worship and singing of the congregation; **metaphor** — "a gale of psalms" — suggests sound of singing, strong and heartfelt — clearly relished by the postman — rising to Heaven, like the wind; "heaving" continues metaphor — strength / power / purpose;
- line 34: "tumult of roofs" — **hyperbole**: the noise is so strong that it seems to be transferred to the roofs; fresh re-working of cliché: raising the rafters; "freighted" suggests transport of heavy goods, reinforcing the strength of the sound; uplifting atmosphere.
- Lines 34–35 — **caesura** — pause before the next **image**: "lovers / Unblessed by steeples . . ." — **synecdoche** focuses on the outward show of the Church, i.e., the steeple; also **metonymy**: steeple used to mean the sacrament of marriage conferred by the Minister.
- Line 36: **metaphor** — homely image — **conceit** — of moon as a buttered oatcake, may suggest that love is simple, natural, rather than the romantic notions associated with lovers and the moon; but, knowing GMB's religious leanings, perhaps he is saying the lovers "unblessed" (a negative) cannot soar spiritually, like the faithful whose psalms fly straight to heaven?
- People in church — working day must be over — and moon, indicate passage of time.

§4: lines 37–45 — poet's tribute to his father.

- Line 37: "He" — back to "My father" of line 1; saving paraffin by putting out light as soon as possible; postman is still working after nightfall, having been all round the district;
- line 38: **oxymoron** — "gay poverty" — did not let his penurious existence get him down; the effect of the oxymoron is to intensify the cheerfulness in spite of the hardship;
- line 39: "seapink innocence" — **metaphor** — sea pink is the name of a plant commonly known as thrift. GMB uses it here, all one word, as an adjective, "-pink" suggesting the child; the whole word meaning that, as a child, he was not constantly made aware of the financial hardship suffered by the family; he was allowed to be carefree, the burden of worry borne by his parents; he is grateful for the food and shelter they provided: line 40: "the worm" — an apt **metaphor** for hunger, and "black wind" = dark and cold; poet / family part of this community;
- line 41: "under equality's sun" — GMB brought up to believe in equality among people, regardless of material wealth; line 42: rich and poor, we all come to the same end.
- Line 43: "in the fire of images" — a **metaphor** within a metaphor! — his writing / this poem, white-hot (another one!) with images; line 44: **pun** — "I put my hand" — I write; also he has forged this tribute to his father out of the fire of his creative genius, not always a painless process?
- Line 45: "save" = record; "for him" = in his honour. Expression of respect, admiration, love.

Looking over the whole poem

- **Poetic Form** — regular line layout: 4-line stanzas, lines 3 and 4 shorter than lines 1 and 2; slight variations in syllable and stress patterns; follows the rhythm of Orkney speech, variations between low and high notes, with frequent silences produced by caesurae. Shorter lines add impact to the images, in the same way that a short sentence makes a good firm conclusion.
- No rhyme + enjambment, appropriate to postman's journey and narrative style / **structure**.
- **Contrast** points up variety of types in population; **juxtaposition** emphasises how they come together, adding up to a whole community.
- **Characters** — apart from father, are types in the community, mostly described in groups.
- **Religious undertone** — father also = Heavenly Father? Always a consideration in GMB.

EVALUATION

- Poem moves from one man > community > human condition.
- Elemental relationship between man and land / sea.
- What poet reveals of himself — not much, but more than in most of his poems.

Using Your Notes for Revision: Checklist

UNDERSTANDING AND ANALYSIS *(Use these questions to revise important parts of the poem.)*

1. **Situation:**
    (a) **Note the situation presented in *Hamnavoe*.**
    - The poet's father, a postman, is delivering letters round the streets of Hamnavoe.

    (b) **Note how the poet uses this situation as a framework for the poem.**
    - Narrative follows postman on his round, providing a moving picture, slide show of the community, noting what he sees and revealing his attitudes.
    - Starts in early morning in streets of Hamnavoe, when postman starts his shift.
    - Sound of gulls, fishing boats already out on the horizon, stallion at the town fountain.
    - Clearly disapproves of the money-grubbing merchants and perhaps too of the old men spitting on the pier.
    - Moving out from the town, he meets a tinker and a crofter lass.
    - Back in town, he passes the pub and we sense his slight disapproval but understanding of the old men, who spend their days drinking.
    - The boats are returning with their catch, which the fisher girls are waiting to process; we sense his admiration for both groups.
    - Passing the harbour, boys are fishing; a close has blinds drawn for a sea-related death.
    - The swelling sound of singing from the church seems to uplift him; he seems to regard the "unblessed" lovers more with regret than disapproval.
    - Finally, he switches off his lantern after his last delivery. His day's work is finished.

2. **Mood / atmosphere: Think about the way the poet uses sound effects and contrast to create atmosphere / mood in his descriptions of the place and people and the way they interconnect.**
    - Morning breaks with loud crying of gulls (**sound**); fishing boats already on horizon; line 5, "salt and tar steps" — this is a working place, sense of activity.
    - Line 10 — stallion at the fountain — brings in the other form of work and it is right in middle of town, a familiar sight in the community, an important part of their lives.
    - At the pier-head — merchants "strolled . . . slow grave jargon" — another layer of the community; old men smoking pipes: though retired, still drawn to the shore; provides **contrast** with activity in earlier lines.
    - Tinker "keening" (**sound**) — suggests unhappy; **contrasted** with "crofter lass" dreaming.
    - Pub The Arctic Whaler — pub is a gathering place in the community — naming it makes it more real; old men at the end of their lives.
    - Fishing boats coming into port; girls singing as they process the heaps of fish: hard ways to earn a living but they remain cheerful.
    - **Contrasted** with carefree boys fishing with cheap rods — the magic of the catch.
    - Their happiness **contrasted** with grief behind the drawn blinds.
    - This silence (sound) **contrasted**, in turn, with **sound** of loud singing in the church,
    - which is **set against** the **sound** of quiet murmurs of "unblessed" lovers.
    - The postman / observer of the scene **contrasted** with the community, but sense of his quiet belonging.

3. **Techniques / devices: The poem is made up largely of a series of snapshots of the community. Revise the effectiveness the techniques / devices used to create each image, and what each adds to the overall impact of the poem.**
    - Details in Suggested Study Points, pages 58–60:
        - (a)   the herring boats. lines 5–9; visual quality; pun / metaphor; compound word / alliteration;
        - (b)   the stallion at fountain, lines 10–12; contrast; lexical choice;
        - (c)   the merchants, lines 13–16; lexical choice, precise detail, metaphor;
        - (d)   the tinker, lines 17–18; lexical choice, sound, simile;
        - (e)   the crofter lass, lines 18–20; lexical choice, oxymoron, contrast, symbolism;
        - (f)   the old fishermen, lines 21–24; number 3, visual quality, synecdoche, sea imagery;
        - (g)   the fishing boats, lines 25–26; sound, simile, metaphor;
        - (h)   the fisher girls, lines 26–28; zeugma, lexical choice, visual quality;
        - (i)   the boys fishing, lines 29–30; lexical choice, synecdoche, personification;
        - (j)   the houses of mourning, lines 30–32; puns;
        - (k)   the singing in the Kirk, lines 33–34; metonymy, metaphor, sound, hyperbole;
        - (l)   the lovers, lines 34–36: synecdoche, metaphor / conceit;
        - (m)   the poet as a child, lines 39–40: metaphors.

    - Note, also, contrasting, juxtaposed images, e.g., merchants v. tinker.

EVALUATION *(Use this question for exam practice.)*

4. **How effective do you think the poet has been in his use of everyday events and simple people to comment on the human condition? You should refer closely to the text to support each point made. (10 marks)**
    - The poem begins and ends with the poet's father and is a personal tribute to him, but it develops into a celebration of this way of life and the implication that this is as life should be.
    - Sense of past in line 2 sets up the universal aspect: poet's father seen as following in footsteps of generations of postmen; messenger, bringer of news an important Christian symbol.
    - Two main activities represented by boats, personified in lines 5–9, and stallion, invested with magical properties: "touched / Fire . . .", lines 11–12 + quote / explain / comment.
    - Characters are types — merchants, old men, fisher girls, boys — and, apart from tinker and the crofter lass, presented in number rather than as individuals.
    - What does he say about the human condition?
    - Importance of simple people like fishermen and crofters, fisher girls and postmen;
    - in spite of hard lives, they remain cheerful — girls sing as they work — they have an innate dignity, personified particularly in the poet's father, through whose eyes we view the community, of which he is very much a part.
    - Close relationship between fishermen and sea: personifies boat, as if men and boat are one; boys fishing, fishermen of the future, seem to have an innate ability to catch fish + quote / explain / comment.
    - Images presented in poem interconnect through syntax, juxtaposition, enjambment and techniques running over from one image to the next — representing the entity that is the community + quote / explain / comment.

    - GMB did not travel far or often from his Orkney home and deplored the "progress" which takes people out of their natural habitats into cities devoid of the community spirit, which he celebrates in this poem.

    + An element of personal response should be incorporated in the answer.

    H – clearly developed discussion of the way the poem moves from man > community > human condition, with good textual support + intelligent personal response; Int. – clear understanding of three stages above, with some textual support + personal response.

Suggested Study Points — *The Old Women*

UNDERSTANDING

1.   The situation
- Old women gossip, know everybody's business and their family history, pass judgment, but change when faced with death.

2.   The themes
- small community life.
- Sanctity of life.
- Mystery of death.

ANALYSIS

Stanza 1, lines 1–4
- Vocative, "Go", line 1 — poet addresses reader; "you", lines 3 and 4: includes reader.
- **Tone** is warning, but not very serious > humorous, flippant:
- line 1, **repetition** of "or"; adjectives are extremes: "sad . . . sweet . . . riotous . . .";
- "riotous with beer" — inflated expression and a little quaint?
- **Hyperbole** adds to humour: "by the hour", "from every close and pier".
- Line 4, "an acid look": **metaphor** — conveys sharpness of their disapproval and links with the rest of the line; "to make your veins turn sour" — a fresh way of conveying the idea of blood-curdling.
- Old women spend hours gossiping; always critical, especially of young people;
- strict Calvinists who do not hold with any form of secular self-indulgence or enjoyment;
- suggestion that the old women can put a curse on you, have supernatural powers.

Stanza 2, lines 5–8
- **Direct speech** — brings the old women down to earth — we realise that the idea of the curse was more hyperbole; they really are just the village gossips, who know everybody's business and their family history.
- Also helps us to imagine the situation, hearing the actual words spoken.
- Line 5 — "No help," they say . . .": typically fatalistic attitude of such people.

- Line 6 — **euphemisms**: ". . . troubled by the same dry-throated curse," — a nice way of saying his grandfather drank too much.
- Line 7 — ". . . he made the ditch his bed.": in other words, he fell, dead drunk, into the ditch and remained there till morning.
- Such euphemisms are common in this sort of community, especially among older women; suggest an unwillingness even to believe that such things happen, or the idea that they might be tainted just by saying the words.

- line 8 — **metaphor**: passing of genes from one generation to the next is compared to water coming from a natural spring. Ties in with the idea of "No help" in line 5.
- "welling", "source" and "cracked" carry the metaphor; "welling" suggests that he has inherited his grandfather's genes in abundance; "cracked" suggests the "source", i.e., grandfather, was faulty, like a cracked spring with water seeping out and being wasted.

- Small fishing port: this kind of community always superstitious; at the mercy of the sea and elements; kind of place where families live for generations.

- **Tone** is mocking; made clear by direct speech, as if the poet is imitating the old women to make fun of them. Strengthens the contrast with the tone of awe to come in the sestet.

Stanza 3, lines 9–14

- Line 9 links back to the first eight lines and intensifies the **contrast** to come.
  - The whole line sums up those women, and indeed their Calvinist religion; they find no joy in life; word order: "frown" at the end of the line emphasises their disapproval. The full stop at the end of the line illustrates that they are intractable, will brook no discussion with any view, which does not coincide with their own.
  - The introduction of the first person in "I have known" lends credence to the poet's less than complimentary description of the old women: he has experienced their disapproval personally, can vouch for their lack of warmth and humour.
  - **Tone** becomes more serious; the old women represent the attitudes of the community, especially the church, in which the poet lives. GMB turned away from those bleak Calvinist attitudes, to embrace the Roman Catholic faith.

- Line 10 — the **contrast** is signalled by "But" and continued in "gray-eyed sober boy" — the opposite of the young man in stanza 1, "riotous with beer". The old women might not have mourned the riotous youth but this boy has none of his faults, and, when he is drowned, they keen over him with "an undersong of terrible holy joy.", line 14.

- Line 11 — comma after "storm" — caesura slows the pace of the narrative, suggesting the poet's awe in the face of death.

- Line 12 — "stones" for this poet are holy, a **symbol** of the Resurrection and its promise.
  - Each death recalls the death of Christ; in this case, being a young man, free of sin, in the eyes of the old women at least, the comparison is clear.
  - The body of the drowned boy, retrieved from the sea, "dripping" on the stones, recalls the emission of blood and water from Christ's side, pierced by the soldier, as recorded in St John's Gospel, chapter 19, v. 34.

- Line 13 — "hags": ties in with suggestion of supernatural powers of the old women in stanza 1.
  - **Alliteration**: "would weave", effect is to intensify the mesmeric feeling of casting a spell.
    Lexical choice: "moans" — the word seems derogatory, continuing the sentiments of first nine lines, as does "hags", but on another level, both words take on a supernatural aura, in line with the new spirituality of the old women presented in the last three lines.

- Line 14 — **oxymoron**: "terrible holy joy" — "terrible" is used in the sense of terrifying; the oxymoron emphasises the combination of fear and love with which Christians face up to the mystery of death.
  - Christians are taught that death is the culmination of life; that our lives on earth are but a small interval in the lives of our eternal souls, and so our time on earth is merely a preparation for death and, as such, is sacred. But all they have to go on is their faith; death, and more importantly what follows, remains a mystery which each individual must face alone when the time comes.
  - GMB was much preoccupied with the mystery of death. In 1961, he converted to the Roman Catholic faith, where he found the ritual transubstantiation of the bread and wine into the body and blood of Jesus, re-enacted in every Mass, in tune with his own beliefs in the mysticism of death and the promise of the Resurrection. He was attracted by the ceremonial of the Mass, believing that by taking part in the ritual — and the Roman Catholic congregation is more involved in responses than that of the Church of Scotland — we are transformed into spiritual beings, and thereby raised above the animal kingdom by virtue of our immortal souls.
  - The whole poem builds to a climax in that word "joy"; given more impact by the delayed rhyme, separated as it is from the first three lines by the rhyming couplet, lines 12 and 13.

Looking over the whole poem

- **Poetic Form — sonnet:**
- fourteen lines of iambic pentameter, with only slight variations from the Petrarchan model.
- He uses the octave (8 lines) and the sestet (6 lines), but the octave is split into two quatrains, each rhyming *abab*, followed by the sestet rhyming *abaccb*;
- the delayed rhyme, separated from the pattern by the rhyming couplet, creates a crescendo on "joy", the last word of the last line.
- GMB uses the sonnet form in the traditional Italian way:
- the octave develops one idea; there is then a turn, or *volta*, and the sestet grows out of the octave, varies it, develops it.
- In this poem, the octave sets the scene, makes a statement about the old women gossiping; in the sestet, he introduces the spiritual element: the old women are transformed into the wailing women who wept over the crucified Christ; their gossiping becomes keening over the dead boy; their semi-jocularly suggested witchcraft in the octave becomes part of the mystery of life and death; their function becomes that of a kind of Greek Chorus.

(Note on Chorus: An essential part of Greek tragedy, sometimes taking part in action, sometimes commenting from a fixed position. T.S. Eliot uses such a Chorus in his *Murder in the Cathedral*, in which the women of Canterbury take part in the action as well as commenting on it and providing mood and atmosphere. Brecht uses the device in his *Caucasian Chalk Circle*, Tennessee Williams in *The Glass Menagerie*, Arthur Miller in *A View from the Bridge*, among others. Used also in some novels, notably in Hardy and, in Scottish literature, "the bodies" in George Douglas Brown's *The House with the Green Shutters*. The same function is sometimes performed by a single commentator, e.g., the Fool in *King Lear*.)

- **Contrast** between the octave and the sestet is also made clear by the contrasting **lexical choice** and **syntax**, which give the sestet a Biblical **tone** in keeping with the sense:
- in the octave, the metaphors are homely, the reworking of a cliché;
- the direct speech, with its euphemisms, mirrors the ways of those so-human gossiping women; the vocative is informal.
- In the sestet, the tone is formal:
- line 9: word order is unusual, with subject and verb at the end of the sentence, introducing the Biblical tone, continued in the formal "I have known . . .".
- Line 13: "Those same old hags . . ." (from the first stanza) are transformed into sacred priestesses; their keening becomes a ritual dirge chanted over the body of the drowned boy.
- The tone is no longer flippant, but holy, full of awe.

EVALUATION

- Discussion summing up the themes and how they are conveyed in the poem.
- Small town or village life — good or bad?
- Points made in the octave show the negative side of this kind of community.
- Good points — closeness, sharing grief, caring for each other are implicit in the sestet.

- Personal response, depending on the level of students, may lead to discussions of old people and their attitudes to young people, genetic inheritance, personal beliefs, experiences with the supernatural . . .

- A discussion of why films which deal with the supernatural are usually horror films — may lead into deeper consideration of the mysteries of life and death.

Using Your Notes for Revision: Checklist

UNDERSTANDING AND ANALYSIS *(Use these questions to revise important parts of the poem.)*

1. **Poet's presentation of the old women:**
    In stanzas 1 and 2, what impression does the poet create of the old women
    - rarely have a good word to say for anyone who does not conform to their own strict Calvinist standards, stanza 1;
    - spend their entire day gossiping, line 2;
    - there is a suggestion that they can put some sort of curse on you, line 4;
    - poke their noses into everyone's business; know everybody's family history, stanza 2;
    - they pass judgments and condemn people, lines 5 and 8.

    and of the kind of community in which they live?
    - Small fishing port, lines 11–12;
    - fishing people notoriously superstitious, possibly because of their reliance on the mercy of the elements and the unpredictable sea, line 4.
    - Impossible to keep one's affairs private, stanza 2.
    - Old women are representative of the community as a whole, greatly influenced by the Church, with Calvinist attitudes to secular enjoyment. As was common in such communities, the two extremes of strict and "riotous" living go hand in hand.
    - Unchanging community where families have lived for generations, stanza 2;
    - close community, though, where everyone mourns a death, not just relatives, lines 12–14.

2. **Techniques / devices:**
    Revise the effectiveness of the devices / techniques used by the poet in the first two stanzas, to bring the old women to life on the page.
    Details in Suggested Study Points, page 63:
    - hyperbole, line 2;
    - metaphor, line 4;
    - direct speech in stanza 2;
    - euphemisms in stanza 2;
    - metaphor, line 8.

3. **Tone:**
    (a) **Identify and account for the tone of the first two stanzas.**
    - Informal — use of vocative, direct speech.
    - Humorous, poking fun at old women but tongue-in-cheek, not unkindly.
    - Talking about everyday occurrences.
    - Exaggerates the way the old women gossip and disapprove of others.
    - Talks of old women, but not seriously, as if they might be witches with power to curse.

    (b) **Identify and account for the change in tone in the third stanza, lines 9–14.**
    - Informal > formal / Biblical.
    - Change from general to particular incident.
    - Change of subject matter: life > death. Tone of awe.

(c) **Revise the effectiveness of the techniques / devices used to bring about this change.**
- ● Change from vocative to first person, line 10.
- - Line 9: word order – formal / rhetoric + "frown" emphasised at end of line.

- ● **Contrast**: signalled by "But", strengthened by emphatic position in line 10:
- - "gray-eyed sober boy" v. "riotous with beer" line 1;
- - line 10, lexical choice — "sober" against almost humorous tone of lines 1–8;
- - gossiping > keening over dead body, lines 13–14.
- ● Comma in line 11 creates caesura; introduces and focuses our attention on the idea of death.

- ● Line 12: visual **image** of drowned boy "dripping on the stones";
- - line 13, "hags" ties in with suggestion in line 4, tongue-in-cheek there — we do not take it seriously; perhaps we should review that reaction?

- ● Line 14: oxymoron "terrible holy joy" — provides climax of poet's fear and wonder in the face of death. Strong contrast with his flippant attitude in stanzas 1 and 2; feeling of vulnerability as he considers the mystery of death.

Poetic Form — see pages 64–65.

EVALUATION *(Use this question for exam practice.)*

4. **Consider your personal response to the old women in the poem and show how the focus of your response changes as the poet uses the old women to make a statement of universal significance. (10 marks)**

- ● Response to old women in stanzas 1 and 2 will most likely be dismissive — nosy, interfering, nothing better to do with their time, living in the past, typical of old people . . . + hyperbole: quote / explain / comment.
- - Suggestion in stanza 1 that they could put some sort of curse on you + metaphor: quote / explain / comment; dispelled in stanza 2 with direct speech, returning the old women to normality, i.e., the village gossips + quote / explain / comment.
- - Euphemisms capture the essence of the old women + quote / explain / comment.
- - Old women are representative of general attitudes of community, led by Calvinist church, still influential in the islands in GMB's youth — summed up in strong statement sentence in line 9.

- ● Response should change as the poet presents old women as some kind of Greek Chorus, confronting death . . . + quote / explain / comment. (See note on Chorus, page 65).

- ● **Poetic form:** strengthened by contrast between octave and sestet, details on page 65 + quote / explain / comment.
- - Focus moves in sestet > poet's statement about mystery of death, sanctity of life.
- - Old women gain status from being part of the religious symbolism + quote / explain / comment. (See Suggested Study Points, page 64.)

H – well-developed discussion of religious symbolism / old women as Chorus / poetic form, with good textual support + intelligent comment. Int. – clear understanding of religious symbolism and how it confers stature on old women, with some textual support + some comment / personal response, perhaps implicit.

Unseen Textual Analysis: Marking Schemes — *The Storm*

Levels: Higher and Intermediate 2

All answers should be supported by close reference to the text.

1. **Describe the situation presented in the poem.**   (2) U
   - Speaker sets out to sea in a fierce storm. His boat tosses on the sea and is finally brought up on a rock; he is saved and finds peace in the monastery on the island.

2. *"How it / Flashed with a leap and lance of nails, / Lurching, O suddenly"*, **lines 1–3. By particular reference to the language used by the poet in these lines, show how he conveys the force of the storm on land in stanzas 1 and 2.**   (4) A
   - "Flashed with a leap", line 2 — sudden lightning flash, firing up the sky, forking to earth;
   - "lance of nails", line 2 — metaphor: sharp, piercing, driving rain, biting into his skin; suggestion of aggressiveness towards him, also in "hounding", line 5;
   - "Lurching, O suddenly", line 3: sudden gusts of wind, against which he had no control, confirmed by "reeled", line 6; exclamation "O" suggests it caught him by surprise.
   - All strong words — "blinding", "lurching" (describes effect on him as well as the storm), "hounding", "reeled" — showing how helpless he was, at the mercy of the storm.

   H – three good points, well explained + intelligent comment; Int. – at least two points clearly understood + some comment.

3. **Referring closely to examples from lines 9–26, show how the poet evokes the sounds of the storm at sea, and uses those sounds to mirror the man's emotions.**   (5) A
   - Line 9, **s**-sound throughout — sound effect of storm: as well as onomatopoeic function, also suggests antagonism of the storm towards him; (cf. "long green jaws", line 10).
   - Line 12, "**s**tammered" — sound of thunder, but also suggests his trepidation. Line 13, **s**- continues. Line 14, "snarling" — sound intensified by personification and alliteration: sea's antagonism.
   - Line 17, "w**ai**led" — long vowel sound + personification: storm howling; despairing, lost, like him; ("miserere": a psalm asking God to have mercy).
   - Line 20, "hi**ss**ing" — onomatopoeia, sound of foaming sea, angry, antagonistic.
   - Line 21, **t**-sounds — onomatopoeia, snapping noise; "stout mast" snaps like matchwood, evidence of force of storm; he is afraid he, too, might snap mentally.
   - Line 26, "ra**sp**" — harsh, grating: synaesthetic image, uniting sound and touch, intensified by alliteration.

   H — at least four good examples, well-explained + intelligent comment.
   Int. — at least three examples, clearly understood + some comment.

4. **From a close examination of lines 10–25, show how the poet creates a vivid picture of the magnitude and the violence of the storm at sea, building up to a climax as he is cast ashore.** *(You may wish to refer to such aspects as ideas, imagery, lexical choice, syntax, enjambment . . .)*   (5) A
   - Line 10, metaphor — "long green jaws" — shark image — danger of stormy sea; might be swallowed up, i.e., drowned;
   - As he gets further out to sea, "scudding", line 14: speed, force of storm driving boat forward;
   - describes clouds as "rampant", line 16 — links back to "heraldic", line 15. Storm clouds racing across the sky, suggests magnitude of storm, on grand scale, legendary.
   - Line 18, "swung": violent, tossing boat into troughs; "fluent": flowing, movement; "valleys": troughs between waves; "poised": held still, like sea's plaything; line 19, "icy": foam-topped, also cold; "yielding", cf. "fluent", changing; "peaks": top of wave, ready to drop again.

- Storm reaches climax, signalled by "until", line 20; **enjambment**: final surge of sea;
- line 22, "billowing": visual image of disaster; "helpless": like him, sail at mercy of storm;
- line 24, **exclamations**! create **caesurae** — punctuating sea's actions as he is tossed up: "seized . . . plunged . . . spun" — all strong movement words, violence of storm.
- Finally, he is cast ashore: line 25, "flung" — violent action, final attempt by storm to dash him against the rocks; two compound words and brackets — suggest total confusion: "wave-crossed" — he is drenched with water; "God-lost" — he is cast into oblivion.

H — at least four good examples + climax, well-explained + intelligent comment;
Int. — at least three examples + climax, clearly understood + some comment.

5. **How does the poet create an atmosphere / mood of peace and tranquillity from line 26 to the end of the poem?** (5) A
   - Lines 26–29 deal with his safe arrival on land: **dots** . . ., line 26, suggest short passage of time, perhaps loss of consciousness, as he is cast ashore and carried to safety;
   - line 27, "stained chancel lights" — lit windows mean safety, light softened by stained glass, suggesting sanctuary of church; line 28, "cluster of mellow bells" — euphonic **sound**, **onomatopoeic**, **contrast** with line 17, "wailed miserere".
   - Line 29, **enjambment** — he is enfolded by peace; cluster of **sensory images**: "crossed hands" — praying, touching his; "scent of holy water" — give impression of an oasis of peace, security; church is always a safe haven, consecrated building.
   - Lines 30–31, flashback to the storm; **contrast** intensifies the peace of the monastery: line 30, "The storm danced . . ." — rejoicing at having dashed him against the rocks or raging at having lost him? line 31, "demons", cf. "evil joy", line 23 — **contrast** with the good Brothers, especially Colm in whose cell he is safely held.
   - Lines 31–34, return to safety he has found in the monastery: line 31, "Safe" at the beginning of the line for emphasis; line 33, "tranced" suggests he is only semi-conscious, but also idea of being happy / delirious; "sunshine" — **contrast**, end of storm.
   - Lines 34–36, the aftermath: line 34, corn ruined — "squashed" — a reminder of the violence of the storm, **contrast**; line 35, seabirds perish but he is saved; **alliteration** and **letter echoes** — corn, tern, strewn — signify mayhem caused by the storm; **contrast** with the peace he has found on the island; line 36, seaweed found "among the highest pastures": evidence of force of storm, suggests abnormally fierce, unnatural, supernatural?
   - Lines 37–40, many years later: line 37, nearly all monosyllables — conveys idea of simple monastic life; "my son" — he has become a monk.

Both levels should deal with contrast: H — at least four good examples, well-explained + intelligent comment; Int. — at least three examples, clearly understood + some comment.

6. **How effective do you find the final stanza, lines 37–40, as a conclusion to the poem,**
   (a) **on the superficial level of the narrative;** (2) UE
   - end of journey started in stanza 1: happy ending: "I find peace here", line 38;
   - time has passed :"These many years", line 39.
   (b) **as the resolution of the poem's deeper meaning?** (7) UE
   - Poet uses storm-tossed journey as **allegory** for mental anguish of spiritual journey.
   - Ends up on the island of Eynhallow, site of 12th century monastery — suggests a return to old religion, pre-Reformation (GMB converted to Roman Catholic faith in 1961, but presumably thought about it for a long time before taking such a huge step.)
   - "Godsent", line 38, is a pivotal word linking the two levels of meaning: **pun**: suggests "godsend" — unexpected piece of good fortune — he has found what he was looking for, happy ending; but also literally sent by God.

- • Physical journey can also be seen as spiritual journey;
- - storm, as his being bombarded with thoughts, feelings, revelations:
- - line 1, **exclamations** — "What . . . !", "How . . . "; **lexical choice**: "blinding": force of storm, in both senses; line 2, "flashed" links back to "blinding": force + visual; suggests that it was not easy, but he does not resist, appears to set out willingly, though driven, drawn;
- - line 9, **enjambment** — inexorable progress: "the sail drew" him over the Sound, line 13; "The sea . . . swung" him into troughs and over crests; and, at the height of the storm, "seized . . . plunged . . . spun . . . And flung" him and his boat; all movements over which he has no control; but "shot out", line 9 — indicates there was no hesitation on his part.
- • Throughout the poem there is **religious imagery** which confirms that the journey at sea is an allegory for the spiritual journey of a tortured soul:
- • Symbols of death:
- - line 2, "lance of nails" — recalls the Crucifixion — death of his old life;
- - line 6, "past kirk and alehouse" — centres of gathering community — renouncing world;
- - line 7, "thousand candles of gorse" — **metaphor** — holy / ritual image, e.g., wake for dead.
- - But there are also symbols of birth:
- - line 4, lambing — birth / lost sheep — spiritual birth?
- - water imagery of whole poem — symbol of baptism;
- - line 8, "mother": he is lost to her, cf. Mary / Christ; "yard": safe place he is leaving;
- - line 9, "hounding" linked to "lambing", suggests he was shepherded to his destination.
- • **Caesura**; "sobbing lungs": **lexical choice**: "sobbing" suggests mental and physical anguish.
- • Line 10, **metaphor**, "long green jaws": signals danger of stormy sea; also recalls Jonah, who was subjected to a great tempest and, having been cast overboard, was swallowed by a great fish and later vomited on the dry land, like the speaker in this poem.
- • Line 15, "heraldic clouds" — proclaiming his new direction? He is going towards ancient faith.
- • Line 17, "organ and harps" — sacred music; "miserere" — prayer asking God to have mercy.
- • Lines 18–19, "valleys . . . peaks" — low / high points, ups-and-downs as he struggles with faith.
- • Line 23, **oxymoron** — "evil joy" — devil fighting God for his soul? Reformers v. old religion?
- • Line 25, **lexical choice**: "flung" — violent, cf. Jonah vomited from fish.
- • **Compound words; brackets** — his thoughts?
- • Line 26, "rasp of rock" — cf. Peter, to whom Jesus said, "..upon this rock I shall build my church . . . "; **alliteration** lends stature to the idea of the rock.
- • . . . in the midst of disaster, he is saved, cf. Jonah — faith conquers death, makes us safe.
- • Line 40, site of 12th century monastery — yet poem starts in contemporary Stromness, cf. kirk, pub; poet travels into past to find peace — pre-Reformation, RC conversion?

H — well-developed discussion of allegory and imagery, good textual reference, well explained + intelligent comment; Int. — same but perhaps less well developed, supported and expressed. Mark on merit.

Level: Intermediate 1

1   **Explain briefly what the poem is about.**   (1) U
- • Man goes to sea in storm; wrecked; ends up staying at monastery.

2.   **Write down two pieces of evidence, from stanza 2, lines 5–8, which indicate where the speaker is at the beginning of the poem.**   (2) U
- • On land, in home town: (1) +
      "kirk . . . alehouse . . . my mother's yard" *(Any two — ½ mark each).*

3. (a) *". . . a leap and lance of nails,"* line 2.
         What exactly do you think the poet is referring to in these words?   **(2) A**
         ●   Wind (1) + rain (1); non-specific, e.g., the storm / weather — 1 mark only.

    (b **What does the word "leap" tell you about the storm?**   **(2) A**
         ●   Wind blowing hard (1) + in sudden gusts (1).

    (c) **Try to explain the effect of the words "lance" and "nails".**   **(2) A**
         ●   Rain stinging (1) + as if face being pierced with sharp pointed object like lance / nails (1).

4. *". . . the long green jaws . . .",* line 10.
    (a) **What is the poet describing in the above phrase?**   **(1) A**
         ●   The sea.
    (b) **Try to explain why this is a good description.**   **(2) A**
         ●   Shark image (1) + danger of stormy sea; might be swallowed up, i.e., drowned (1).

5. **Pick out and explain three separate words from lines 13–20, which convey the sound of the storm.**   **(3) A**
    ●   Line 14, "snarling" — growling, like a wild animal; dangerous. (1) +
    ●   Line 17, "wailed" — storm howling; despairing, lost. (1) +
    ●   Line 20, "hissing" — onomatopoeia, sound of foaming sea, also suggests angry, antagonistic. (1)

6. (a) **Pick out and explain two separate words from lines 21–24, which show the force with which the boat was wrecked.** *Any two from:*   **(2) A**
         -    line 21, "snapped" — p and t sounds mimic the noise of the "stout mast" snapping like matchwood with force of storm; "billowing" — **visual** image of disaster; "helpless" — like him, sail at mercy of storm;
         -    line 24, "seized . . . plunged . . . spun" — all strong movement words, violence of storm.

    (b) **Write down and explain two separate words from lines 25–26 which show the violence with which the boat was cast ashore.** *Any two from:*   **(2) A**
         ●   "flung" — violent movement; "wave-crossed" — compound word intensifies force of the waves battering the boat and him; "rasp" — grating noise as the boat is thrown against the rocks.

7. **How does the poet create an atmosphere of peace and calm from line 26 to the end of the poem?**   **(2) A**
    ●   *See marking of question 4 in H. / Int. 2 level — any two examples, with some attempt to explain.*

8. **What do we find out about the speaker in the last stanza?**   **(2) U**
    -    Middle-aged / elderly / old man.
    -    Now lives in monastery / has become monk.
    -    Is happy / at peace now. *Any two for I mark each.*

9. (a) **Do you think the story of the speaker's experience in the storm has a happy or a sad ending?** *Either can be justified.*   **(1) E**
    (b) **What makes the ending happy / sad?**   **(2) E**
         ●   Happy — safe from storm; peaceful life . . . *or any other reasonable point.*
         ●   Sad — left family, friends; cut off from normal life . . . *or any other reasonable point.*

10. **Think about the violent storm which the speaker experienced and where he ended up:**
    (a) **What do you think the symbolic meaning of the storm might be?**   **(2) U**
         ●   *Should get idea of mental anguish (1) + religious aspect. (1)*
    (b) **Explain how the poet's description of the storm has helped you to appreciate the symbolic meaning of the poem.**   **(2) UE**
         Mark on merit — violence of storm, his suffering, contrast with later peace . . .

Suggested Outline Plans for Critical Essays

1. **Many poems depend for their success on the poet's skill in employing the devices of poetry. Choose a poem in which more than one poetic device contributes significantly to its impact and show how the use of such devices helped you to understand the ideas in the poem. (You might consider imagery, lexical choice, point of view, contrast and any other literary or linguistic techniques the poet has used effectively.)** *(Hamnavoe)*
    §1   Title, poet, brief statement of situation; postman's round as framework: point of view — how we see through father's eyes; reveals his attitudes.
    §2   Contrast, juxtaposition, counterpoint — creates atmosphere of place and community + quote.
    §3   Imagery, esp. fishing linked with crofting in simile, metaphor; three linked images of boats coming in, fisher girls and boys fishing — essence of community working together + quote, etc.
    §4   Conclusion — celebration of way of life; importance of simple people; personal response.

2. **Many memorable poems leave the reader with a powerful impression of a person, a place or an era. Using a poem which has left you with such an impression, explain what techniques / devices are used by the poet to convey this impression.** *(Hamnavoe)*
    §1   Title, poet, brief mention of place / community; indications of coastal situation; postman's round used as framework.
    §2   Hamnavoe morning, stanzas 1-3: sense of past, imagery, lexical choice, two main occupations in fishing boats and stallion, linked through imagery and continuation of techniques + quote, etc.
    §3   Apart from the poet's father, characters presented are types rather than individuals, referred to by title: merchants, tinker . . . linked together to form community, interdependent, by imagery, juxtaposition and contrast + quote / explain / comment.
    §4   Conclusion: celebration of way of life; importance of simple people; personal response.

3. **By looking closely at a poem written in a particular literary form . . . sonnet, dramatic monologue, ballad . . . consider to what extent its particular techniques enhance the impact of the subject matter.** *(The Old Women)*
    §1   Title, poet, brief statement of literary form and of situation presented in the poem.
    §2   Deal with presentation of old women in octave: vocative, tone and how created, imagery, use of direct speech, euphemisms + quote / explain / comment.
    §3   Presentation of old women in sestet: change of tone and how created, contrast, symbolism, building to climax in oxymoron of final words, assisted by delayed rhyme + quote / explain.
    §4   Conclusion: octave sets scene, old women as gossips; sestet introduces spiritual element, old women > symbols — ideas enhanced by traditional sonnet form; personal response.

4. **By referring closely both to the ideas and to poetic techniques / devices used in a poem which you know well, show whether your appreciation of the poem depends more on the ideas or on the techniques / devices.** *(The Old Women)*
    §1   Title, poet, brief statement of situation; how poet uses literary form to give contrasting views of the old women.
    §2   Deal in more detail with techniques / devices used to provide contrast, in tone and presentation of old women, between octave and sestet + quote / explain / comment.
    §3   More detail of how focus changes in sestet from old women to poet's ideas of sanctity of life and mystery of death: graphic picture of dead boy, religious symbolism + quote / explain.
    §4   Conclusion: change from humorous, disrespectful tone of octave to hushed reverence in sestet has shocking effect, mirroring poet's sense of shock and awe in face of death; impact of climax in "terrible holy joy", personal response.

CHAPTER 5 — Iain Crichton Smith

Suggested Study Points — *Old Woman*

UNDERSTANDING

1. **The situation**
   - The poet recalls a visit to an old couple; the old woman is helpless and dying, but slowly. She is cared for by her husband, who prays for her release from this life.

2. **The themes**
   - Old age and decay.
   - Meaning / pointlessness of life.
   - Euthanasia.
   - Critical of Calvinism / indifference of God to the plight of the individual.
   - Poet's feeling of being trapped in his native island culture.

ANALYSIS

Stanza 1, lines 1–4
- **Lexical choice** shows the degradation of the old woman: line 1, "fed" — suggests automatic nature of eating, simply keeping alive; also animal connotations, which continue in following lines;
- "mashed plate" — **hypallage**: the food is mashed, not the plate; concision suggests lack of interest in food; baby / animal "feeds"; sloppy food / bran mash (fed to an old / sick horse);
- line 2, **simile**: compares her to an old mare, useless, fit only to be put down; introducing, implicitly, the idea of euthanasia, whose adherents argue that we put animals out of their misery but not human beings; note "its", line 3, not "her" — old woman similarly dehumanised;
- line 2, the horse "might droop"; line 4, the old woman is "held upright by her husband";
- line 3, "dull . . . ignorance" suggests total loss of interest in and understanding of surroundings;
- line 4, husband "prayed" — certainly for his wife's release from her suffering through death.
- Line 1, "And she, being . . ." — Biblical **tone**, solemn, immediately sets old woman in Calvinist religion — slightly ironic — but universalises the theme of decay / dying.
- **Mood** is sympathetic, compassionate, pitying old woman.

Stanza 2, lines 5–8
- **Enjambment** suggests repeated prayers which go unanswered; also, together with **juxtaposition** of lines 5–7 with lines 1–4 and 8, suggests problem / cause relationship;
- line 5, important — no suggestion of euthanasia here on part of old man; he awaits God's will.
- **Tone**: poet's **irony** comes through in "all-forgiving" — poet questions faith of old couple; what can this old woman possibly have done to bring such suffering on herself?
- Line 6, **irony** and **tone** of scepticism continued in the unspecific "some . . . somewhere", the uncertain "might . . . perhaps"; suggests old man's ambivalence — cannot bring himself to be more precise; also his respect for God in not being too demanding on his wife's behalf.
- Line 7, "foreign" referring to angel in line 6 — compare MacDiarmid's "trashy bleezin' French-like folk" *(Crowdieknowe)*; angels would appear to be foreign to Calvinists, especially angels of mercy; people are born to suffer. Poet is satirising Calvinist faith here — Calvinism is shown as blind to social needs, responsible for the old woman's degradation.
- "gradual crops", sense of life taking its own time, with people as with crops; cf. Ecclesiastes iii, 1: "To everything there is a season and a time to every purpose under heaven: A time to be born and a time to die."
- Line 8 comes back to the old woman's helpless state, continuing the degrading / dehumanising animal comparison in the **lexical choice**: "munched" recalls horse munching oats; also suggests old woman's noisy eating; "blindly searching the spoon" — suggests baby being fed.

Stanza 3, lines 9–12
- In stanza 3, the focus is on the poet's reaction to the scene:
- line 9, **contrast** with lifelessness, despair inside — "Outside, the grass was raging" — **pathetic fallacy**: poet's own feelings ascribed to the grass; he is raging at the old people for adhering to their cruel God, and at the Calvinist religion for teaching such blind faith and stoicism;
- **contrast** with their patient acceptance of the situation, represented by "gradual crops", line 7.
- Line 10, poet's **mood** — pity, for the suffering of the old people; and shame, bred in him ("imprisoned"), that he was once part of this culture, which he cannot quite throw off; but, more importantly, in the sense of feeling it was shameful that people should suffer so;
- lines 11–12 clearly point to euthanasia as alternative: those people have had a hard time throughout their lives and should not be subjected to such indignity in death;
- line 12, poet's feelings and the distressful nature of the situation are here intensified by the **alliteration**, and by the **repetition** of the phrase "in such a . . ." and echoed in line 16, "such decay"; idea of euthanasia is continued in stanza 4.

Stanza 4, lines 13–16
- **Enjambment** continues the idea of the poet being trapped in this Calvinist culture;
- line 13, "wished to be away . . ." — but he cannot break free of his early conditioning;
- intensified by "yes" and **repetition**, with the addition of "far".
  (The poet was alienated from his community, and even from his mother, by his education and by his "indulgence" in something so manifestly impractical as poetry.)
- Enjambment also links "wish to be away" with the old woman "in such a state", line 12. "To be away" is a common **euphemism** for death, especially among older people of that time.
- Lines 14–16, poet would like to escape into a more civilised society, represented here by classical literature, where great heroes, faced with the degradation of being killed by their enemies, fell upon their swords — "bitter spears", **hypallage** emphasising that it was difficult for those heroes to inflict death on themselves and therefore even more heroic, but they did it to conserve their honour.
- No such preservation of human dignity is allowed to the old woman: the poet is clearly advocating euthanasia here, but it would go against the Calvinist religion, which believed that God's Will would be done, and man has no say in the matter; cf. The Lord's Prayer.

Stanza 5, lines 17–20
- **Contrast** with classical culture seen in **juxtaposition** with the **direct speech** of the old man's prayer: that was a story; this is reality. We hear his actual words.
- Line 17, the humility of the old man's prayer is in keeping with Calvinist ways.
- **Repetition**: "Pray God . . . we ask you God" and "he said" — suggests his desperation but also — the poet's **irony** — that God is not listening;
- **lexical choice**: "said" rather than a more fervid, emotive word like begged or pleaded might suggest that he knows there is no point, that he cannot influence God's Will.
- Line 18, "The bowed back was quiet." — **caesura** emphasises the finality; the prayer is over; they must wait God's pleasure; **synecdoche** focuses on the back bent under its burden, gives a visual image of the old man, attracting our pity for the old couple in their distress.
- Lines 18–19, **metaphor** — death's-head image:
- line 18, "teeth" recalls old woman feeding in stanza 1; also the jaws of death closing on her.
- She is so wasted that her head looks like a disinterred skull; line 19, "a delicate death" suggests the fragility of the old woman; her skull would easily crumble. Line 20, "And nothing moved" — very little life left in her; "knotted head" — focus still on the head; "knotted" literally, her hair was pinned up in a "bun", but also that her brain cells are fused together, no longer functioning; "within" also suggests her brain is confused; links to "veins" in next line.

Stanza 6, lines 21–24
- Enjambment here suggests life drags on relentlessly.
- Line 21, "a few poor veins" links back to "knotted" to give us a visual image of the veins standing out in the old woman's forehead, contrasting with the paper-thin skin covering.
  - **Simile**: veins compared to seaweed; visual image;
  - "vague wishless . . . floating": continues the idea of the old woman's confused state, her loss of interest in life, over which she has no control, as she exists at the mercy of time / God, just as the seaweed floats, without direction, controlled by the tide.
- Line 23, "all the salty waters" — **metaphor** for the bitter lives which people have to endure;
  - line 24, "too many waves" — compares human lives to waves of the sea; the implication is that God is indifferent to the plight of the individual: we are no more to Him than so many waves in the ocean — ties in with the Calvinist suppression of individuality, the same doctrine which disapproved of people like Iain Crichton Smith, who "did his own thing" by becoming a poet; such nonconformist behaviour was regarded as vanity;
  - also here **visual image**: cinematic technique of waves lapping on the shore, suggesting the continuity of the human condition, cf. "gradual crops", line 7 — growing, seasonal, cyclical nature of life: as old people die, babies are born.
- The **mood / tone** is one of despair; oo-sound in line 24 suggests life drawn out beyond endurance; ICS perhaps thinking here of his mother: might she come to the same end in her unstinting Calvinism? Although this poem was written after visiting elderly relatives on Lewis, there is always something of his mother in his many poems about old women.

Looking over the whole poem
- **Poetic Form:** four-line stanzas with fairly regular metre, five strong stresses.
  - Variations, e.g., in lines 6 and 8, where extra strong syllable slows up the line, mirrors the endless, fruitless prayers, the pointless, seemingly-endless life.
- Rhyme is generally para-rhyme or assonance, or a mixture of the two; appropriate to the discordant situation and the confusion and turmoil in the poet's mind. The pattern is *abba*: e.g., stanza 1 — *a*-lines, "plate / prayed" — assonance but very little difference between final sounds of the two words; *b*-lines, "fence / ignorance" — para-rhyme;
  - in stanzas 4–5, the rhyme in the *a*-lines is perfect, and the *b*-lines are very close, while in stanza 6, the rhymes are perfect, suggesting the acceptance by the old people of the cross they must bear, and by the poet, the gradual acceptance of their stoicism and his admiration for their endurance.
- Title: Old Woman — no definite article; stands for all people in such situation;
  - throughout the poem, they are referred to as "she" and "her husband / he";
  - generalises in line 11, "men and women" — makes theme universal;
  - introduction of classical references in stanza 4 also helps to universalise the situation.

EVALUATION

- Old couple representative of human condition in general: ageing process, frailty / limitations of human body. (Note no names given to couple.) On positive side, stoicism, faith in God and lasting human love: the old man shares his wife's burden, without complaint.

- Almost inevitably there will be a discussion on euthanasia, which might be good for talk assessment and for an argumentative, persuasive or report essay.

- If *The Old Women* by George Mackay Brown (Chapter 4) and / or Norman MacCaig's *Visiting Hour* have been studied, comparisons could be made at this point.

- Impression of poet: cannot throw off native culture; his education has taken him away from it but his upbringing remains a strong force in his psyche. He hates the hold Calvinism has on its adherents but admires their stoicism, which stands against the classical examples he cites. Though personal dignity is lost, the old people are admirable in honouring their faith.

Using Your Notes for Revision: Checklist

UNDERSTANDING AND ANALYSIS *(Use these questions to revise important parts of the poem.)*

1. **Summarise, in your own words, details of the old woman,**
   - She is very frail, close to death but death is a long time coming. Her head like the skull of a dead person; hair pinned up in a bun; gnarled veins stand out on her forehead.

   and her situation.
   - She is completely helpless: husband feeds her mashed food from a spoon; she chomps automatically, with no apparent relish for her food and opens her mouth for the next spoonful to be shovelled in.
   - She is not really aware of what is going on around her; cannot sit up by herself — husband holds her as he prays for her release from her suffering.
   - She cannot pray, so he prays in both their names, patiently waiting for God to act for the relief of both of them.

2. **Poet's presentation of the old woman: Revise the effectiveness of the poetic devices / techniques, which have helped to form your impression of the old woman,**
   - Stanzas 1 and 2 — show degradation / dehumanisation of old woman:
   - **lexical choice** — "fed", line 1; **hypallage** — "mashed plate", line 1; **simile**, compares her to an old mare — lines 2–3; image continued in line 8.
   - Stanzas 5 and 6 — show how close she is to death: **metaphor** — death's-head image, lines 18–19; **lexical choice** — "within the knotted head", line 20; "a few poor veins", line 21; **simile** — seaweed image, lines 21–22.

   and her situation.
   - Line 3, "dull pastures of its ignorance" — continues simile, suggests old woman is mentally confused;
   - line 8, image of animal or baby seeking food instinctively;
   - line 12, **alliteration** and **repetition**; **enjambment**, line 13 + **ambiguity** of "wished to be away" + **euphemism**;
   - patiently awaiting God's will — **direct speech**, line 17; prayers not answered — **lexical choice**, line 17; **repetition**; **metaphor**, lines 23–24 — God's indifference to individuals.

3. **Mood.**
   (a) **Trace the changes in mood and tone throughout the poem.**
   (b) **Make sure you have evidence of the reasons for the poet's feelings.**
   (c) **Note how you are made aware of each mood change.**
   - Stanza 1: sympathetic towards old man; compassionate, pitying old woman;
   - reason: old man's burden of looking after his wife; her degrading condition and situation;
   - awareness: Biblical tone of first three words gives woman stature.
   - Stanza 2: irony, scepticism;
   - reason: old couple's blind adherence to their Calvinist faith;
   - awareness: "all-forgiving", line 5; vagueness in line 6: "some . . . somewhere . . .might . . . perhaps".
   - Stanza 3: angry impatience;
   - reason: angry that Calvinists teach such blind faith and suffering without complaint;
   - awareness: **contrast** — reactions of old couple and those of poet; **pathetic fallacy**, line 9.
   - Poet feels trapped in his native culture;
   - reason: he disapproves of the old couple's blind faith, but he cannot condemn them;
   - awareness: line 10, "Imprisoned".

- • Pity, humbled by their stoical acceptance, but also feels it is shameful that they should suffer;
- reason: old people like them, who have had hard lives should not have to suffer such indignity (woman) nor bear such a burden (man) in the end;
- awareness: **alliteration** and **repetition**, line 12 and line 16.
- • Stanza 4: desire to cast off this culture, replace it with classical culture;
- reason: finds the outcome of his native culture too distressing; prefers to control his own fate; upset by the degradation of the old woman and by the burden on her husband;
- awareness: admiration for the classical heroes, lines 14–16; echo of line 12 in "such decay".
- • Stanzas 5 and 6: compassion for the old couple;
- reason: old man's heavy burden; he pleads with God to bring relief; old woman so near death, mind confused, yet life drags on;
- awareness: **direct speech** and **repetition**, line 17; **synecdoche**, line 18.
- • Despairs of Calvinist culture; his own mother might come to same fate;
- reason: in spite of their faithful adherence to Calvinist beliefs, God makes them suffer;
- awareness: line 22, "vague wishless . . . floating"; line 24, oo-sound.

EVALUATION *(Use this question for exam practice.)*

4. *(a)* **Explain the importance to the poem of lines 14 and 15: "with athletes, heroes, Greeks or Roman men / who pushed their bitter spears into a vein".** (5)
- • Introduces the idea of euthanasia:
- heroes fell on their swords to preserve their honour;
- line 15, "bitter spears" — not the easy option or coward's way out; those were the cream of men;
- Calvinist religion preaches that man must await God's will; no control over his fate;
- poet introduces classical heroes in the very heart of the poem, flanked on either side by the degradation of the old woman and her husband's heavy burden of caring for her;
- contrasts between classical and Calvinist cultures highlights the ignorance of the old people and the backwardness of Calvinist religion.
- • Introduction of classical references helps to universalise the theme; not just one particular couple but all old people;
- also suggests that not just age decay but any terminal condition might be relieved by mercy-killing; classical heroes faced certain death from enemies, not old age; important to be in control of one's own fate.
- • Classical references also bring in the poet's personal alienation from his native culture through his education and his writing; the two sides can be seen as Calvinist community, and more particularly his mother, versus the culture of education and literature, the poet.

(b) **Referring closely to the poem, discuss the extent to which you agree with the ideas expressed in those lines.** (5)
- • Personal response should be well-supported by references to the plight of old people like the couple in the poem; might also consider termination of suffering at any age.

Suggested Study Points — *Iolaire*

Background to the poem: *In the early hours of New Year's morning, 1919, Admiralty yacht* Iolaire *was wrecked in a rough sea on the Beasts of Holm, just outside Stornoway harbour. She left Kyle about 7.40 p.m. with 260 Royal Navy ratings, who were looking forward to bringing in the first peaceful New Year with their families, the first time many had been together for four and a half years. The island had already lost around 800 men; now 200 more were added to the list. An enquiry found that the officers in charge had not exercised sufficient prudence in approaching the harbour and slowing down; no-one was on lookout except the First Officer on the bridge; an inadequate number of lifeboats and lifebelts; and, after the accident, no orders were given by the officers with a view to saving lives. They were satisfied, however, that no one on board was under the influence of intoxicating liquor, as testified by all of the survivors, but not believed by most islanders. Iain Crichton Smith was born on 1 January, 1928, exactly nine years later. The poet wrote three poems on the subject:* The Iolaire, After the War *and* Iolaire *(note: no definite article), the poem we are looking at here.*

UNDERSTANDING

1.   **The situation**
   - A Free Church elder stands watching the aftermath of the disaster. Midway through the poem, he addresses God and finally turns away from Him. He appears to drown himself.

2.   **The themes**
   - Fate; accidental / casual nature of catastrophe.   • Loss of faith.

ANALYSIS

§ 1, lines 1–12
   - Line 1, short statement sentence sets stunned **tone**, **mood** of disbelief, continued in the succession of **short sentences** and **caesurae** in first five lines ; caesura in line 1 mirrors finality of disaster. Lines 1–2, second short sentence, **enjambment** — appropriate to elder's confusion; introduces tone of **irony**: young men were coming home to celebrate the New Year, so the sentence is literally true; New Year is a time for new beginnings: the War was over, they could begin to resume their lives; but "brought them home" is a common euphemism for bringing a dead body back to its home for burial.
   - Lines 2–3, introduce the "enigma" of the situation; the sun's coming up brought no answers, emphasised by end-stopped line, one of the few in the poem. **Lexical choice**, "orbed" gives a visual image of the sun rising, showing the magnitude of the disaster even more clearly. The idea of the enigma continued in **repetition** of "seemed" — also suggests his feelings of confusion, beginning of his uncertainty and conveys the nightmare quality of the scene.
   - Lines 4–5, **metaphor** — "men buzzed" creates an image of the men swirled round in the rough sea, like insects: noise of sea + their size and helplessness against the might of the sea;
   - the name, Beasts of Holm, suggests monsters; there is an irony too in "Holm" / home.
   - (Line 5, "fire" — the ship's boiler exploded.) Line 6, "thin and white" — seems harmless by the time it reaches shore; heightens the perplexity;
   - line 7, **lexical choice** — "unravelling": tide brings in bodies, disentangling them from the wreckage but ironic level of meaning: did not solve the puzzle of how it could happen.
   - Lines 7–8, he touches his hat out of respect; it "seemed to float" — reflection in moving water;
   - but also **metaphor** here; hat is symbol of his office as elder; "fixed" in sense of fixed ideas, narrow-minded; "float" suggests movement of those ideas, doubts.
   - Lines 9–10, "fish" are the bodies, floating in the water; "caps" links to his hat in previous line; those, too, are the symbols of office, bearing the names of the ships in which they served and, in some cases, whose sinking — "vanished" — they had survived. One of the victims of the *Iolaire* had been the sole survivor of his ship — a further natural **irony** of the situation.

- Lines 10–11, **lexical choice** — "sloppy waves . . . the fat of water" — the idea of "waste" in line 24 (slops); they were washed up like flotsam; feeling of pity for the waste of young lives.
- Line 12 — "bruising against their island" — visual image of the effect on the bodies of being dashed against the rocks; "their" holds the powerful **irony**; wrecked so near home.

§ 2, lines 12–21

- Line 12, "It is true" — **contrast** with "it seemed" in previous section;
- **tone** even more incredulous: truth, that man could wreak such havoc, not God.
- Line 13, "a minor error" — human / navigational error; enquiry blamed officers; line 14, "that star" — seamen navigate by the stars; also star in the sense of Fate; "not responsible", not its fault; but also in sense of irresponsible — Fate / God should have been guiding them. **Caesura** — sense of finality of the judgment; "It (Fate / God) shone"; watched but did not care.
- Line 15, "puffy . . . flapping" — suggest helplessness of sailors cast into the sea; strong visual **image** of bodies, dressed in naval uniform, wide shirts, bell-bottomed trousers.
- Lines 16–17, **alliteration** suggests the smoothness of seagulls swimming on rough sea; "bonded" — as if attached to the water, being their natural medium; but those men were sailors, also their natural element. **Caesura** intensifies the question in line 17: **irony**: do seagulls mean more to God than Man? — first doubts / criticism of God's treatment of man.
- Line 18, **alliteration** — l- and t-sounds, similarity of the words, suggest movement, bustle — but also feeling of bitterness at dashed hopes — and slow the line, as if in a dream, far off . . .
- "hoarded food" — war shortages and rationing; food had been saved for welcome feast.
- Lines 19–21, desire to see boys again; recalls God's Will — He did not "will the ship to port".
- **Irony** of New Year, new beginning: "errant . . . unpractised" — war is unnatural, an aberration.

§ 3, lines 22–26

- Line 22, **tone**: present tense and direct speech (although no inverted commas) make question more poignant, more heart-rending; becomes clear in line 27 that he is addressing God.
- Lines 22–26: body "fixed", a semblance of the moving debris, i.e., the lifeless bodies washed ashore — distorted image created by the moving water — a favourite with ICS — suggests things are not as they appear; succinctly conveyed in "simulacrum"; line 24, "mobile" — **contrast** with "fixed", his fixed ideas may be changing; "plants that swayed" — things rooted in time, figuratively the foundation of his life, his faith; line 25, "keeling ship" — **metaphor** for his life, foundering; "exploding" suggests the suddenness and the force of this change in him.
- Lines 25–26, "splayed" — lifeless — limbs spread, recalling Crucifixion; "cold insect bodies" — image recalls "buzzed" in line 5; cold = dead; "insects" — to God we are like insects; recalls *King Lear* IV.i.36: "As flies to wanton boys, are we to the gods; / They kill us for their sport."

§4, lines 26–32

- Addressing God directly now, present tense to end of poem; note "your" church — in the past, church has been the foundation of his life, now dissociating himself; "solid" — cf. rock.
- **Contrast** between fixed and moving continued in "solid"; line 27, "This" is reality, truth, not the church — **short sentences** and **caesurae** – emphasises his feeling of certainty now;
- lines 27–29, **image** of shipwreck conveys the way the truth dawns on him; sudden, unexpected, impact of the experience: "pours" — force with which certainty hits him; "parting timbers" — his mind, beliefs, breached by this experience; "where I ache" — it is a painful process to renounce the beliefs of a lifetime; "globular eyes"- now unblinkered, sees truth.
- Lines 29–32, "slack" — lifeless; "ringing" — **pun**; circling, swirling, but linked to "mortal bells"; "without sound" — because dead, but also without church bells. Contrast in these lines between God and human, "mortal", whose power appears now to be greater than God's: "exuberant" suggests full of a life of their own, and "flower" — growing, blossoming, a pleasant **image**; "unknown to our dry churchyards"; "dry" — **contrast** with "water", also suggests devoid of feeling, love, nurturing care.

§ 5, lines 32–37
- Line 32, "I look up." — literally and figuratively — short sentence intensifies meaning;
- lines 33–35, **tone** of surprise that day breaks as usual, despite the tragedy; **alliteration** emphasises ordinariness of the day;
- line 34, "remorseless amber": the sun comes up, no matter what happens; life goes on;
- "the bruised blue"; cf. line 12, "bruising"; the sea has patches of dark colour, bodies; "erupting"; spewing bodies on the shore; suggests force and sound of waves breaking on rocks.
- Addresses God again, directly: "not as the playful one" — ICS said the tragedy was "almost a black comedy . . . a macabre joke" — reference to the **irony** of the whole situation;
- lines 36–37, "black / thunderer from hills." — the Calvinist God, hard taskmaster venting his wrath from above; line layout emphasises "black" and "thunderer".

§ 6, lines 37–45
- Line 37, "I kneel"; shows respect to man; especially in view of line 40;
- line 38, "this dumb blonde head"; "dumb" — cannot speak, dead; "blonde" — contrast with "black thunderer", line 37; the two together, usually derogatory, has shocking effect — the drowned men used as God's playthings, "dumb blondes"; sees God now as sadistic.
- Lines 38–40, touching the dead man's hair fills him with new feeling of love for humanity;
- "scorched" conveys the force of his realisation; he is shocked at this discovery in himself; "confuses" — it is a new experience for him to love mankind before God.
- Line 41, turns away from God; echo of line 37 and unusual preposition emphasise deliberate action.
- Lines 42–45, unclear: they seem to say that he drowns himself, and that would make sense as his whole life has been shattered. On the other hand, and more likely I think, water **imagery** can be seen as a sort of reverse baptism into a new humanist faith, loving his fellow-men.
- Lines 42–45, **repetition** of "I am" at start of each sentence, suggests rebirth; "running", he is filled with new feeling; "tart sharp joy", **oxymoron** focuses on the mixture of feelings he has gone through (Calvinists were hostile to joy), intensified by the **tautology** of "tart sharp".
- Lines 43–44, puts himself on the side of human beings, his old self is cast into the water, old way of thinking discarded with his "black uniform", symbol of Calvinist office;
- "embraced" by his new understanding; "ignorant" — **personification**, mindless, not knowing God, as he now feels he no longer does; loss of lives mirrored by loss of faith which was his life; unclear ending, knows what he rejects but not what might be put in its place; poet's own feeling, having rejected religion and culture of island and mother but unable to fill gap fully with his education and poetry? Line 45, "I am calm." — final statement of certainty, short, direct.

Looking over the whole poem
- **Poetic form** — Blank Verse — appropriate to the workings of the elder's mind;
- generally five strong stresses per line; speech rhythms; no pattern of rhyme, but occasional, e.g., lines 23, 24, 25 — rhyme / pararhyme holds image together; last two words — lend finality.

EVALUATION

- Fate: to what extent do we control our lives? "What's for you won't go by you." "Que sera sera." Until now, Elder has followed life mapped out for him; now he appears to take his Fate into his own hands. An important concept for young people to consider.
- Why would God allow such a tragedy to happen? Young men who had risked their lives for their fellow men; surely the very basis of Christianity.
- Use of **persona** — how / why effective?
- How realistic as response to the situation? Poet's own response?
- How effective in conveying the tragedy / irony of the situation?

Using Your Notes for Revision: Checklist

UNDERSTANDING AND ANALYSIS *(Use these questions to revise important parts of the poem.)*

1. *(a)* **Summarise what happens in the poem.**
    - An elder of the Free Church stands on the shore, watching the aftermath of the disaster. Midway through the poem, he appears to be talking to God. In the end, he turns away from God. The ending is not clear; he appears to drown himself; he is calm.

    (b) **Make sure you understand the enigma**
    - He cannot understand how such a thing could happen; asks God if it is a punishment for wrongdoing.
    - Experienced crew; minor error of navigation has such dire consequences;
    - Beasts of Holm a well known hazard; no-one under the influence of drink;
    - why no more survived since wreck so near shore.

    and the irony of the situation.
    - So near home; all had survived horrors of World War I;
    - many had survived earlier shipwreck, one was sole survivor;
    - many hadn't seen families for four and a half years;
    - end of war; looking forward to peace they had helped to win;
    - New Year, time of new beginnings.

2. **Mood / Tone:**
    Trace the development of mood and tone through the poet's skilful use of syntactical and poetic techniques.
    - **Short sentences** and **caesurae** in lines 1–5 — stunned tone, mood of disbelief.
    - **Enjambment** — suggests elder's confusion.
    - Line 2 introduces sense of the **irony of the situation:** New Year, War over, etc.
    - Lines 4–8, **repetition** "It seemed . . ."; conveys puzzled feeling introduced in "enigma", line 3;
    - also conveys nightmare feeling of the experience.
    - **Irony** — "vanished ships", line 10 — some were already survivors of other shipwrecks.
    - Lines 10–12: pity — idea of waste of young lives;
    - **irony** of "their" — so near home.
    - Line 12, "It is true" — tone even more incredulous because of **contrast** with "It seemed".
    - Line 17, first doubts, questioning God's treatment of man + effect of **caesura**.
    - Lines 18–21, sense of bitterness at dashing of hopes.
    - Line 22, soul-searching, looking for reason + effect of **present tense** and **direct speech**.
    - Line 26, addresses God directly — tone of certainty — **short sentence** + **caesurae**.
    - Lines 27–29, describes the pain of his dawning realisation.
    - Lines 32–35, tone of surprise that things go on as normal, despite the disaster and his massive change of direction + effect of **short sentence** in line 32.
    - Lines 37–41, **short sentences** and **caesurae** — tone of wonder mixed with confusion — caused by his discovery of his love for humanity before God.
    - Line 41, **repetition** of "I kneel" + impact of unusual preposition "from" — tone of certainty.
    - Lines 42–45, **short sentences** and **caesurae** — tone of certainty mixed with joy of seeing truth.
    - **Blank verse** and **speech rhythms, no rhyme** — appropriate to mood of poem.

3. **Revise the effectiveness of the imagery used to help us picture the scene, which confronts the elder after the shipwreck.** Details in Suggested Study Points, pages 78–80:
    - Lines 4–5, "men buzzed . . ." — metaphor.
    - Lines 9–10, ". . . fish . . . caps . . ." — image of floating debris.
    - Lines 10–11, "sloppy . . . fat . . . bruising . . ." — continues previous image + suggests waste of lives.
    - Lines 14–16, "puffy . . . flapping . . ." — suggests helplessness of the men.
    - Lines 23–26, "transient waste . . . insect bodies" — continues idea of flotsam . . ."splayed" like insects.
    - Lines 29–30, "slack heads ringing . . ." — pun, link to "mortal bells".
    - Lines 33–35, ". . . remorseless amber . . . bruised blue" — sun . . . sea.
    - Line 38, ". . . dumb blonde head . . ." — shocking effect.

EVALUATON *(Use this question for exam practice.)*

4. *(a)* **The ending of the poem can be understood in two ways. Briefly outline the two possible interpretations, giving evidence for each one from lines 42–45. (2 marks)**
   - First literal / superficial interpretation: elder drowns himself + evidence from lines 42–45, second / metaphorical interpretation: his baptism, change to more humanist attitude + evidence from lines 42–45.

   (b) **In more detail, state clearly which is your preferred ending, drawing evidence from the whole poem to support your claim. (6 marks)**
   - Should choose second interpretation but a convincing case made for the first should be given credit; e.g., elder may feel, as one of God's representatives on earth, he has let people down + clear evidence from rest of poem.
   - More convincing evidence for second interpretation: gradual loss of faith and movement towards humanist beliefs.
   - Line 3, "enigma" — beginning of his uncertainty; his inability to accept such an accident with such dire consequences develops into his turning away from his Calvinist religion, and from God.
   - Lines 7–8, he touches his hat out of respect to the drowned men; **metaphor** — "fixed / float" — quote / explain / comment.
   - Link made between his hat and naval caps in the water; his hat seems to be moving with the caps, all symbols of office.
   - Lines 10–11, **lexical choice** brings in idea of "waste" in both senses — no mention of God's Will.
   - Line 14, "star": not responsible / irresponsible — this is man's doing, human error; at the same time, suggests God's indifference to fate of his creatures; God is not responsible but should have been watching over those men; continued in lines 16–17, **contrast** seagull / man;
   - line 22, question — natural reaction for Calvinist.
   - The following movement **imagery** suggests he has doubts about God's justice here;
   - insect image (also "dumb blonde", line 38) suggests we are no more to God than his playthings; doubts continue in shipwreck imagery, showing the suddenness and force of his loss of faith in the goodness of God; distorted mirror imagery.
   - Lines 31–32, **contrast** between man and God in lexical choice — "exuberant flower . . . dry churchyards" — man seems more important than God; Humanism complete when he kneels to touch human head — "My hand is scorched."; line 41, he turns his back on God; lines 42–45: powerful baptism **image** completes his rebirth; "I am calm."
   - The fact that **persona** used is an elder of the Calvinist church makes his loss of faith significant and gives impact to the magnitude of the tragedy. It would be more likely for an ordinary person to turn from God in such circumstances.

   H – preference clearly explained with good textual support + intelligent comment. Int. – preference made clear, some textual support + some comment.

   (c). **Explain how your interpretation affects the impact of the poem. (2 marks)**
   - Supports themes: casual nature of catastrophe, mystery and irony part of human life.
   - In line with ICS's criticisms of Calvinists' beliefs and control over adherents of that faith.
   - Reaffirms importance of human life.
   - Mirrors poet's own loss of faith and his alienation from community and mother.

Unseen Textual Analysis: Marking Schemes — *You Lived in Glasgow*

Levels: Higher and Intermediate 2

All answers should be supported by close reference to the text.

1. **What can you deduce from the first verse (lines 1–11) about**
    (a) **the purpose of the poet's visit to Glasgow** (1) U
    - His mother lived in Glasgow many years ago (line 1); she is now dead ("your breath", line 2);
    - he is searching for traces of her in the city ("I do not find", line 2).

    (b) **and how successful this visit is?** (2) U
    - In line 2 we are told that he can find no trace of her. (1) +
    - Glasgow has changed, she is rooted in her time and he in his. (1)

2. *(a)* **What is your impression of the thirties from reading lines 4–5?** (1) U
    - Mass unemployment. (1)

    (b) **Discuss the effectiveness of the language and devices used in line 5.** (3) A
    - The metaphor combines visual image with cause: literally — picture of men hanging about street corners, chewing unlit cigarette ends; cannot afford to smoke whole cigarettes; (1) +
    - metaphorically — they are the dregs of a society, innocent victims of economic problems;
    - "failed culture" — recession which led to unemployment; link (cause / effect) made with idleness and poverty in **metaphor**, intensified by **alliteration**. (1) +
    - "fag-ends" — colloquial expression has shock effect. (1)

    H — full explanation of effects of language and devices + intelligent comment; Int. — clear understanding of language and devices + some comment.

3. **Show how the sentence structure and line layout of lines 9 – 10 effectively convey the impact made on the poet by the "maxi-skirted girl".** (2) A
    - His memories are stirred on seeing the young girl but of course it cannot be his mother; she was a young woman in 1930 and it is now 1970.
    - Line 10, **short sentences; caesurae** — mirror the impact on him; "But no." — **non-sentence, end-stopped lines** suggest his sadness, loss, yearning to find some trace of his mother.

    H – 4 x ½; Int. – one example of sentence structure + end-stopped lines.

4. *(a)* **Discuss the effectiveness of the poet's use of contrast in lines 12–13.** (2) A
    - He **contrasts** stone statues with living beings. He is sitting in George Square bordered by statues memorialising dead heroes; line 12, **caesura,** intensifies the two-word sentence.
    - "The mottled flesh" is the living being, whose flesh has varied tones and changes e.g., by blushing, with cold, etc.; also suggests the idea of imperfect, the mark of human beings; **unlike** the constant colouring of the stone, made perfect under the sculptor's hand; (1) +
    - "transient" is **set against** "remains", line 12: living beings short-lived but stone long-lasting. (1)

    H — full explanation of both sides of contrast, at least two textual references + intelligent comment.
    Int. — clear understanding of both sides of contrast, at least two examples + some comment.

    (b) **Comment on the ambiguity in "Stone remains", line 12.** (1) A
    - Those statues are all that is left of those people (the word "remains" used in the sense of a corpse); or stone endures, lasts — which points up the contrast of the next sentence.

(c) **Explain the importance of the contrasting ideas in those lines, in the context of the poem.** **(2) UA**
- Contrast between stone remains and transient flesh central to his search for his mother's spirit; now she is dead, he feels a gap. (He had become alienated from her through education and writing, but mostly his rejection of her Calvinist religion.)
- The country's dead are remembered by erecting stone statues and memorials but he is looking for something more personal, more spiritual; the essence of his mother.
- The statues, contrasting with what he is looking for — her "breath", line 2 — serve only to remind him of his loss and his inability to bridge the gap between them, now that she is dead.

H — full explanation of importance in context, good textual support + intelligent comment.
Int. — clear understanding of importance in context, some textual support + some comment.

5.　*" 'There was such warmth,' you said."* (line 16).
Discuss the effectiveness of three of the following techniques / devices used by the poet to evoke that atmosphere of "warmth" in lines 16–35: **(6) A**
(a) grammatical features; (b) sound; (c) rhyme; (d) imagery; (e) lexical choice; (f) contrast.
- *(a)* **Grammatical features,** line 16, **direct speech,** brings mother to life as witness to that warmth; lines 16–17, **present tense,** brings scene to life; lines 33–35, **reported speech,** mother's view comes through again, as witness to warmth; line 33, **comparative** in "happier"; line 34, emphasis of adverb of Degree, "Such".
- *(b)* **Sound,** line 16, "gaslight hums" — **onomatopoeia** — *m*-sound creates cosy atmosphere;
- *(c)* **Rhyme,** suggests harmony: lines 15–16, "slums" / "hums"; lines 34–35, "child" / "Wildes", neighbours helping each other.
- *(d)* **Imagery,** line 17, detail of shadows; "large caped (30s fashion) . . . tremble" (because of flickering of gas flame); line 22, "a black figure" — creates larger-than-life image of his mother; line 25, bright picture of colourful fruit.
- *(e)* **Lexical choice,** line 22, "gaslit blue", soft, warm light; (also effect of transposing functions of words: "blue gaslight" might be expected; "gaslit blue" focuses on the soft glow.)
  - line 24, "Flat-capped Glaswegians" . . . suggests friendly, approachable; "Music Hall" — live performance as opposed to cinema, TV; more personal in those days;
  - line 25, "open stall" suggests cheerful stall-holders, personal interest in customer;
  - line 26, "sparkling" suggests clean, pleasant (but spoiled by the "local sewage" in next line!);
  - line 34, "fine . . . helping"; "pleasant", line 35.
- *(f)* **Contrast,** "gaslit blue" warmer than the glare of the "fiercer voltage" of 1970.

H — full explanation of three devices / techniques + intelligent comment. Int. — clear understanding of three devices / techniques + some comment.

6.　*"The past's an experience that we cannot share."* (line 23)
Show how this statement is central to the main ideas raised in the poem,
- Line 23 is the conclusion reached by the poet as a result of his search for some trace of his mother; in it he acknowledges the differences between his mother and himself — generation gap; culture gap; and also conveys his sense of loss.
- **Contrast** between past and present throughout the poem, starts in first 2 lines:
- line 1, **past tense,** "many years ago", "You"; **end-stopped line** appropriate — mother dead;
- line 2, **present tense,** "I"; can find no trace of her; "breath": she is dead, looking for her spirit.
- Line 3, "long-skirted thirties" — **hypallage,** emphasises her in her time, which he cannot share;
- line 5, "failed culture", suggests a different outlook, way of life,
- Line 6 — firmly rooted in present; contrast between dark days of depression and present — "yellow . . . glows bright" + substance — War Memorial v. fag-ends;
- line 9, "maxi-skirted girl" — gives us a glimpse of 30s fashion in 70s.

- Line 11, "a 1970 sky" — 40 years since she lived here; he is in his time;
- line 16, **direct speech**, emphasises that he knows those things only from her telling him.
- Line 18, "Now everything is brighter", **contrast** with "shadows", line 17; **caesura** emphasises the break between then and now; the past is "Pale ghosts" — faint, ephemeral; line 20, changes in lifestyle, represented here by "lights of fiercer voltage"; the present has wiped out traces of the past; **paradox** of lines 20–21, "fiercer voltage . . . less / visible" intensifies the loss of contact; "less" emphasised by being placed at end of line;
  "flickering soul" suggests he cannot pin down his memories of her; links to gaslight, line 16;
- line 32, "constant" — contrast with "transient" — she hovers at the back of his mind; "tenant of my tenement" — links to her time in Glasgow slums — **metaphor**; **word play** adds to "flickering".
- From this point in the poem to the end, the loss of the past is linked firmly to the knocking down of the old tenements of Glasgow: "fallen rubble", visual image; people were housed in suburban schemes and led a new way of life; line 37, housing replaced but cannot replace the camaraderie of the people; picking up here the ideas in lines 12–13, stones / people;
- line 38, present-day Glasgow — **comparatives** unite but also separate them: "cleaner . . . better"
- line 39, ICS poking fun at himself a little, Lewis boy in his city clothes — but also **contrast** is made with her black clothes, symbol of Calvinism in his poems, cf. *Iolaire*; "paler hands", mother was a fisher girl who followed trawlers to gut the catch, hence red hands — his life is quite different, and soft by comparison; line 40 may be his own publication or just symbol of his education which separated them most effectively, her Gaelic culture being largely oral — note superlative here, "latest".
- Line 41, he addresses the ghosts of the tenement dwellers; feels affection for them because she was one of them; likes the feeling of the past in the present, but it stays in the past; "sunlit winds" — part of air / breath / **ghost references** throughout poem, which contribute to the idea of the transience of human existence.
- Line 44, **dichotomy** between two cultures — Calvinism of Lewis / more liberal Glasgow — the root of their differences; line 45, continues religion theme: Celtic / Rangers, Catholic / Protestant divide, similar to that between him and his mother, cannot be bridged.
- Line 46, "constant", echoes line 32, longing to make some contact, to lay his mother's spirit peacefully to rest; line 47, **assonance** — o-sound suggests hollow echo in the close — she's not there; line 48, accepting her culture as part of her, but also as separating them.
- Line 49, break in **line layout** mirrors the gap between then and now, the final fruitlessness of his search — the Glasgow in which she lived has gone; "bulldozer breaks" — strong violent words, intensified by **alliteration**; line 50, "powder" — "dust-to-dust" connotations; **caesura** emphasises break with past; "Boyish workmen" — new generation; he is getting older — "young policemen" syndrome; suggests naturalness of generation gap — another is forming behind him;
- lines 50–51, **simile** and **metaphor** — going forward into the future; Glasgow is moving on, progress is inevitable; line 51, old songs — symbol of her Gaelic culture, oral, traditional; line 52, giving way to modern pop culture; **pun** — "scale" = music; also magnitude of change; "dizzying" — reference to multi-storeys as well as rate of technological progress.

making clear the extent to which you agree with those ideas. (10) E

- Personal response will almost certainly come down on the side of the present, need to move with the times, but good answers might be expected to consider accepting / respecting each other's differences, generations living together in harmony; may pick up on the Catholic / Protestant divide in Glasgow or even in Northern Ireland.

H — fully developed discussion of past / present, well-supported by textual references + intelligent response; Int. — clear understanding past / present, some textual references + some personal response. Breakdown of marks: 7 + 3.

Level: Intermediate 1

1. **The poet mentions the thirties in line 3 and 1970 in line 11.
    What is the significance of those dates in the poem?**   **(2) U**
    - Mother lived there in 30s (1) + poet visiting city in 70s (1).

2. **Describe, in your own words, your impression of city life in the thirties, from lines 3–5.** **(2) U**
    - Ladies wore long skirts (1) + men unemployed / hung about street corners smoking (1).

3.   *"There was such warmth," you said.* (line 16)
    (a) **What is meant by "warmth"?**   **(1) U**
    - Friendliness / neighbourliness.
    (b) **What is the effect of using direct speech in this line?**   **(1) A**
    - Brings mother to life / makes her seem more real / as if he is hearing her words in his mind.
    (c) **How does the rest of the line add to the atmosphere of warmth?**   **(2) A**
    - Light / heat (1) + pleasant noise (1).

4. *(a)* **Who are the "pale ghosts" in line 18?**   **(1) U**
    - People who lived in old tenements / 30s.
    (b) **What are the "lights of fiercer voltage", line 20?**   **(1) U**
    - Electric lights / fluorescent strip lighting.
    (c) **How does the word "fiercer" help to make the contrast between then and now?** **(2) A**
    - Some attempt to explain contrast between hard glare of "fiercer" and softness of "warmth".
    (d) **What does the poet mean by "you are less / visible", lines 20–21?**   **(2) UA**
    - Literally, cannot see her (1) + idea of different time (1).

5. *(a)* **In your own words, describe the pleasant aspects of Glasgow, mentioned in lines 24–35.** **(3) UA**
    - Line 24, "Flat-capped Glaswegians" . . . suggests friendly, approachable; (1)
    - "Music Hall" — live performance as opposed to cinema, TV, more personal; (1)
    - line 25, "open stall" suggests cheerful stall-holders, personal interest in customer; (1)
    - line 26, "sparkling" suggests clean, pleasant, shining river (1) — *Any three.*
    (b) **What unpleasant aspect of the city does he mention in those lines?**   **(1) UA**
    - The "local sewage" in next line.

6. *(a)* **What is the poet describing in lines 49–50, from "The bulldozer . . .?** **(1) U**
    - Knocking down old tenements.
    (b) **Why is there a gap between "Highland Gaelic", line 48, and "The bulldozer", line 49?** **(1) A**
    - To show the gulf between then and now in the city.

7. *(a)* **Explain the comparison in lines 50–51, from "Boyish workmen . . .**   **(2) A**
    - Workmen on huge cranes / scaffolding (1) + compared to sailors high up in rigging / crow's nest (1).
    (b) **Why is this a good comparison?**   **(2)A**
    - Crane / high scaffolding like tall masts of sailing ships in height, shape (1) + some attempt to explain idea of progress, moving forward, like ship on a journey (1).

8.   *"The past's an experience that we cannot share.",* line 23.
    (a) **Explain, in your own words, what that statement means.**   **(2) U**
    - Attempt to explain different experiences of succeeding generations (2); cannot turn the clock back (1).
    (b) **To what extent do you think the poet has proved the truth of that statement in this poem? (Refer to the poem in your answer.)** **(2) E**
    - *See marking for question 6, Higher / Int. 2. — any attempt to make two points — mark on merit.*
    (c) **Do you agree with the statement? Why / why not?**   **(2) E**
    - Any attempt to make two points. — *Mark on merit.*

Suggested Outline Plans for Critical Essays

1. **Choose a poem which has something important to say to you. By closely referring to the poet's language, briefly explain why you consider the subject matter to be important, and go on to analyse how the language conveys the importance of the subject.** *(Old Woman)*
    §1   Title, poet, brief statement of situation presented in poem and what is important — euthanasia.
    §2   Starts with degradation / dehumanisation of old woman — lexical choice, hypallage, simile; comparison with mare + comment: animals can be legally relieved of suffering, not humans.
    §3   Poet's reaction to the situation: impatient with old couple, angry with Calvinist religion + quote from stanza 3; behaviour portrayed in classics + quote from stanza 4; education has led him away from the narrow outlook of his native community.
    §4   Conclusion: condemnation of Calvinism + refer to imagery in stanzas 5 and 6; poet advocates euthanasia + personal response to the idea.

2. **Poetry is often written as a result of reflecting on an intense emotional experience or on a significant event. Examine the techniques used by one poet to convey the significance of an experience or event which gave rise to a poem or sequence of poems.** *(Old Woman)*
    §1   Title, poet, brief statement of situation presented in poem, written following visit to elderly relatives on Lewis, and poet's reaction to it.
    §2   Poet's compassion for the old woman's suffering, degradation, and for the husband's burden; lexical choice, hypallage, simile, stanzas 1 and 2, juxtaposition; irony, scepticism – quote, etc.
    §3   Poet's feelings: anger: pathetic fallacy; pity and shame — stanza 3; he was brought up like them in Calvinist faith but has escaped through education; still affected though: "imprisoned"; seems to advocate euthanasia, comparison with classical heroes — quote, etc.
    §4   Conclusion: ends with compassion for old couple: direct speech, repetition, lexical choice, synecdoche, seaweed imagery in last stanza + personal response (including to euthanasia).

3. **Sonnet, Dramatic Monologue, Ballad . . . By looking closely at a poem with one such form, consider to what extent its particular techniques enhance the impact of the subject matter.** *(Iolaire)*
    §1   Title, poet, form, persona, brief description of the disaster, enigma and irony of the situation.
    §2   We witness the reactions of the elder — quote / refer to and comment on mood and tone of disbelief §1: syntax, repetition; description of scene: metaphor, lexical choice, irony — quote.
    §3   Start of doubts, questioning, lines 12–17; bitterness, lines 18–21; gradual turning from God, lines 27–29; talks directly to God: comment; final rejection: water imagery, baptism — quote / explain.
    §4   Conclusion: choice of persona makes impact, because generally narrow-minded, follow doctrines doggedly, believe God determines each individual's fate; unclear ending.

4. **Many poems are concerned with a sense of loss or deep sadness at a particular event. Examine the techniques / devices by which a poet, in one poem, conveys either of those emotions.** *(Iolaire)*
    §1   Title, poet, explain disaster, enigma and irony of situation; mention persona.
    §2   See aftermath of tragedy through eyes of persona: mood and tone §1: disbelief, puzzled, nightmare — syntax, repetition; description of scene — metaphor, lexical choice, irony — quote.
    §3   Preparations made, new start, end war: irony; further descriptions: man as God's plaything, helpless; day breaks as usual in spite of loss — quote / explain / comment.
    §4   Conclusion: loss of lives mirrored in elder's loss of faith, which was his life; unclear ending perhaps suggests he knows what he is rejecting but not what he is putting in its place; poet's loss of faith and alienation from native community + personal response.

CHAPTER 6 — Norman MacCaig

Suggested Study Points: *Assisi*

UNDERSTANDING

1. **The situation**
   - A beggar sits outside the Church of St Francis in the Italian town of Assisi.
   - He is ignored by the priest and tourists who are being shown Giotto's famous frescoes.

2. **The themes**
   - The plight of the disabled / isolation.
   - The injustice of fate.
   - The hypocrisy of the Church.
   - The apathy of society towards the less-fortunate.
   - Rich v. poor / social injustice.

ANALYSIS

Verse 1, lines 1–9, introduces the **beggar**: abnormally short, severely disabled, with deformed limbs.
   - **Tone**: created by casual use of **brutal language**: line 1, "dwarf": in non-medical context is derogatory; "with his hands on backwards": casual tone; no hint of sympathy or compassion for the plight of the man or the pain which almost certainly accompanies his disability; line 2, "sat, slumped": no sympathetic tone (**onomatopoeia** suggests the heaviness of his body and his lack of control over it); "like a half-filled sack": comparison with inanimate object, emphasises non-human shape; line 3, "tiny twisted legs": idea of limpness, like a rag doll; not just small but "tiny" emphasises the grotesque nature of his deformity; lines 4–5, "from which / sawdust might run": non-human, like a piece of furniture or bonfire guy, filled with sawdust.
   - **Effect**: dehumanises the beggar.
   - **Purpose**: to shock his readers into a reaction — poet considers that we, like tourists in the poem, may be apathetic to the plight of poor and disabled people who require our help just to exist, so he verbally thrusts the disabled beggar in our faces defying us to withhold our pity.
   - **Tone**: created by **sarcasm**:
   - lines 7–9, (St Francis) "over whom / he had the advantage / of not being dead yet"; continues the brutal tone, **ironical**. Clearly, the poet thinks the beggar would be better off dead. The tone helps us to realise that the poet does not mean to be brutal in his descriptions of the beggar; reveals his pity for the beggar and anger at the way he is neglected.
   - **Irony of situation**: The fact that the beggar is ignored outside this church which is dedicated to St Francis, "brother of the poor".
   - **Juxtaposition**: grotesquely disabled beggar is placed outside architecturally elaborate and beautiful church. The first four lines describe the beggar followed by line five: "outside the three tiers of churches" — description sounds very ornate, like a wedding cake. Emphasises the hideousness of the divinely created beggar in contrast with the man-made church and criticises the Church, which will spend a lot of money on lavish buildings and furnishings but give nothing to the poor; intensified by the **syntax** (both ideas in a single sentence).
   - **Alliteration**: "tiny twisted legs" — intensifies the grotesque extent of the beggar's deformity.

Verse 2, lines 10–17, introduces the **priest**:
   - proud: shows off his church and the valuable paintings;
   - superior / pompous: explains how Giotto's paintings were designed to tell stories to "the — illiterate", whom he obviously regards as inferior to himself but perhaps not to the tourists;
   - condescending: "how clever it was of Giotto", as if he is superior to Giotto;
   - commercial / materialistic: acting as some kind of tourist guide, no doubt collecting tips, when he should be more spiritually-inclined;

- self-indulgent: more interested in aesthetic quality of paintings than in pastoral duties;
- hypocritical: talks about "the goodness of God and the suffering of His Son" but ignores real human suffering, which he should be trying to alleviate himself, as well as bringing it to the notice of the people whom he is instructing.
- **Tone**: lines 15–17, "I understood / the explanation and / the cleverness";
- dry, sarcastic tone suggests the poet's scepticism and criticism of the priest (and of the Church), who, in the poet's opinion, should be trying to alleviate the suffering of the living, like the beggar outside his church door, and teaching people their Christian duty to such people instead of telling them about paintings of the dead Christ and how clever the artist was.
- **Syntax** adds to the tone; emphasis on "cleverness" at end of verse, suggesting double meaning — the poet has understood the cleverness of Giotto but has also "twigged" what the priest is up to. The full stop in the middle of line 15 ending the long sentence from the start of the verse necessitates a pause in which you can almost hear the poet's sceptical "Huh!"
- **Irony**: The priest spends his time talking to tourists when he might be expected to be administering to the needy of his parish; his instincts seem to be commercial rather than pastoral; by implying what should happen, the poet criticises priest and Church in general.

Verse 3: lines 18–27, introduces the **tourists**, who follow the priest, happily swallowing every word — line 18, "clucking contentedly"; walk past the beggar, ignoring his plight — lines 20–21.

- **Extended metaphor**; lines 18–20, "A rush of tourists . . . the Word.": the tourists are compared to chickens; "clucking contentedly (they) fluttered after him as he scattered the grain . . ." Chickens are proverbially brainless and when they are being fed, they fall on the grain, fluttering over each other to get at it; suggests that the tourists are equally undiscriminating as they "swallow" the priest's Word. (Note: the capital "W" means the Word of God, i.e., the teachings of the Church in general). The priest, like the farmer feeding chickens, spreads the dogma of the Church and expects the people to accept it in blind faith, without question.
- **Juxtaposition**: here emphasises the apathy of society;
- tourists walk past beggar to view frescoes which depict suffering of Christ whilst ignoring the real suffering of the beggar. "It was they who had passed the ruined temple outside".
- The **syntax** suggests the scorn felt by the poet towards the tourists. "It was they who" rather than simply "they", as if accusing them, verbally pointing his finger at them.
- **Metaphor**: poet refers to the beggar as a "ruined temple", line 21; Christians believe that the body is the "tabernacle" (or temple) of the soul and should be treated with respect. The beggar is disabled, hence "ruined". Clearly this poor creature is not respected by the priest and tourists, who are more interested in the stone temple and its treasures. The metaphor draws attention to the neglect by the priest and tourists. **Irony** — a temple is generally beautiful and the disabled beggar is grotesque but, as a human being, he deserves respect.
- Adds to description of beggar: hunch-backed, with mattery eyes and a twisted mouth, from which comes a piping, childlike voice.
- **Tone**: return to brutal language in description of beggar: lines 21–22, "whose eyes / wept pus"; the word "pus" gives an unpleasant picture of poisonous green matter oozing out of his eyes;
- lines 22–23, "back . . . higher than his head": technically accurate but not a sympathetic description, almost as if poking fun at the hunchback.
- **Simile**: lines 24–25, (the beggar's voice is) "as sweet / as a child's when she speaks to her mother" — "child" suggests innocence, the use of the female suggests gentleness and the child / mother relationship suggests love and respect.
- Lines 26–27, "or a bird's when it spoke to St Francis" — a bird is devoid of the baser instincts that human beings display and communicating with a saint adds to the purity of the image.
- The poet is saying that the beggar is as innocent and as harmless as a child or a bird. He is drawing our attention to the injustice suffered by the beggar, who cannot help being disabled. He has to beg, not because he is too lazy to work but because he is physically incapable of supporting himself in any other way.

Looking over the whole poem

• **Poetic Form — Free Verse**:
- three verse paragraphs; no rhyme or regular metrical pattern;
- allows poet freedom to use beginnings and ends of lines and to vary line lengths for emphasis; natural narrative rhythm gives credibility to incident and to poet's feelings.

• **Structure**:
- each verse begins with introduction of one character / character group — seems to emphasise the lack of real contact between them and particularly the isolation of the beggar;
- begins and ends with beggar; brutal language at start, sweetness emphasised at end.
- Comes back to St Francis in the last line of the poem to remind us of the ironic position of the beggar and to intensify poet's criticism of a priest (and a religion) which places more value on fine buildings and valuable paintings than on the well-being of its parishioners.

• **Contrast** intensifies the difference between the beggar and more fortunate members of society, highlighting the themes of the poem: Rich tourists who can afford to take holidays v. poor beggar who does not even have the means to live — rich v. poor / social injustice.
- The contrast also draws attention to the tourists' lack of interest in the plight of the beggar, despite the severity of his disabilities — apathy of society and injustice of Fate. They are on holiday and are carefree, having the leisure to enjoy the wonderful art work on display inside the church, while the beggar is outside painfully begging for the means to exist.
- Their mobility is contrasted with his immobility; in verse 3, "a rush of tourists . . . fluttered after . . ." whereas he "sat, slumped" [verse 1] — physical disability / injustice of Fate.
- The tourists move round in a group while the beggar is isolated, on his own, shunned by society because of his grotesque appearance — isolation / injustice of Fate.

EVALUATION

• To what extent have conditions improved for disabled? Facilities, attitudes . . .?
- What are our responsibilities towards less fortunate people in society?
- Pros and cons of releasing mental hospital patients into society. NIMBY syndrome?

• **Poet's attitude**
- Compassion and concern — the last four lines of the poem — see above under simile.
• Concerned and wants to draw our attention to such people by his shockingly graphic descriptions of the beggar's physical defects — brutal language.
• Pity for the beggar, obvious in the sarcastic tone of last three lines of verse 1 — sarcasm.
• Angry at the way people neglect the needy members of our society who require our help. He mocks the tourists in the chicken metaphor in verse 3 and makes clear his opinion that they should be attending to the living who need their help instead of looking at paintings of the dead Christ. His scorn is clear in the syntax of the sentence in verse 3, lines 20–21.
• The poet seems to put most blame on the priest / the Church in general. His bitterness against the Church comes through in verse 2, where he shows the priest behaving more like a tourist guide than a spiritual director, especially in the dry tone of the last three lines of that verse — see under **tone — sarcasm** — and again in the chicken metaphor.

Using Your Notes for Revision: Checklist

UNDERSTANDING AND ANALYSIS *(Use these questions to revise important parts of the poem.)*

1. **Summarise the situation presented in the poem.**
   - A beggar sits outside the Church of St Francis in the Italian town of Assisi.
   - He is ignored by the priest and tourists who are being shown Giotto's famous frescoes.

2. **Characters: the beggar.**
   - The beggar is abnormally short, severely disabled, hunch-backed, with deformed limbs, mattery eyes and a twisted mouth, from which comes a piping, childlike voice.

3. **Poet's presentation of the beggar in lines 1–4:**
   (a) **What kind of language is used in these lines?**
      - Brutal language, which dehumanises the beggar.
   (b) **Examples:** See Suggested Study points, page 88, for details.
      - "dwarf", line 1; "with his hands on backwards", line 1; "sat, slumped", line 2; "like a half-filled sack", line 2; "tiny twisted legs", line 3; "from which sawdust might run," lines 3–4.
   (c) **Note the effects of onomatopoeia and alliteration in these lines.**
      - "slumped" — heaviness of body; no control.
      - s-sound — suggests sadness of beggar's life, mimics sound of sawdust running out.
      - t-sound intensifies grotesque nature of deformity.
   (d) **Tone:** Matter of fact; derogatory; no hint of sympathy — but ironic.
   (e) **The poet 's purpose:** To shock readers into a reaction; poet considers that we like tourists in the poem may be apathetic to the plight of the poor and disabled people who require our help just to exist, so he verbally thrusts the disabled beggar in our faces and defies us to withhold our pity.

4. **Characters: the priest. What characteristics of the priest are suggested in verse 2?**
   Evidence:

Characteristic:	*Evidence:*
• proud	shows off his church and the valuable paintings;
• superior/ pompous	explains how Giotto's paintings were designed to tell stories to "the illiterate", like the tourists perhaps ;
• condescending	"how clever it was of Giotto", as if he is superior to Giotto, giving him a pat on the head!
• commercial / materialistic	acting as some kind of tourist guide, no doubt collecting tips;
• self-indulgent	more interested in aesthetic quality of paintings than in performing spiritual duties of a priest;
• hypocritical	talks about "the goodness of God and the suffering of His Son" but ignores real human suffering, which he should be trying to alleviate himself, as well as bringing it to the notice of the people whom he is instructing.

5. **Characters: the tourists.**
   (a) **What do we learn about the tourists in verse 3?**
      - Ignore the beggar; swallow the priest's words; empty-headed; thoughtless.
   (b) **Extended metaphor:** See Suggested Study Points, page 89, for details:
      Tourists compared to chickens swallowing grain (the priest's words) at feeding time.
   (c) **What is MacCaig saying about the tourists and the priest?**
      Priest expects people to accept his teachings without question as hens accept corn feed, and they do.

6.   Irony:

(a) • **The irony of the situation**: lies in the implied contrast between what might be expected to happen and what does happen: instead of ministering to the poor of his parish, priest acts like tourist guide; Church dedicated to St Francis, "brother / of the poor", lines 6–7, yet beggar, sitting outside it, is ignored.

(b) **Use of contrast and juxtaposition to convey Irony and to put across the themes of the poem.**
   • **Contrast**: rich tourists who can afford to take holidays v. poor beggar who does not even have the means to live (theme: rich v. poor).
   - MacCaig criticises the tourists by showing them as apathetic to the plight of the beggar, despite the severity of his disabilities (theme: apathy); they are on holiday and are carefree, having the leisure to enjoy the wonderful artwork on display inside the church while the beggar is outside painfully begging for the means to exist (theme: injustice of Fate);
   - their mobility is contrasted with his immobility in verse 3, "a rush of tourists . . . fluttered after him" (theme: physical disability);
   - the tourists move round in a group while the beggar is isolated, on his own, shunned by society because of his grotesque appearance (theme: isolation).
   • **Juxtaposition** (emphasised by syntax): grotesquely disabled beggar is placed outside architecturally elaborate and beautiful church — "three tiers of churches", line 5 — emphasising the hideousness of the "God-made" beggar in contrast with the beauty of the man-made church (themes: physical disability and hypocrisy of Church, which will spend a lot of money on lavish buildings and furnishings but give nothing to the poor);
   - tourists walk past beggar to view frescoes which depict suffering of Christ whilst ignoring the real suffering of the beggar — "It was they who had passed the ruined temple outside" (theme: apathy of society).

EVALUATION *(Use this question for exam practice.)*

7.   Explain, in detail, and justify by close reference to the poem, what you consider to be the poet's attitude to the scene he observes, (7)
   • The poet's attitude towards the beggar is one of compassion and concern.
   - Lines 24–27 — beggar innocent, harmless; he describes the beggar's voice — quote, etc.
   - He draws our attention to the injustice suffered by the beggar + explain / comment.
   - The poet is concerned and wants to draw our attention to such people by his shockingly graphic descriptions of the beggar's physical defects (verses 1 and 3) — quote, etc.
   - The poet feels pity for the beggar. Evidence — sarcasm (lines 7–9) + comment.
   - The poet is angry at the way people in general neglect the needy members of our society who require our consideration and help (tourists) — quote / explain / comment (verse 2 and chicken metaphor, syntax, line 20).
   - Metaphor, line 21, poet refers to the beggar as a "ruined temple" — explain.
   - He seems to put most of the blame on the priest and on the Church in general — (verse 2 and tone, lines 15–17; chicken metaphor) — quote / explain / comment.

H – well-developed discussion of poet's attitude to three character groups, with good textual support + intelligent comment. Int. – clear understanding of poet's attitudes, some textual support + some comment.

making clear in your answer the extent to which you agree or disagree with him. (3)
   • Personal response may touch on several themes or concentrate on one. *Mark on merit.*

Suggested Study Points — *Visiting Hour*

UNDERSTANDING

1. **The situation**
   - Visiting hour in hospital. The poet is making his way along the corridors towards Ward 7, where his seriously ill relative lies.

2. **The themes**
   - Facing death, both from the point of view of the dying person and that of the surviving relative; dealing with feelings.
   - Inexorability of death.
   - Problems of communication.

ANALYSIS

Verse 1, lines 1–4. The **scene** is set in verse 1 by reference to the poet's senses: line 1, "The hospital smell"; line 4, "green and yellow corridors", accord with most people's experience of hospitals.

- The poet **creates mood / atmosphere** through **lexical choice**: line 2, "combs my nostrils": smell is so pungent and so unpleasant to him, as if it reaches the roots of the hairs in his nostrils; line 4, "green and yellow": colours of vomit, pus; suggest unpleasantness, his discomfort / unease in this place; he finds the visit distressing.
- **Synecdoche**, lines 2–3, "nostrils / . . . bobbing along": obviously his whole body is moving along the corridor, not just his nostrils. The **synecdoche** focuses attention on the nostrils in order to strengthen the idea of the "hospital smell" being so overpowering that all other impressions are blanked out, thus intensifying his feeling of unease in the situation.

Verse 2, lines 5–7

- **Mood / atmosphere**: first indication of what is on his mind comes when he sees a trolley bearing a body: line 5, "What seems a corpse" – he immediately assumes it is a dead body — "vanishes heavenward" — in fact, it goes up in the lift, but as far as the poet is concerned, it is on its last journey. He is obviously worried about his sick relative – has he come too late?
- There are many examples of **enjambment**; the effect is usually to emphasise the last word on the line: in lines 5 / 6 / 7, the focus is on "corpse" and on "vanishes", in line with his thoughts of death and its finality; also suggests his progress along the corridors as well as the confused state of his mind.
- His concern shows too in the **lexical choice**: "trundled" implies lack of care by the porter; as if the poet thinks there is no point taking care as the person is dead; supports his general feeling of hopelessness at this stage of the visit.

Verse 3, lines 8–10

- **Repetition**: the poet appears to be talking to himself. The repetition intensifies the control he is trying to impose on himself, denying his feelings as they are too painful.
- Together with the staccato **rhythm** of this short verse, with its monosyllabic words, and the **enjambment** on lines 8–10, the repetition heightens the **atmosphere** of tension.
- The rest of the verse "until / I have to" shows the poet making a conscious effort to be detached. He knows he will have to face up to the situation eventually, but not yet.

Verse 4, lines 11–18

- Creates **mood / atmosphere** by recording details of the nurses:
- how they walk: "lightly, swiftly"; appearance: "slender waists"; expression: "eyes . . . clear".
- **Syntax**: in line 12, unusual word order — one would expect "here and there" — highlights the ubiquitous nature of the nurses, as if they are everywhere, upstairs and downstairs at once.
- "and . . . and . . . and" drags the line out, emphasising the distance the nurses cover and gives the impression of the speed at which they move around.

- An implied contrast here with himself and the way he is (or is not) coping as he drags himself reluctantly to his dreaded destination: "slender waists" suggests young women and he marvels at the way they cope — "miraculously carrying their burden" — compared with the struggle he, a mature man, has with his feelings. "Burden" conveys the extent of his anguish, and "farewells" in the last line anticipates the last unbearable goodbye to his dying relative; yet the nurses seem able to deal with so many deaths, "their eyes still clear."

- **Repetition** — "so much pain, so/ many deaths . . . so many farewells."; emphasises the extent of the burden the nurses carry, intensified by the **enjambment** on the second "so", and strengthens the contrast with his own response to the situation.

Verse 5, lines 19–30

- **Caesura** in line 19 is unexpected; signals a long pause, in line with the narrative. He has arrived outside the ward and comes to an abrupt halt. He has to stop, take a deep breath and pull himself together, steeling himself for the ordeal ahead.
- The numeral "7" stands out from the surrounding words, a visual reminder to us of where the poet is; this is how it would appear on the actual door, so we can see what he sees and feel his dread on reading those words.

- **Imagery / Metaphor**
- *"She lies, / in a cave of white forgetfulness."*, lines 19–20. *(This example is explained in the pupils' book.)*
  The bed, screened off by a white curtain, in the centre of which she lies, is compared to a cave; it is a "cave of forgetfulness" because she is barely conscious.
  The **metaphor** is appropriate as she is cut off from the rest of the ward as effectively as if she were in a cave in the side of a cliff. The curtains are well above the level of her head, adding to the cave impression. Because she is in a coma, she cannot communicate with the poet, nor he with her. "white" adds to the feeling of inaccessibility, as if the poet is seeing her through a white haze or snowstorm, a white-out or "white noise" which impedes communication. There are connotations of other cultures in the past where old people, when they became a burden, were left in caves in the hillside to die.
- *"A withered hand / trembles on its stalk"*, lines 21–22:
- "withered" appropriate to dying woman; "stalk" suggests thinness / weakness of her arm.
- The trembling hand and eyes moving behind eyelids are her fluttering uncontrolled attempts to reach him, so he, too, is alone with his pain. The **enjambment** emphasises the heaviness of the patient's eyelids and the effort she is making to open them, to communicate with him. The flower **image** gives the sense of fragility and her beauty in the eyes of the poet, who looks on her with love.
- *". . . Into an arm wasted / of colour a glass fang is fixed, / not guzzling but giving."*, lines 24–26.
- The vampire **image** intensified by the **alliteration** conveys his abhorrence at the sight of the drip feeding blood into the patient's veins. He sees the needle as a fang biting into her arm, like a vampire greedily drinking her blood — "guzzling" makes this picture almost obscene and the arm "wasted of colour" adds to the impression that that the blood is being taken out rather than given. Effectively conveys his pity for the suffering of the patient, his distress, and the feeling that the whole process is intrusive and pointless.
- *"And between her and me / distance..../....that neither she nor I / can cross."*, lines 27–30.
- He bends to kiss her but she does not respond. She is alone with her pain which has formed an invisible barrier between them; he cannot reach her. The image conveys his feeling of desolation and hopelessness at this inability to reach her; his isolation is emphasised by the **enjambment** — "I", poised at the end of the longest line of the poem, intensifies his isolation and the lack of communication between them.

- The imagery in this verse effectively monitors the gradual opening of the floodgates to the feelings he was trying so hard to control earlier.

Verse 6, lines 31–38

- When the bell rings at the end of the visiting hour, he leaves in a highly emotional state.
- **Metaphor**, line 34: *"(he) clumsily rises / in the round swimming waves of a bell."*
- He escapes from his distress like a drowning man to dry land.
- **Synaesthesia**: "round" and "swimming" are visual images unusually here describing a sound; "round" signals the intensity of the effect the ringing of the bell has on him; "swimming" suggests his eyes are filled with tears, his head swimming with the emotion of the experience, confirmed by "dizzily" in the next line. His self-control has collapsed now as he stumbles "clumsily" out of the ward.
- **Pun**, line 35: the poet would grow fainter with distance from the patient; he is so upset he feels faint.
- **Paradox**, line 37, and **oxymoron**, line 38: she is beyond his reach; he can do nothing for her; he has brought books and fruit but knows she is past reading and eating. He has gone through the motions of visiting but knows his presence has made no difference to the final outcome. His distress and confusion are intensified by the paradox and oxymoron.
- **Alliteration**, line 38: the futility of the situation is intensified by the fricative "f" sound.

Looking over the whole poem

- **Poetic form:** Free Verse — appropriate to narrative and to confusion in poet's mind / feelings.
- The overall **structure** contributes to the **atmosphere / mood**:
- Verses 1–3: short, staccato; create sense of place, atmosphere and poet's feelings in the situation. Verse 4: sense of bustle in busy hospital, leading into verse 5: main action, sense of hush in presence of dying woman; post-action verse 6: opening of floodgates of poet's emotions in face of his inevitable loss.
- The structure follows the **narrative** shape with introduction / setting / character in setting in verses 1–3; followed by further development / detail in verse 4; building up to climax in verse 5; and ending with a kind of epilogue in verse 6.
- The content of the verses helps us to place the poet and accompany him on his journey:
- verse 1 — entering the hospital; verse 2 — passing the lift; verse 4 — passing stairs and wards, populated by nurses going about their work; verse 5 — ward 7; verse 6 — back in corridor, bell ringing.
- We also follow the build-up and gradual release of the poet's feelings.
- By writing in the **first person**, the poet can express his feelings from the inside, which an observer would have been unable to detect. Those feelings come across as genuine, as the feelings experienced by the poet himself.
- N.B. In verse 6, where he has lost control of his feelings, he writes in third person.
- **Stream of consciousness** style lends immediacy and gains our sympathy: helps us to put ourselves in the poet's position / identify with his feelings. We arrive with him, walk the corridors and leave with him, thus increasing the poem's emotional impact.

EVALUATION

- Themes: taking two points of view together, less of an ordeal for dying person than for person left behind? But in the poem, we are given only the surviving relative's point of view; we do not know what is going on in the mind of the dying woman.
- Dying is something we have to do on our own, even if surrounded by loved ones. Poet's inability to communicate with patient, as if she has already begun the process of dying.
- Highlights need to communicate while we can, not leave things unsaid.
- Personal response to poet's feelings — realistic, convincing?

Using Your Notes for Revision: Checklist

UNDERSTANDING AND ANALYSIS *(Use these questions to help you revise important parts of the poem.)*

1. **Situation:**

    (a) **Summarise the experience which inspired this poem.**
        - The poet enters hospital to visit a close relative who is near to death.
        - We accompany him on his journey along corridors and into the ward.
        - He is unable to communicate with her but she seems to know he is there.
        - At the end of visiting, he stumbles out in a very emotional state.
        - She smiles: suggests when time comes one is ready to die? Or trying to reassure him?

    (b) **Theme: How the poet has used this experience to convey his ideas about death and dying.**
        - Facing death from the point of view of dying person:
        - isolation of death; something we must do alone, even if family is present:
        - her attempts to communicate — eyes moving behind closed eyelids, fluttering hands.
        - Facing death from point of view of surviving relative:
        - worrying about condition of relative before he gets there — still alive / too late?
        - Denies situation in attempt to control feelings, for sake of sick person as well as his own;
        - feelings of inadequacy in coping with situation;
        - upset at seeing sick person attached to drips, machines, etc.;
        - impossible to make contact with loved one; her smile is no comfort to him;
        - situation so abhorrent, he rises as soon as the bell rings for the end of visiting.
        - Taking two points of view together, seems to suggest death is more of an ordeal for those left behind than it is for the dying person;
        - but we are not given dying person's point of view from the inside.

2. **Setting the Scene:**
    (a) **Note the details in lines 1–18, which help us to imagine the scene.**
        - Gives details of what he sees: corridors, trolley with patient, lift, nurses . . .
        - **Syntax** in line 12, word order and "and . . . and . . . and" suggests bustle, urgency.

    (b) **Use of sensory observation:**
        - the scene in verse 1 is set by reference to poet's senses: smell, colours.

3. **Atmosphere / mood:**
    (a) **Lexical choice and synecdoche in lines 1–4.**
        - "combs my nostrils"; connotations of "green and yellow".
        - **Synecdoche:** lines 2–3, "nostrils . . . bobbing along . . ."

    (b) **His reactions to what he sees:**
        - The first indication of what is on his mind comes when he sees the trolley bearing a body;
          — "What seems a corpse vanishes heavenward";
        - **enjambment; lexical choice:** "trundled"

    (c) **Repetition, rhythm and layout:**
        - Repetition: poet talking to himself; effort of trying to hold back feelings;
        - staccato rhythm and enjambment on lines 9–10 create tension.

    (d) **Reaction to the nurses:**
        - implied contrast here between himself and nurses.
        - Repetition, lines 15–18 — emphasises extent of burden.

4.   **Imagery:**
   (a) **Syntax in line 19** — full stop, numeral, **caesura** — show his reaction on arriving at the door of the ward.
   (b) **Revise the effectiveness of the imagery and metaphors in verse 5.**
   - Culmination of journey and of theme — poet's feelings build to climax: he is forced to face up to the situation.
   - Cave image, lines 19–20: isolation of dying woman.
   - Flower image, lines 21–22: we witness his love and tenderness towards the patient.
   - Vampire image, lines 24–26: his horror at the sight of her wired up to drips, etc.
   - Barrier image, lines 27–30: his feeling of helplessness at their inability to communicate.

5.   **Last verse, lines 31–38:**
   (a) **Note the ways in which the poet has changed by this point.**
   - Faced up to situation; no longer in control of emotions.
   (b) **Devices / techniques used to show the changes in him:** metaphor, lines 33–34; synaesthesia, line 34; pun, line 35; paradox, line 37; oxymoron and alliteration, line 38.

EVALUATION *(Use this question for exam practice.)*

6.   Discuss the extent to which you consider *Visiting Hour* to be an *effective* and *credible* portrayal of a person's reactions to such distressing personal circumstances as these, making clear whether or not the poet gained your sympathy.   **(10 marks)**

   - **Effective?**
   -   The narrative **structure** traces the emotional journey of a man through hospital corridors to the ward where his dying relative lies and back out again:
   -     verse 1   uneasy in hospital setting — smell — quote / explain / comment;
   -     verse 2   morbid thoughts of death, about what he will find — quote / explain / comment;
   -     verse 3   refuses to allow himself to feel, saving himself from the pain of feeling, but knows he will have to face it eventually — quote / explain / comment;
   -     verse 4   allows himself to be distracted momentarily by admiration for the nurses, marvelling at the way they cope — quote / explain / comment; feels inadequate because of his comparatively poor showing. Dread of what is to come is still there, seen in lexical choice: "burden", "pain", "deaths", "farewells".
   -     verse 5   Dread as he halts outside ward door; tries to pull himself together and summon up strength to go in — quote / explain / comment;
                     Imagery conveys feelings of love, pity, distress, helplessness — quote, etc.;
   -     verse 6   communication is almost achieved as she "smiles a little at this / black figure". She seems to know he is there but the smile serves only to point up the frailty of the link between them — he is a "black figure" (already in mourning?). When the bell rings, he stumbles out, clumsy with emotion — quote / explain / comment; futility of the situation — oxymoron — quote, etc.
   - Stream of consciousness style allows us to share his experience and feelings at first hand.
   - **Credible?**
   -   Writing in first person allows the poet to convey feelings from the inside, more genuine.
   -   Description of hospital corridors accords with most people's experience of hospitals;
   -   inability to face up to / take in death of loved one is very natural;
   -   feelings of abhorrence at loved one wired up to machines, frustration at inability to make contact, feelings of helplessness and loss are all very normal reactions.
   - **Sympathy?** (May be subsumed in treatment of credible.)
       Personal response but must be backed up by reference to the poem. Might suggest poet over-reacting in verse 5, or being selfish in his reaction to drip, etc., as it is helping patient; or that he is over-critical of himself in verse 4 . . .
       Rough breakdown of marks: 4 + 3 + 3

Unseen Textual Analysis: Marking Schemes — *Hotel Room, 12th Floor*

Levels: Higher and Intermediate 2

1. **Referring closely to verse 1, lines 1–9, show how the poet creates . . .**
    (a) **a sense of time,**   **(1) U**
    - "This morning", line 1 (½) + "now midnight has come in", line 6; "darkness", line 7. (½)

    (b) **and a sense of place.**   **(1) U**
    - Title — hotel room; 12th floor (½) +
    - names real buildings — "Empire State Building", line 3; "PanAm skyscraper", line 5. (½)

    (c) **Explain how the setting contributes to the mood of the poem.**   **(2) A**
    - "This morning . . . now" — lends immediacy.
    - "midnight . . . darkness" suggests evil, contrast with "a million lit windows"; evil seems to come with the darkness "from foreign places" — poet's anxiety is almost tangible.
    - Title suggests impersonal surroundings, isolation;
    - naming real buildings lends credibility.

    H — two examples of each (time and place), well explained + intelligent comment re effect on mood;
    Int. — at least one example of each (time and place); link to mood clearly understood.

2. *(a)* **Explain the effectiveness of the simile in line 2 and of the metaphor in line 4, making clear what, together, they reveal of the poet's reaction and attitude to the Empire State Building.**   **(4) A**
    - Simile: "helicopter . . . like a damaged insect";
    - size suggested by comparison with insect, even from 12th floor;
    - noise made by helicopter sounds like a bluebottle which has been sprayed with insect killer; going round and round is another feature of sprayed insect;
    - unpleasant connotations.
    - Metaphor: "that / jumbo size dentist's drill":
    - dentist's drill refers to the shape, jumbo size to the height of the building.
    - Poet's attitude: Those two images are generally referred to as **conceits**; the comparisons certainly do not enhance the images, rather they are disparaging. They reveal the poet's contempt for what he sees as the American desire to have the biggest of everything. The ESB is regarded as a monument to the American way of life, which the poet is attacking.

    H — devices fully discussed + intelligent comment re poet's attitude;
    Int. — devices identified and understood + some comment re poet's attitude.

    (b) **Consider the common theme in these two devices, and show how they form an effective introduction to a main concern of the poem.**   **(2) A**
    - Both devices depict suffering: the damaged insect, the dentist's drill (a common metaphor for pain!) (1) + the poem goes on to identify causes of suffering and the effects. (1)

    (c) **Explain how the image in lines 8–9 adds to the theme in lines 2–4.**   **(2) A**
    - "a million lit windows, all / ups and acrosses";
    - the window frames are in the form of The Cross; the suffering of Christ on The Cross, dying to save civilisation (compare light trying to fight off "uncivilised darkness");
    - suggests that religion (light) makes a vain attempt to counteract the evil, symbolised by the darkness. ("But midnight is not / so easily defeated.", lines 10–11.)
    - The poet's anxiety in the situation is clear; he feels society is beyond redemption.

    - Civilisation symbolised here by the ESB, pride of the USA, attacked by the poet;
    - evil symbolised by darkness leads into verse 2 which deals with human suffering and isolation, in the midst of ostentation and wealth, such as the ESB.

    H — should see the link clearly and how it leads into verse 2; Int. — some awareness of both.

3. *(a)* **Referring closely to lines 13–14, show how the poet uses Wild West imagery to take his argument forward.**   **(3) A**
   - Wild West imagery: the police and ambulance sirens are "the wildest of warwhoops . . . ululating": the fearsome shrieks (really needs to be demonstrated!) which emit from the Braves in war paint as they attack with axes and arrows in the cowboy and Indian films;
   - intensified by alliteration; suggest the uncivilised nature of the street violence.
   - The streets are referred to as "glittering canyons and gulches" — the high buildings on both sides of the streets resemble those areas favoured by the film Indians for ambush purposes; the implication is that the streets in the city are just as dangerous.

   H — WW imagery fully understood; individual words / phrases well-explained + intelligent comment.
   Int. — WW imagery recognised; some individual words clearly understood + some comment.

   (b) **How does the poet's situation / position at this point in the poem add to the effectiveness of this imagery?**   **(1) A**
   - Poet is in bed, on 12th floor, with both radio and TV switched on (½) + ;
   - makes us realise how loud those noises must be if he they can still disturb him in that position (½);
   - **or** he seems to be frightened, trying to blot out the violence with radio and TV (½).

4. **Show how the device, which the poet uses in lines 16–18, serves to illustrate the truth of his argument.**   **(4) A**
   - **Synecdoche**: refers to "broken bones" — not the person who has broken bones; "harsh screaming" — not the hurt person who is screaming in fear or pain; "blood glazed" — not the person who has been attacked and injured:
   - in each case, part of the person is used to represent the whole person. Two effects: focuses on and therefore highlights the pain and suffering and depersonalises the suffering.
   - Continues the idea of **suffering** introduced in verse 1;
   - and the **isolation** of people in the city. In the midst of wealth and show (ESB), people fight and kill each other on the streets; poor people — the kind of people who live in "coldwater flats"; i.e., they cannot afford the luxury of hot water — are suffering;
   - and **nobody cares.** The police and ambulancemen who come to remove them from the streets or to break up the violence of which they are victims see only the "broken bones" to be strapped up, the blood on the pavement which is "glazed" because the victim has lain unattended and ignored by passers-by, and hear only the screams to be quietened, without taking any interest in the human being who has suffered the violence.

   H — device identified; examples fully discussed + intelligent comment re illustration of argument;
   Int. — examples identified and clearly understood + some comment re illustration of argument.

5. **To what extent do you consider the last 3-line verse to be an effective conclusion to the poem? Justify your answer with reference to the whole poem but do not treat in detail any points already used in earlier answers.** (You may wish to refer to such areas as structure, imagery, narrative stance . . .)   **(10) E**
   - **Structure**:
   - anxiety in verse 1, where he attacks the materialistic attitude of society;
   - grows into fear in verse 2 as he tries (unsuccessfully) to hide under the bed-clothes from the noise of the violent streets.
   - "But" forges the link between the two verses, suggesting that the violence is a product of the materialistic society.
   - Verse 3 is a strong conclusion — three short lines; two strong statement sentences; decisive words: "never", "no".

- **Narrative stance**:
- verse 1, poet describes the sights seen from his hotel room window;
- verse 2, he describes the noises heard from his room;
- verse 3 is his comment on what he has seen and heard; the fact that he is there and can see and hear for himself what it is like makes his pessimistic ending more convincing.
- **Imagery:**
- It is a good conclusion — continues the **imagery** used earlier — extended **Wild West metaphor** which the poet has used throughout the poem to represent the uncivilised nature of the violence on the city streets:
- verse 1 — ". . . uncivilised darkness / is **shot at** by a million lit windows . . ."; the idea of light (religion) trying to fight against darkness (the evil of the world);
- verse 2 — already discussed in question 4, but may make additional comment or passing reference to show continuity;
- in verse 3, he returns to the idea of darkness / midnight as symbols of evil;
- in verse 1, he has said "midnight has come in from foreign places", literally true in terms of time zones but there may also be a suggestion that the violence / evil is a result of the multiracial nature of American society.
- In his conclusion, the poet makes his comment in wild west terms: "The frontier is never / somewhere else." He is saying the evil is within us and we are no more civilised now than the cowboys and Indians were in the days depicted in western films. The basic principle underlying those films was the triumph of good over evil; reality is not so black and white. "And no stockades / can keep the midnight out." — The evil in men's souls is worse than the tomahawks and arrows of the Indians because it is unseen and cannot therefore be avoided.
- In this concluding statement, no solution is put forward; he seems to be saying religion has failed (Cross image in lines 8–9) and he can express only pessimism about the nature of human beings that these conditions prevail in a supposed-Christian, prosperous society. The despair of his final statement is a logical conclusion to the suffering, expressed in figurative terms in verse 1, and the pitiful reality of the underclass described in verse 2.

H — fully developed discussion, covering at least two of the above categories + intelligent comment.

Int. — should show clear awareness of structure and imagery + some comment.

Level: Intermediate 1

1. **Write down the following, giving two pieces of evidence from the poem for each one:**
   (a) **the time of day <u>when the poem is being written</u>;**
      - "now midnight" (1) + "darkness" (1).   **(2) U**
   (b) **the place (inside) where the poet is;**
      - "Hotel Room" / "12th Floor" / "in bed" — *any two.*   **(2) U**
   (c) **the place (outside) where the poet is.**
      - New York — " ESB" (1) + Pan Am. (1)   **(2) U**

2. (a) **Write down a phrase from verse 1 which describes the Empire State Building.**   **(2) U**
      - "that / jumbo size dentist's drill", lines 3–4: "jumbo size" (1) + "dentist's drill" (1).
   (b) **Explain how this phrase lets you know what the poet thinks of the Empire State Building.**   **(2) A**
      - Attempt to explain, e.g., this is insulting / making fun of it / dentist's drill causes pain (1); +
      - does not approve of it / does not like it (½) + thinks too big / ridiculously big (½)

3.   (a)   **To what does the poet compare the helicopter in lines 2–3?**   **(1) U**
     ● Bluebottle which has been sprayed / accept lift — "a damaged insect".

     (b)   **Write down two ways in which those two things are alike.**   **(2) A**
     ● Both fly (1) + fly that has been sprayed makes buzzing noise / flies round and
       round like helicopter (1).

     (c)   **How does this comparison help us to appreciate the height of the Empire State
           Building?**   **(1) A**
     ● If helicopter appears insect-sized (even from 12th floor), it must be very high.

4.   (a)   **Name two sources of the sounds, which the poet hears outside.**   **(2) U**
     ● Police sirens (1) + ambulance sirens (1).

     (b)   **Write down two words from line 13, which help you to imagine what those sounds
           are like.**   **(2) A**
     ● "warwhoops" (1) + "ululating" (1).

     (c)   **What do you think the poet wants these words to remind you of?**   **(1) A**
     ● Wild West / cowboys and Indians.

     (d)   **Try to explain why this is a good way to describe those sounds.**   **(2) A**
     ● Some attempt to link war cries with uncivilised nature of street violence. — *Mark
       on merit.*

5.   *". . . the broken bones, the harsh screaming
                 from coldwater flats, the blood
                 glazed on the sidewalks."*

     (a)   **What is the poet concerned about in these lines?**   **(2) U**
     ● Street violence / domestic violence / people left lying in street. — *Any two.*

     (b)   **How do you think the poet feels about the situation described here?**   **(2) UA**
     ● Thinks it is wrong / uncivilised / authorities should do something about it (1) +
       people should not have to live in poverty / people should care more for each other
       (1).

6.   **The poet gives us a vivid description of life in New York. Write about some of the
     things he mentions, which you find particularly sad or frightening or which make you
     think about some aspect of life, trying to explain why they have this effect on you. (You
     may deal with any one or more than one of these areas.)**   **(5) E**
     ● **sad:**   people in "coldwater flats" — lonely, unhappy, needy, can't get
                            out of situation;
                            people so scared that they do not try to help people lying
                            injured in street;
                            even police / ambulancemen do not care; just pick up the
                            pieces.

     ● **frightening:**   violence in streets;
                            reference to Wild West imagery;
                            poet conveys his own fear as he lies in bed.

     ● **thought-provoking:** US society / rich businesses spend a lot of money on big
                            buildings like ESB and PanAm; money better spent on
                            relieving the poor in their midst.
                            US society considered height of civilisation yet really no more
                            civilised than in the days of Wild West;
                            poet says there is no solution but there must be a way to make
                            things better.

*Any reasonable points made about one or more of the categories, with even tenuous
reference to the ideas in the poem — mark on merit.*

Suggested Outline Plans for Critical Essays

1. **A poem is often inspired by an intense emotional experience. Choose one such poem and examine the techniques used by the poet to convey the significance of the experience or event which gave rise to the poem.** (Suitable for either of the poems in this chapter: *Assisi; Visiting Hour* is covered in question 3.)
    §1   Title, poet, **brief** description of experience / event which inspired poem.
    §2   Presentation of characters: brutal language, alliteration, metaphor, simile (beggar), chicken metaphor (priest and tourists) — all reveal poet's attitude to characters — quote, etc.
    §3   Contrast, sarcasm, irony, juxtaposition — reveal poet's attitude to situation — quote / explain.
    §4   Personal response to characters and situation.

2. **Select a poem, which has genuinely shocked you. Explain which aspects of the poet's ideas and of the devices he uses provoked this strong response in you.** *(Assisi)*
    §1   Title, poet, brief statement of what shocked student.
    §2   More details of one of ideas which shocked: e.g., conditions in which beggar lived — quote / explain techniques used deliberately to shock — brutal language, metaphor, sarcasm.
    §3   Other ideas: e.g., hypocrisy of church — quote / explain — juxtaposition, presentation of priest; apathy of society — quote / explain — chicken metaphor, juxtaposition, contrast.
    §4   Personal response: e.g., result of ideas + techniques + poet's feelings.

3. **Choose a poem in which the poet's feelings are revealed. By close reference to the poem, explain how the literary and linguistic techniques, used by the poet, help to convey the theme(s) and the extent to which the poet was successful in engaging your sympathy.** (Suitable for either of the poems in this chapter: *Visiting Hour; Assisi* is covered above at question 1, feelings less personal, more social.)
    §1   Title, poet, situation presented in poem and feelings revealed.
    §2   Trace feelings from entering to leaving hospital (including control): follow narrative pattern, verse form + staccato rhythm (§3), enjambment — quote / explain / comment.
    §3   Mood created by lexical choice, synecdoche, repetition, caesura, imagery, paradox, oxymoron — quote / explain / comment.
    §4   Sympathy — may prefer to include this aspect in discussion of each (stage of) feeling in §2 and §3; if so, short concluding statement of poet's experience / student's response.

4. **Compare and contrast two poems by the same writer and, by close reference to the techniques / devices used in both poems, explain which, in your opinion, has put across the stronger message. (*Assisi* and *Visiting Hour*.** Also suitable for *Assisi* and *Hotel Room* if the unseen poem has been studied closely.)
    §1   Titles, poet, **brief** statement about situation presented in each poem.
    §2   Points of comparison: both have narrator, deal with suffering, isolation — quote / explain.
    §3   Points of contrast: [Assisi] — social outrage against society and Church — quote / explain.
    [Visiting Hour] — personal distress, self criticism — quote / explain.
    [Hotel Room] — poverty more general; violence in streets: quote / explain / comment;
    Italy / USA — Old World / New World; USA supposed to right the wrongs of debased European society but same underclass, same apathy of more fortunate: quote, etc.
    §4   Which has put across stronger message / had most effect on student + reasons.

CHAPTER 7 — Edwin Morgan

Suggested Study Points: *The Starlings in George Square*

UNDERSTANDING

1. **The situation**
   - The poem is about a plague of starlings in Glasgow, particularly in George Square, in the 1960s; buildings were defaced and the newspapers debated how to deal with them.

2. **The themes**
   - Man's cruelty / insensitivity to lesser creatures.
   - Appreciation of the beauty and mystery of the birds.
   - Communications.
   - Sanitisation / order v. compassion / beauty.

ANALYSIS

§I. lines 1–23
- Line1 — invocation; **tone** of wonder, amazement, excitement; introduces the Western **imagery**:
- **lexical choice**: "Sundown . . . high stonefields" — high buildings surrounding George Square, but compare with high chaparral, dense, tangled brushwood of western films.
- Line 2 introduces the starlings: large number of birds: "roofscape" — packed together so closely — "thick", line 3 — look like part of the buildings; when they move, the building seems "alive".
- Line 4, noise "singing" — this was part of the trouble, dealt with in more detail in section 2; the starling is a very garrulous bird with a harsh grating call but it also mimics other birds' songs.
- Line 5 continues the Western **imagery**: the **simile** suggests that George Square is under attack from the birds; good visual image too: bird in flight resembles an arrow-head.
- line 6: sun sets in the west, hence the flash as the birds fly through the rays of the setting sun.
- Line 7, necklace **image** — again suggests number, close together, size (small) but the **metaphor** also reveals something of the poet's attitude to the birds, suggesting their beauty — jet is black and shiny; also quite valuable, showing the poet's appreciation of their worth.
- Lines 8–10, **lexical choice** and **layout**: all precise words describing actions of birds — nestle, preen, sidle;
- verbs and present participles, letters and sounds echo and intermingle, like the birdsong, and the way they swoop and rise, diving through each other with their amazing precision flying, which man can only wonder at.
- Along with the **repetition** of "by the lamps" is further indication of huge number of birds;
- lines 10–11, reaction of people going home from work — **alliteration** in "homeward hurrying" seems to draw the people together against the birds, two sides in battle. Indeed, people were badly affected by the birds; according to local anecdote, many people walked under umbrellas, even on dry days, to avoid being "bombed"!
- Line 12 introduces two characters in close-up — film technique. The man "looks up and points";
- no words spoken — they would not be heard over the "clamour" of the birds;
- lines 15–20, we see through the child's eyes — lines 15–23 convey the poet's attitude to the birds; the child is "wide-eyed" at the exhibition of aerobatics in the sky.
- line 14, **alliteration** in "clamour . . . cliffs", draws birds together to form one mass; "cliffs", echoing back to "stonefields", line 1; the birds transform the Square; continued in "waves", line 15;
- **sound** level varies: loud > low > loud > low conveyed in "clamour > sinks> shrills > murmur > scatters > stab" as the birds move on the roofs, dive and swoop;

- "arcs" suggests their gracefulness in flight; "confused sweetness" — how the boy hears the "clamour"; "stab" suggests a short burst of song, continued in line 19 with "pierces" — effect of the scene on boy — "like a story" — it communicates something to the boy, he understands something of the beauty and mystery of the birds, unlike most of the adults; "He will never forget", line 21; the picture is engraved on his mind, like a story of magic and wonder.
- Lines 22–23 end the section with a romantic visual image: the roofs in silhouette, spotlight on the starlings, continuing the film technique, the closing shot.

§II: lines 24–44

- Juxtaposed with this romantic view of the starlings through the child's eyes, section 2 has hilarious, **surrealist descriptions** of the effect of the birds on the people who work in the buildings around George Square. The **juxtaposition** makes those people and their attitudes to the birds seem ridiculous, and yet it must have been a considerable problem.
- Line 24, **lexical choice**: "hopping" is a "bird-word" indicating that birds dominate the scene.
- **Visual humour** throughout this verse — e.g., line 24, **metonymy** gives us a cartoon image of the City Chambers heaving up and down with rage; line 25, exclamation marks add to the **hyperbole**; line 26, presumably secretaries were known as fresh air freaks? "protection and danger money" — further hyperbole; line 28, apparent confusion of genders mirrors chaos caused by birds; in fact, the Lord Provost at the time was Dame Jean Roberts;
- lines 29–30, **repetition** exemplifies the problem of hearing over the noise; like the joke about hearing aids . . . pardon? Technique repeated in last two lines of each verse in this section.
- Line 31, The GPO — hub of communications; the rest of this section deals with a theme which crops up frequently in Morgan's work: the breakdown or difficulty of communication.
- Again the birds dominate the scene, showing the effect on the minds of the workers, as the clerks write "Starling" for sterling. **Simile** in line 33: people trying to telephone cannot hear for the noise of the birds, as if they are standing in an aviary; line 34, the humour gets more and more surreal, with confusion between "Kerry" and "Cairo; line 35, "fankled" is a very expressive Scots word to describe the muddle caused by the birds; line 36 again reminds us of the noise which is causing all this trouble; the **gap** after line 37: complete breakdown of communication.
- Lines 38–44 become hilariously nonsensical with the substitution of **onomatopoeic** bird sounds for human speech words, as people become "bird-brained", culminating in the ludicrous "When's the last boat to Milngavie".

§III: lines 45–70

- In this section of the poem, in which he deals with the solutions put forward the **tone** is heavily **ironic**; the **satirical purpose** of the poem becomes more obvious, as the good-natured fun of the previous section develops into a tone of ironic censure:
- lines 45–46, scaffolding erected, the "bird-men" are summoned; as if there is a whole profession dedicated to getting rid of birds; proprietary names of products lends credence to lines 47–48, tangible proof that people actually did those things — the poet disapproves.
- Line 49, **inflated language**, "Armour our pediments": as if defending themselves against wild animals; **humour** in **pun** on "eavesdroppers" — here literally bird-droppings on the eaves.
- Line 50, back to the wild west imagery: "outpost"; **caesura** coupled with **alliteration**, lends comic emphasis to "Save our statues."; **hyperbole** in "Send back the jungle."
- Lines 52–58, **irony** stronger: quotation from newspapers; clearly Morgan does not find it at all comical; questions in lines 54–55: people ease their consciences, consider themselves civilised compared to Peking where shooting birds, supposedly for hygienic purposes, is a profitable business. **Ironic** "So": far from being humanitarians, the poet regards the treatment of the starlings as barbaric: "locked in our cliff dwellings"; "encased" — heads-in-the-sand attitude, the visual **alliteration** of "guano...guilt", line 58, humorous but with a heavy undertone of scorn as he tricks us into reading "gwilt".

- **Irony** continues with the Lord Provost singing in "her marble hacienda", like a song-bird in a fancy cage, poking fun — not quite so good-natured now — at the grandeur of the City Chambers; the P-G can hear himself licking the stamps in the starling-free silence, a slightly undignified picture, suggests slurping; but Sir Walter (Scott) is lonely without the birds on his statue: as a poet, sensitive writer, he would appreciate the beauty and mystery of the birds.
- Lines 62–70, the **poet's own voice** comes through: line 62 is **ambiguous**: (1) Are we good enough for the starlings? or (2) Are we so bad that we deserve to be harassed by them?
- Line 63 is remarkably prosaic in its expression, suggesting logical deduction. Do we ordinary mortals lack poetry in our souls, leading to our banishment of the starlings? Morgan sees them as "joyous messengers" — if only we could understand the message: we come back to the theme of communications. In our obsession with cleanliness and hygiene, we turn away those beautiful birds, without appreciating their beauty and mystery: he uses harsh words to describe our behaviour — "repel . . . indignant";
- line 65, for the poet, the birds are beautiful and spiritually uplifting; line 66, he thinks some day we might be able to decode the message they bring with their "sweet frenzied whistling" (cf. "clamour" of line 14); line 67, a reminder of their skill and grace in flight; line 68 suggests we should, rather, feel honoured to have those birds settle on our buildings;
- lines 69–70, the birds can communicate one thing: they like "the warm cliffs of man" — they want to be part of our lives, so we should respond with the humanity and social warmth of our race; "cliffs" takes us back to the idea of primitive man as part of Nature in line 57; also links back to line 14, suggesting that the starlings belong in our city just as much as we do.

Looking over the whole poem

- **Poetic form:** free verse, appropriate to the sense of chaos caused by starlings.
- **Structure:** written in three sections — 1. description of birds swarming on rooftops; 2. effect of birds on people working in vicinity of George Square; 3. solutions put forward and poet's own attitude to birds + comments on how they were treated.
- **Style:** combines comedy with sensitive appreciation of beauty of birds and gratitude for unknown forces which have led them to associate themselves with the city. **Juxtaposition** of sections: they set each other off.
  - (I)   — descriptive, lyrical: figurative language, **enjambment**, manipulation of words and letters;
  - (II) — hilarious, surrealist effect of birds in **lexical choice**, **sound effects**, **hyperbole**;
  - (III) — prosaic, serious, reflective, **satire**, **irony**.

EVALUATION

- Discussion of themes:
- man's cruelty / insensitivity to lesser creatures — §III, satire, irony;
- appreciation of the beauty and mystery of the birds — §I, using child's view + §III, poet's attitude; reflection, comment; contrasted with ridiculous antics of human beings in §II;
- communications — §II, GPO and Information Bureau + §III, line 63 to the end;
- sanitisation / order v. compassion / beauty — §III, solutions, irony, lines 63–65.
- Poet's attitude to birds;
- §I: beauty and mystery of birds — like child, hasn't lost sense of wonder; also Scott, line 61;
- §II : makes human beings appear ridiculous; he has no sympathy for them;
- §III: shows disapproval of solutions tried; we should feel honoured that the birds have chosen to come to our city; their presence should be regarded as an accolade, not a plague.
- Poet's success in creating a sense of place: square is named; high buildings, roofscape; City Chambers, Lord Provost, GPO, City Information Bureau; Milngavie; statues, Sir Walter;
- crowds going home from work, streetlamps, silhouette.

Using Your Notes for Revision: Checklist

UNDERSTANDING AND ANALYSIS *(Use these questions to revise important parts of the poem.)*

1. *(a)* **Summarise what is dealt with in each of the three sections.**
   - §I — Presents situation; describes starlings, numbers, sounds and activities;
   - §II — describes effects on people working in area;
   - §III — solutions for getting rid of birds and poet's attitude and comment.

   (b) **What could a stranger learn from the poem about this area of the city**
   - High stone buildings, flocks of starlings, street lamps.
   - Magnificent building housing City Chambers, statues.
   - Busy central area: GPO, City Information Bureau.

   and its citizens?
   - Large number of people work in this area (line 11).
   - Busy workers: secretaries, window cleaners, polite post office clerks ("sir").
   - Councillors, female Lord Provost.
   - Impression of warmth from picture of man smiling, pointing out birds to his son in §I.
   - Most people not lovers of nature: do their best to get rid of birds.

2. **Section I: the starlings. Revise the effectiveness of the devices / techniques which Morgan uses to describe the starlings.** *Details in Suggested Study Points, pages 103–104.*
   - **Wild West imagery**, suggesting ambush, attack by starlings — starts in line 1, "Sundown . . . high stonefields!"; line 5, "a shower of arrows"; line 6, "western window".
   - Lines 2–3, number of starlings — **lexical choice**: "roofscape . . . thick . . . alive with".
   - Line 5, in flight — **simile**.
   - Line 7, necklace image — **metaphor**.
   - Lines 8–10, **lexical choice**, **word layout** and **repetition** — combine to indicate large numbers of birds.
   - Line 14, **alliteration** draws birds together in one huge mass.
   - Lines 14–18, **sound effects** — sound level varies, "clamour > sinks > shrills > murmur".
   - Lines 15 and 19–20, **lexical choice** shows effect on boy – "wide-eyed"; "stab . . . confused sweetness . . . pierces".
   - Lines 22–23, final romantic **image** of birds — "silhouette . . . lamps" — film technique.

3. **Section II: people in George Square**
   (a) **Note the change of tone in this section.**
   (b) **Identify the tone throughout this section.**
   (c) **Revise the techniques / devices which contribute to that tone.** *Details in Suggested Study Points, page 104.*
   - Complete change of tone from that in §I — **juxtaposition** creates shock effect; makes human beings seem ridiculous and small-minded.
   - Tone is hilarious, becoming hysterical, with surrealist description of effects of birds on people working in vicinity of George Square.
   - Line 24, visual humour: **metonymy** — cartoon image of City Chambers.
   - Lines 25–30, **hyperbole**: exclamation marks.
   - Apparent confusion of genders, line 28 — mirrors confusion caused by starling noise.
   - Lines 28–30, (and lines 35–37 and 42–44), "What's that?", **repetition** of words, phrases seems to exemplify the problem caused by noise of birds; lines 34–35, word play on "Cairo / Kerry" and **alliteration**.
   - Line 33, **simile** — adds to the general exaggerated picture.
   - Lines 38–44, much of humour achieved by using "bird" words to replace human speech, creating effect of birds dominating the scene; becoming increasingly ludicrous, **sound effects** reaching a hilarious climax in line 44.

4.   **Section III: solutions . . . and recriminations**
    (a)   **Note the different solutions, which were tried, to get rid of the starlings.**
        ● Lines 47–48, "Scarecrow Strip . . . Cameron's Repellent".
    (b)   **Note the further changes of tone in this section.**
        Identify the tone in lines 45 – 61.
        Revise the techniques / devices which contribute to that tone. *Details in Suggested Study Points, pages 104–105.*
        ● Tone immediately one of grim reality, as if Morgan saying, "Enough hilarity. This is real".
        ● Heavily ironic, shocks after apparently light-hearted, skittish tone of section II, as if he has tricked us into laughing and now makes us feel guilty about it.
        ● Exaggerated tone of desperation in lines 45–48 > inflated language, line 49.
        ● Touch of humour in **pun**, line 49, but it is grim humour.
        ● Lines 50–51, back to Wild West; caesura and staccato rhythm of short sentences intensify **hyperbole**.
        ● Lines 52–58, **irony** > scornful censure, intensified by comic / ironic **alliteration**, line 58.
        Identify the tone in lines 62 – 70.
        ● Tone is reflective, matter-of-fact in lines 62–64:
        ● straight rhetorical question; long prosaic line 63: "There is something to be said for . . ." becoming lyrical from line 65 when he starts to talk about starlings: "lift up the eyes . . . lighten the heart . . . sweet frenzied whistling."
        In what way is the tone in these lines different from anywhere else in the poem?
        ● This is the poet's own voice coming through.

EVALUATION *(Use this question for exam practice.)*

5.   **What have you understood about Edwin Morgan's attitude to the starlings**
    The poet comes down firmly on the side of the starlings:
    ● §I, descriptions bring out the birds' beauty and skill in flight — quote / explain / comment;
    - attitude of child evokes the mystery and wonder of the birds, which the poet shares, unlike the majority of the population of Glasgow: quote / explain / comment.
    ● §II, makes human beings seem ridiculous as they are dominated by the birds, becoming "bird-brained" — quote / explain / comment.
    ● §III, **satire**, **irony** — inflated language, line 49 — quote / explain / comment;
    - **pun**, line 49 — quote / explain / comment;
    - lines 50–51, **caesura**, **alliteration**, **hyperbole** — quote / explain / comment;
    - lines 52–58, quotation from newspapers, questions, "So" , visual **alliteration** — quote, etc.
    ● Lines 59–61, after the starlings have gone — quote / explain / comment.
    ● Lines 62–68, asks if we deserve the starlings; ambiguous — quote / explain / comment;
    - line 63, "joyous messengers" set against line 64, "our indignant orderliness — explain / comment;
    - introduces idea of communications — they have something to say to us but, unlike the child in §I, we cannot decode the message; poet thinks some day we might.
    ● Lines 69–70, strong reproach to people of Glasgow who got rid of the starlings — quote, etc.

and to what extent has his presentation of the situation led you to agree or disagree with his view? (10)
    ● Personal response: may be implicit in discussion of the poet's attitude; may come down on side of orderliness and hygiene but some appreciation of the beauty and mystery of the birds should be shown.

Both levels should show clear understanding of poet's attitude.
H — should cover all three of the poet's ways of presenting the problem, making personal response clear in intelligent comment; Int. may concentrate on section that had greatest influence on personal response.

Suggested Study Points: *Trio*

UNDERSTANDING

1. The situation
- Records an incident witnessed by the poet: three young people walking up Buchanan Street, possibly on Christmas Eve, carrying a baby, a dog and a guitar.
- They pass on, lost to his view, and the poet reflects on what he has seen.

2. The themes
- Human warmth / happiness / relationships.
- Spirit of giving between human beings at Christmas more important than religious aspect, the birth of Jesus.

ANALYSIS

§1: lines 1–8
- Line 1 immediately establishes a real location: Buchanan Street;
- "quickly" suggests the liveliness, energy of the trio;
- "on a sharp, winter evening", establishes time of day and season; the cold of the evening **contrasts** with the warmth of the people;
- present tense adds to the immediacy, reality of the situation.
- Line 2 expands on the title: their youth adds to their freshness, vigour;
- "Christmas" establishes season more precisely and introduces the religious element; the three young people are like the Magi, on their way to see the newly-born Jesus; they immediately gain stature, importance; the "lights" are the stars above Bethlehem.
- Line 3, "a new guitar" introduces the idea of bearing gifts, as the Magi did, confirmed by line 8.
- Line 4, the girl with "a very young baby" recalls Mary with Jesus.
- Line 5, the chihuahua: tiny, exotic; reminds us of the beasts in the stable at Bethlehem.
- Line 6, they are laughing — happy because it is Christmas, but their pleasure is human, the joy of loving relationships, of giving; nothing to do with religious aspect of Christmas.
- Lines 6–7, **metaphor** — because of the cold atmosphere, their breath is visible, like a cloud; but it is "a cloud of happiness": their warmth is almost tangible, infectious; the poet feels their love like a wave of warm air as they pass.
- Line 8, **direct speech** — brings them to life; construction, adding "but" at the end of the sentence, is peculiar to Glaswegian dialect, so they are established as Glaswegians, and their warmth is shown as the warmth of all Glaswegians, especially at this time when even those with the smallest incomes do their best to make Christmas magical for their children.

§2: lines 9–11
- Those lines expand the references above to what each is carrying, as their love is expansive, touching all around them, including the poet.
- The chihuahua: the exotic name makes it special; wearing a tiny, red, tartan coat;
- line 9, **simile**: "like a teapot-holder" — suggests size, shape, but most of all, warmth, cosiness.
- The baby is wrapped in a white shawl — suggesting innocence and again warmth, cosiness;
- line 10, **synecdoche**: "all bright eyes and mouth" — focuses on the eyes which reveal the soul, in this case "bright" — clear, fresh, pure, seeing things for the first time; and the mouth which sucks its sustenance, as far as the baby is concerned, the most important part of its body;
- **simile**: "like favours" — decorations on wedding and christening cakes, later given to close relatives and friends as tokens of love; "fresh, sweet" also have pleasant connotations.

- The guitar is also protected from the cold in its "milky plastic cover" — "milky" makes the connection with the baby, as if it too is being nurtured with love; "swells out" suggests shape but is also in line with the idea of expansiveness, well-being which surrounds it;
- tinsel and mistletoe make it special and obviously a gift, the mistletoe perhaps representing the myrrh of the third Wise Man; "brisk" here meaning alive, living, real rather than artificial; the **alliteration** on letters s and t holds it all together in a third snug parcel.
- **Line layout**: the long, over-running lines in this section are appropriate to the human love overflowing from the trio.

§III: lines 12–19

- Line 12, change of **register** here; the invocations and exclamation marks reflect the poet's reaction to the scene:
- "Orphean sprig!" — Orpheus, the Greek God of Music, the guitar; sprig, a small shoot or twig, the mistletoe;
- "Melting baby!" — takes us back to the favours, icing on the cake; sweetness, warmth, love;
- "Warm chihuahua!" — again, love, warmth; it is well cared for, cosy in its tartan coat.
- **Apostrophe**: the poet addresses the trio.
- Line 13, "The vale of tears" — **metaphor** — the world, chiefly the unpleasant aspects; this is **Biblical language**, in keeping with the analogy. The poet is saying here that human love can conquer all of the world's problems, hardships.
- Lines 14–16 continue the idea that human love is more important than the love which, according to the Christian faith, was brought to earth with the birth of Jesus;
- line 15, "put paid to": a very secular phrase in this context, supporting the idea of the superiority of human happiness / love over religious faith;
- "it abdicates": it (fate) is chased off by the force of the secular, represented here by "the Christmas lights"; the power of "fate", usually written with a capital F, is reduced by use of lower case; the Leonine / middle rhyme intensifies the power of the trio;
- **lexical choice**: "abdicates" links "fate" to the idea of the newborn king, Christmas, strengthening the humanist message; the **line layout** here reflects the sense of the words.
- Lines 17–18, "Monsters of the year": the troubles, problems of the past year and any which are lurking in the future; "go blank": lose the ability to frighten, in the face of this human happiness and spirit; they are defeated by the shared love, mutual caring of human beings.
- Line 19, "this march of three": they sweep into the future, a new year with new hope, new beginnings, the baby, the tiny dog, the guitar which will open new vistas for the recipient.

§IV: lines 20–24

- Line 20, the **dash** marks the closing of the parenthesis opened at the end of line 2: emphasising that this was a brief interlude; the three young people have passed by, lost to the poet's view in the Christmas Eve crowd.
- Lines 21–23, another parenthesis, this time indicated by brackets, in keeping with the sense of their being insulated from harm; also to show that the poet has been embraced by their warmth;
- line 21, **repetition** of "vanished....not vanished" illustrates that their spirit remains with the poet, suggestion of the indestructibility, the immortality of human love.
- Lines 21–22, "in their arms they wind" — they are carrying, but also they embody "the life of men" (the baby) "and beasts" (the chihuahua) "and music" (the guitar): those three "items" represent for Morgan all that is important in life, presumably seeing music in its general sense of all creative art, the products of man's finer spirit;
- linking the nouns with "and" supports the idea of their indestructibility, survival, immortality;
- line 23, "laughter", the outward sign of happiness; **simile**: their mutual love keeps them safe, insulates them from all perils; the image is of a halo of light surrounding them — this is an optimistic, if rather romantic, humanism!
- Line 24 completes the statement begun in line 20; the poet is left to the cold winter evening, but his spirits have been raised by the picture of warmth and happiness he encountered albeit briefly in Buchanan Street. **Tone** of joy, confidence in and hope for future of human race.

Looking over the whole poem
- **Poetic form:** free verse, in keeping with the outwardly prosaic nature of the encounter with three ordinary people in an ordinary Glasgow street.
- The over-long lines in lines 9–11 are appropriate to the idea of expansiveness in those lines;
- from line 12 onwards, the metre is more regulated and the language more "poetic", appropriate to the underlying spirituality of the message those ordinary people have brought to the poet.

- **The title:** "Trio" suggests three people working or playing together in harmony with each other, sharing, each playing his / her part for the benefit of the whole.

- **Irony:** Morgan is using the conventions of the Christmas story, the "very young baby", the animal, the three Wise Men bearing gifts, to show the superiority of human love over God's love. (cf. MacDiarmid: *Lo! a Child is Born*, discussed in chapter 2.) Usually the commercial side of Christmas is condemned but here he shows the real human warmth underlying the spirit of giving at Christmas time. This is very much a secular trinity.

EVALUATION

- Discussion of **themes**:
- Human warmth / happiness / relationships: embodied in the trio, and the general sense of well-being surrounding them; seen also in the effect of the encounter on the poet, touched by their warmth which stayed with him even after the three had disappeared into the crowd.
- Spirit of giving between human beings at Christmas more important than religious aspect, the birth of Jesus: seen in the whole Christian analogy in which the human beings are seen as vibrant, alive, warm, loving, real . . . while the Christian story is presented as just that, a story;
- the human gifts encompass all that is important to human life, as far as Morgan is concerned; whether they are given as a reminder of God's greatest gift to mankind, His Son, is totally irrelevant for Morgan: it is the human love behind the gifts which is important.
- The **effectiveness of the Christian analogy** in conveying the themes:
- readily recognisable symbols: baby, Three Wise Men, gifts; but poem is dominated by the human love in the form of the vibrant trio, walking together, invincible, real.
- **Poet's attitude** very clear:
- he apostrophises the trio, as if they are Gods themselves;
- he makes clear statements of their power against Fate, usually written with a capital when used in this sense but here written with lower case, an indication that is "powerless" before the combined force of three loving human beings;
- poet clearly touched by the experience.
- Poet's **use of an everyday situation** as basis for poem:
- the very ordinariness of the people and the encounter is its strength; all over the country, the western world, other ordinary people are behaving in the same way as the trio in Buchanan Street, giving us hope for the essential goodness of the human race.
- Is this an **over-romantic view** of the human race?
- Personal response: many wicked people, in history and today: consider examples;
- and yet the human race persists and we, like the poet, continue to see the goodness in people.
- Where does this goodness spring from?
- Some people may be offended by the poet's assertions here but faith in humanity does not have to exclude God and some students may want to read the poem on this basis.

Using Your Notes for Revision: Checklist

UNDERSTANDING AND ANALYSIS *(Use these questions to revise important parts of the poem.)*

1. **Situation: In his introduction in *Worlds,* Edwin Morgan writes: "I think of poetry as . . . a special way of recording moments and events."**
   (a) **Summarise the "moment" recorded in this poem.**
   - Three young people walking up Buchanan Street, possibly on Christmas Eve, carrying a baby, a dog and a guitar; they pass on, lost to his view, and the poet reflects on what he has seen.
   (b) **Note the ways in which the poet makes the event real for us.**
   - Real location: Buchanan Street.
   - Time of day and season: "sharp, winter evening", Christmas.
   - Present tense.
   - Direct speech — "but" at end of sentence is common in Glasgow vernacular.
   - Christmas lights, crowds.

2. **Characters:**
   (a) **Note who they are and what each is carrying.**
   (b) **Christian analogy.**
   - Three young people, baby, dog and guitar — The Magi, bearing gifts to Jesus.
   - Young woman with baby — Mary and Jesus.
   - Christmas lights — star over Bethlehem.

3. **Techniques / devices: Revise the effectiveness of the techniques / devices used by the poet in his description of what each person is carrying.** *Details in Suggested Study Points, pages 108–109.*
   - **Profusion of adjectives** and **lexical choice** appropriate to the feeling of expansiveness and well-being surrounding the trio; mirrored by **line layout**: long overrunning lines.
   - Chihuahua: exotic choice, "tiny" links it to baby, Royal Stewart tartan is a bright red tartan;
   - **simile** line 9 — size, shape, warmth.
   - Baby : "very young" — new, represents future; in "white" — Innocent, pure; wrapped in shawl — well cared-for, compare with dog in coat; "bright" eyes — clear, fresh, pure;
   - **synecdoche**, line 10 — focuses attention on eyes and mouth;
   - **simile**, line 10 — tokens of love; pleasant connotations.
   - Guitar: "swells" suggests shape, also ties in with expansive idea; it too is protected from the cold by plastic cover; "milky" makes connection with baby — nurtured with loving care;
   - tinsel and mistletoe make it special, obviously a gift; mistletoe perhaps represents myrrh;
   - **alliteration**, line 11 — holds it together in snug parcel.

4. **Register:**
   (a) **Note the change of register which occurs in line 12.**
   - Lines 1–11: record the facts in everyday sort of register, allowing for the similes which are the kind of comparisons made in normal speech; even the synecdoche is a popular form of description, cf. "all fingers and thumbs".
   - Change of register in line 12 to invocation, more poetic form, exclaiming — over the top?
   (b) **Explain how the change is made clear to you.**
   - Line 13, **Biblical language**: "vale of tears", with occasional insertions of secular language, e.g., "put paid to", line 15, which point up the contrast and assert the superiority of the secular over the religious.
   - Change in **poetic form** helps to convey register:
   - shorter lines; more regular line length and metre; "poetic" line layout;
   - figurative language more "poetic", more complex, as in lines 17–19.

(c) **How appropriate is this change to the sense of the poem?**
- Line 12, invocation — in keeping with the assertion, which is to follow, that the young people, in their spirit of love and warmth, represent a force superior to that of God's love.
- Line 13, Biblical language in keeping with the Christian analogy being made.

5.   How effective are lines 20–24 as a conclusion to the poem?
- In terms of structure: end of parenthesis;
- poem begins with trio approaching and ends when they have passed.
- Line 20, "vanished in the crowd": they are three ordinary people but they symbolise the whole of the human race;
- final statement of theme: power of human love and its superiority over Christian ideas of God's love; details in Suggested Study Points, page 108–109.

EVALUATION *(Use this question for exam practice.)*

6.   How effectively has the poet conveyed his ideas about Christmas to you (7)
- Human warmth, happiness, relationships:
- title — quote / explain / comment; embodied in the young people;
- their happiness is clear, walking quickly, laughing, direct speech;
- warmth, love shown in care for baby, dog and guitar, all protected from cold, carried carefully;
- effect on poet is obvious, particularly in line 12 and line 21 — quote / explain / comment.
- Spirit of giving:
- guitar obviously a present — tinsel, mistletoe;
- young man's obvious delight in gift — quote / explain / comment;
- general air of happiness surrounding trio.
- Use of Christian analogy:
- recognisable symbols — quote / explain / comment;
- poem emphasises the human over the religious — quote / explain / comment;
- effectiveness of irony in use of Christian analogy to prove superiority of human love — quote / explain / comment.
- Use of ordinary people > all people — quote / explain / comment;
- ordinary street, chance encounter;
- lines 14–16, "fate" with lower case f; Leonine / middle rhyme — quote / explain / comment;
- power of human love dominates the poem from this point to the end — esp. lines 17–19 — quote / explain / comment;
- summed up in parenthesis, lines 21–23 — quote / explain / comment;
- use of parenthesis adds to effect — explain / comment.
- Effect of incident on poet:
- he is struck immediately by their warmth;
- they eclipse the story of Bethlehem in his mind; they are real, vibrant, living.

and to what extent do you agree or disagree with his views? (3)
- Personal response must acknowledge the poet's feelings, even if arguing against it;
- possible to see goodness of humanity without excluding God;
- may cite examples of evil in human beings from history or present day.

H – well-developed discussion of ideas with good textual support + intelligent comment / response;
Int. – clear understanding of main idea with some textual support + some comment / response

Unseen Textual Analysis: Marking Schemes
From the Domain of Arnheim

Levels: Higher and Intermediate 2

All answers should be supported by close reference to the text.

1. (a) **Briefly outline the story told in the poem.** **(1) U**
    - Two members of an advanced class of human beings with the ability to cross time barriers visit Earth at the time of the Ice Age. Earthmen, celebrating the birth of a baby, sense their presence; one throws a firebrand. Space couple return to their own planet and time zone with rock samples and seeds.

    Both levels should cover three main areas of narrative.

    (b) **Show how the structure helps to make the narrative clear.** **(2) A**
    - Lines 1–3: introduction — space couple depart from their planet.
    - Lines 4–36: separated by a gap to show passage of time and change of scene;
    - main part of story — what happens when space couple arrive on earth.
    - Lines 37–40: conclusion — gap shows time lapse as space couple collect rock samples and seeds and space ship comes to collect them; space couple back on their planet.

    Both levels should recognise three areas of structure, justified by general statement of content.
    Int. — accept beginning, middle and end if general content of each area is suitably described.

2. (a) **Comment on the effectiveness of the simile in lines 2–3.** **(2) A**
    - *"like the smoke-clouds / dragged back into vacancy when the rocket springs"*, lines 2–3.
    - Describes how they move out of their own time zone, leaving their own time behind, like the exhaust vapours as rocket is launched (1) + connotations of speed and high technology (1). This is a familiar sight on our TV screens, so easily understood by readers.

    (b) **Explain how the simile effectively encapsulates the nature of the visitors to the domain of Arnheim.** **(1) AU**
    - Other planet: advanced beings with ability to travel across time barriers, lines 1–2;
    - **Simile** is appropriately hi-tech; indicates high level of technological development: they can take off through time with the effortless ease of a rocket, shedding the backward jet of hot gases which propels it into Space.

3. **From a close examination of the language and ideas in lines 5–25:**
    (a) **What can you deduce about the nature of the domain of Arnheim?** **(3) A**
    - Contrast: between planet left by space couple and land they arrive at.
    - After gap denoting time lapse, we are in the domain of Arnheim:
    - very primitive, undeveloped land; the word "domain" — small independent settlement;
    - line 5, yellow light would indicate oil lamp;
    - "icefield" — indication of time / development of human beings and world; "white" (and "snow" line 4) suggests purity, man not yet corrupted; line 8, pure air allows sound to travel clearly;
    - lines 11–12, **alliteration** and **sound effects:** give idea of space — sound magnified;
    - line 13, primitive fuel, mammoth's bones, sets time in Pleistocene age; line 16, "ice crystals".

    H — at least three examples of language, well-explained + intelligent deduction;
    Int — at least two examples of language, clearly understood + some attempt at deduction.

    (b) **What impression does the poet give us of the people of Arnheim?** **(3) A**
    - Line 6, huts — pine trees — primitive earth people; laughter — first sound — happy people;
    - line 7, "white" (and "snow" line 4) suggests purity, man not yet corrupted by civilisation;

- line 14, primitive — "naked", natural state; "kissed in smoke" — followed instincts;
- line 15, cannot distinguish between child and animal — suggests primitive state of man.

- Lines 19–22, primitives have strong sense of the supernatural — "a displacement of the air, a sudden chill"; sense presence of visitors — feeling of being watched is familiar;
- **syntax**: commas suggest the reactions of earth people; hesitance, fear in face of "ghost".
- Lines 24–25, celebrate the birth of child with music — trumpets, drums, song;
- line 26, **short line** and **question mark** intensify "joy", give stature to those primitives.
- Line 29, brave; earth people stand their ground, in spite of fear, "sweating", line 30;
- line 31, one of them tries to ward off invisible presence with firebrand — primitive element.
- Line 32, indication that presence is real to earth people — aimed where visitors were.

H — should cover at least three of above points, well-explained + intelligent comment;
Int. — at least two of above points, clearly understood + some comment.

4. (a) **Referring closely to lines 25 – 35, show how the poet contrasts the people of Arnheim with the visitors.**   (3) A

- **Contrast** between primitives, very much in the flesh, and the ghostly space couple.
- Line 28, **contrasts** dismay of space couple / joy of primitives; space couple are the outsiders / intruders.
- Line 33, brand cannot touch them — insubstantial nature, contrast with very real substance of earth people; like the space people, we are impressed with the courage of the earthman.

H — at least two examples, both sides of contrast well-explained + intelligent comment;
Int. — at least two examples, both sides of contrast clearly understood + some comment.

(b) **Which of the two groups does he appear most to admire? (Justify your answer.)**   (1) A

- The **contrast** throughout between the warm, living, substantial earthmen and the ephemeral, ghostly space people, and the respect shown to the earthmen by the space couple, show the poet's attitude to, and win the reader over to the side of, the earthmen.

5. **Look carefully at lines 19–33:**

(a) **What is the narrative function of those lines?**   (2) A

- Those lines contain the **climax of the narrative** (1) + the point at which the earthmen become aware of the presence of the space people, stand their ground and fight to defend themselves from possible attack by, to them, an invisible force. (1)

Both levels — climax (accept an explanation of climax from Int.) + explanation / comment.

(b) **Comment on the poet's skill in building up to and achieving this effect.**   (4) A

- From the start of the poem, **readers are aware** of the aliens' journey back through time. We witnessed their departure from their planet in lines 1–3.
- Straight away a **dramatic tension** is created in the reader's mind because we are not told the purpose of their visit; we have in mind other stories of aliens attacking Earth, kidnapping earth people, conducting experiments on them, etc.
- From their arrival in the Domain in line 4 to line 18, we see the earth people through the eyes of the aliens, witness the **gradual approach** of the aliens in lines 9–11 and their arrival amongst the earthmen in line 17 — all the time, wondering what the aliens will do.
- Line 18, we know that the earthmen are unaware of the aliens in their midst and the **tension** builds; superior, arrogant **tone** of lines 17–18 adds to the tension, makes us fear for the safety of the earthmen.
- The **climax** comes in line 19 when the earthmen sense the presence of the aliens and the **tension** mounts as the reader realises this is the point at which something will happen.
- **Commas** create **caesurae**, suggesting the hushed breath of the earthmen, at the height of the **tension**; the **dash** before "even into our eyes" — we sense the danger, increased by the fact that the aliens are invisible to the earthmen.

- Lines 21–23, only now are we told that the aliens have "no power" over the earthmen, and we are relieved to know they are safe, but the earthmen do not know that and, although we know the subsequent attack with the firebrand is unnecessary, we are proud of the courage displayed by the earthman in defence of his people.
- The way is clear to a **happy ending** for the earth people.

H — development of tension building up to action, techniques well-explained + intelligent comment; Int. — some awareness of tension, moment of action, techniques clearly understood + some comment.

6. **How effective do you find the last short section, lines 37–40, as a conclusion to the poem? (You might like to consider such aspects as structure, resolution of the narrative, theme . . .)** **(8) E**
   - In terms of the **structure**, lines 37–40 form a conclusion, perhaps more of an **epilogue**;
   - lines 1–3, prologue to the main story, departure of the aliens from their planet.
   - The main part of the narrative lies in the long, middle section of the poem and deals with the time spent by the aliens on Earth; in lines 37–40, aliens return to their planet.
   - **Resolution of the narrative**: we see the effect on the aliens of their visit to Earth.
   - Line 37 records the bare facts: they made contact with their space ship and returned home.
   - The **semicolons** in this line show the automatic nature of those actions, as if they were in some sort of trance. The following lines indicate that they have been profoundly affected by their visit; they resume their normal day to day activities — "but" at the end of line 38 is a strong indication that things have not gone back to normal:
   - they are "haunted" by their memories of the earthmen, cannot stop thinking of them.
   - In line 39, we finally learn why they went to Earth in the first place: to gather rock samples and seeds; the word "souvenirs" suggests samples eclipsed by the aliens' impression of and reaction to the earth people.
   - Line 40, they have been impressed by the heroic courage of earthmen; suggests that they went to Earth with a superior attitude, a conceit of their own advanced stage of development and have returned considerably chastened by the display of courage by one primitive man.
   - Those lines drive home the **theme** of optimistic Humanism for us:
   - indicated in main narrative by the reactions of the aliens; line 33, "we felt nothing but his courage" — the **zeugma** and the **double negative** in "nothing but" intensify the admiration felt by the alien for the brave earthman's springing to the defence his people.
   - Lines 34–35 are a declaration of faith in the courage and integrity of human beings, and confidence in their powers of survival, even under attack by an unseen force.
   - Line 36, "There are no gods in the domain of Arnheim." is a conclusive ending to the main narrative: they are celebrating the birth of baby, but it is very much a human baby — no Jesus — a strong statement of Man's inherent ability to survive without help from any outside force.
   - The last lines, showing the admiration felt by the aliens, an obviously advanced class of beings, light years ahead of the primitive earthmen of Arnheim, confirm lines 34–35, reinforce our pride in our ancestors and give us hope for the survival of the human race;
   - Morgan's reversal of the usual aliens-come-to-Earth story adds impact to the theme (cf. his reversal of the usual Christmas story in "Trio").

H — should cover all three aspects in well-developed discussion + intelligent comment;
Int. — should show awareness of at least two aspects, though they may be less explicit + some comment.

Level: Intermediate 1

1. (a) **Who is speaking in the poem?**   • Aliens (who have come to visit Earth). **(1) U**
   (b) **Explain *in your own words* what is described in lines 1 – 3.** **(2) U**
       • Aliens leaving their planet (1) + going back through time (1).
   (c) **Why is there a gap between lines 3 and 4?**   • To denote passage of time. **(1) A**
   (d) **Line 4, *"we were there"*: where were they?** **(1) U**
       • The domain of Arnheim (1); Earth (½).

2. **We are not told the reason for the aliens' visit to Earth.**
    Why might the poet want to keep this information from us at this point?   (2) A
    - Suspense (1) + we don't know whether they come in peace (½) + or to harm earth people (½).

3. **Lines 4 to 8 describe the domain of Arnheim.**
    (a) **What kind of place is it?**   (2) U
    - Very primitive, undeveloped land (1) + high in hills / mountains (1).
    (b) **Write down the details which help you to picture what it is like there.**   (2) UA
    - The word "domain" — small independent settlement; line 5, yellow light indicates oil lamp. (1) +
    - "Icefield" — indication of time / development of Earth; line 7, sound travels: indication of space, openness of area; "white" (and "snow", line 4). (1)

4. **Look at lines 11 to 16: What do we learn about the people who live in the domain of Arnheim?**   (2) U
    - Line 6, live in huts — pine trees — primitive earth people; laughter — first sound — happy people.
    -   Line 14, primitive — "naked", natural state.
    -   Lines 19–22, primitives have strong sense of the supernatural — "a displacement of the air, a sudden chill"; sense presence of visitors — feeling of being watched is familiar.
    -   Lines 24–25, celebrate the birth of child with music — trumpets, drums, song.
    -   Line 29, earth people brave — stand their ground, in spite of fear, "sweating", line 30.
    At least two points clearly understood.

5. *"A child, or one of their animals, was crying"*   (line 15)
    (a) **What does this line tell you about the attitude of the aliens to the earth people?** (2) UA
    - They look down on earth people (1) + consider them primitive / not much higher than animals. (1)
    (b) **Give a reason for your answer.**   (2) A
    - Cannot distinguish between human child's and animal's cry. *Mark on merit.*

6. **Look at lines 19 to 33.**
    (a) **Explain, in your own words, what happens in those lines.**   (2) U
    - The earthmen sense the presence of the aliens (1) + one throws a firebrand (1).
    (b) **Explain how the punctuation in line 19 helps to create tension.**   (2) A
    - **Commas** create **caesurae**, suggesting the hushed breath of the earthmen (1) + **dash** before "even into our eyes" — like a gasp. (1) We sense the danger, increased by the fact that the aliens are invisible to the earthmen.
    (c) **Why is this an important part of the story?**   (2) A
    - Confrontation / earthmen aware of aliens for first time (1) + what will happen? (1).

7. **What point is the poet making about human beings in lines 34–36?**   (2) A
    - Don't need help from outside force / God (1) + can survive on their own. (1)

8. **Look carefully at lines 37 to 40.**
    (a) **Where are the aliens in those lines?**   (1) U
    - Back home.
    (b) **What effect has their visit to Earth had on them?**   (2) U
    - Cannot stop thinking about Earth people (1) + impressed by their courage (1).
    (c) **Explain how their reaction to what happened on Earth helps you to understand the ideas about mankind raised by the poet.**   (2) E
    - Poet shows faith in the courage and integrity of human beings, and confidence in their powers of survival, even under attack by an unseen force like the earthmen here.
    - Admiration felt by the aliens, an obviously advanced class of beings, light years ahead of the primitive earthmen of Arnheim, should give us hope for the survival of the human race.
    Mark on merit.

Suggested Outline Plans for Critical Essays

1   **Scottish poets often use humour or satire to deflate pomposity or simply to ridicule. By referring to one Scottish poem, show how effective you find use of humour / satire or both. (The Starlings . . .)**
    §1   Title, poet's name, brief description of situation dealt with, as presented in section I of poem.
    §2   Humour in surreal treatment of effects of starlings, poking fun at councillors, Lord Provost, clerks in GPO and Information Bureau in section II — quote / explain / comment.
    §3   Satire in section III of poem, against the general public, the press – quote, etc.
    §4   Personal response to situation — should refer to serious message in lines 62–70; sum up how humour and satire leading up to those lines made them more effective.

2. **It is often thought that poetry is solely about serious and sad subjects. Choose a poem which deals with a happy occasion or incident and write about the techniques which helped you both to appreciate the joy of the occasion and to understand the poet's message.   (Trio)**
    §1   Title, poet's name, brief description of happy occasion, as presented in lines 1–5.
    §2   The happiness and warmth of the trio made clear to us lines 6–8 — quote / explain / comment. Also in descriptions of what they are carrying — quote / explain / comment.
    §3   Message conveyed, ironically, via analogy with the birth of Jesus – quote, etc.
    §4   Personal response should refer to poet's response to situation + personal comment / view.

3. **Choose a poem which either *(a)* communicates, very strong feelings or *(b)* creates a mood of reflection and, by close analysis of the language of the poem, show how this has been achieved.**
    (a)   ***The Starlings in George Square***
         §1   Title, poet's name, brief description of situation in poem and strong feelings communicated.
         §2   Appreciation of beauty and mystery of birds in descriptions, section I and child's view — quote, etc.
         §3   Poet's anger at man's cruelty to birds shown:
              ridiculing of people around George Square in section II — quote / explain / comment;
              irony / satire in section III — quote / explain / comment.
         §4   Personal response to poet's attitude to birds shown in serious message in section III.

    (b)   ***Trio*** §1–3 as for question 2 above.
         §4   Poet's reflection from line 12 onwards: change of register; proclaims Humanist message; warmth remains with him after they have gone — quote / explain / comment + personal response.

4. **Choose two poems,which deal with the same subject matter. Explain briefly what the common theme is and, by analysing how the language in each poem helps to convey the poet's ideas, discuss which of the two poems puts its message across more strongly.**
    (***Trio*** and ***From the Domain of Arnheim***; *Trio* covered adequately above. ***Trio*** and ***Lo! a Child is Born*** by Hugh MacDiarmid. *See Suggested Study Points, page 33.*)
    §1   Titles, poet(s), brief account of situation in each poem and common Humanist theme.
    §2   *Trio* celebrates mutual human warmth / love — quote / explain / comment;
         Domain celebrates primitive man's courage — quote / explain / comment;
         Lo! celebrates human love for newborn child in strong contrast to God's indifference to his creation — quote / explain / comment.
    §3   Each poem uses Christian story ironically — quote / explain / comment.
    §4   Choice will be personal but should justify, for example:
         Trio, real location and experience, ordinary people, effect on poet;
         Domain, space element adds interest; contrast between aliens and earthmen, persona;
         Lo! makes direct comparison between human and divine; imagery.

Suggested Study Points: *Revelation*

UNDERSTANDING

1. **The situation**
    - Young girl taken to look at the bull at the farm, where she has been sent to collect eggs and milk; frightened, she runs away.

2. **The themes**
    - Girl's transition from innocence to experience.
    - Gender stereotyping.
    - Female condition.

ANALYSIS

Verse 1, lines 1–14

- Line 1, "I remember . . ." — mature woman looking back on childhood experience.
- "the black bull" — symbol of male sexual prowess / procreative function.
- Line 2, "eggs and milk" — introduces female symbols; **contrast** continued in next three lines.
- Lines 3–5: the idea that male sexual aggression ("monster" line 4) may hide behind an apparently benign exterior ("Bob . . . charm . . . friendly name."); the experienced woman talking; line 4, "reduce" introduces idea of size as part of the male threat; continued in following lines.
- Lines 6–7, "threshold" — **lexical choice**: the girl is at the threshold of adulthood; ties in with title. A woman was traditionally carried across the threshold by her new husband; there is, perhaps, an underlying reference to the high incidence of domestic abuse suffered by women at the hands of men in the "safety" of their own homes;
- "someone / held my hand" suggests the male should be approached with trepidation.
- Lines 8–14 describe the bull through the eyes of the young girl, her observations mirroring her progressively improving sight as her eyes become accustomed to the dark interior of the shed; at the same time her growing fear develops; lines 1–7 have been building up to this point.
- Lines 8–9, **syntax** — no verb in sentence, suggests girl holding her breath; her first impression is black, followed by line 9, ". . . the hot reek of him" — his smell; the **synaesthesia** in "hot reek" intensifying her impression by coupling the two senses of touch and smell; "of him" rather than "his" — makes the bull loom large in the dark shed; the **caesura** represents a gasp as she makes out his size. Line 10, he seems to fill the whole shed, to be part of the darkness.
- Lines 11–12, "a big bulk" — **alliteration** gives extra force to the commonplace "big".
- **Synecdoche** in "a big bulk and a roar" focuses on his size and his frightening bellow;
- continues in line 12 in "a trampling and a clanking", focussing on his powerful hooves and the chain restraining him, indicating that he is dangerous; the present participles add movement, making him more threatening as he pulls on the chain, "jerk" suggesting the force he is exerting.
- **Lexical choice / pun** on "tense": his force stretches the chain to its limit, as if he is trying to get to his observers; also describes the feelings of the watching child.
- Line 13, as the child's eyes adjust to the darkness, she makes out his eyes; "swivelled" suggests madness, lack of control, strong emotion; "wedge" gives shape of his head, the solidity of it; "tossed" indicates he is angry, continued in next line.
- Line 14, **alliteration** intensifies his "rage" and the frightening roar; the **caesura** represents the child's gasp of fear as she notices the flaring nostrils — "gaped" suggests their size. The two short statement sentences emphasise the power of the bull; strong conclusion to verse 1.

Verse 2, lines 15–23

- Line 15, **contrast** in place — "outside"; reintroduces the male / female contrast, with the idea that if the bull could get out of his shed, he would trample over the hens, break the eggs, kick over the jug of milk.
- Line 16, "hens" — female; "picked their way about" suggests dainty movements; contrasts with "trampling", line 12; "oblivious" — unsuspecting, unaware of the raging bull nearby.
- Lines 17–18, "faint . . . festive tinkling" suggests sleigh bells, innocence of child's Christmas story; contrasts with "clanking", line 12; **alliteration** intensifies the **irony** in "festive" — same idea as " the charm of a friendly name", line 5; suggests women are blissfully unaware of the dangers posed by the male; continued in line 18, "mellow" — idea of pleasant gentleness; contrast with the reality of the bull's force and power, "straining at his chains", line 19.
- Line 19, "Black Mass" — **pun**, more sinister with capitals: literally the bull is black and large; but underlying evil force, the Black Mass is a travesty of the Mass practised in devil-worship.
- Line 20, female instinct, but only half-aware of the danger posed by male.
- Line 21, **alliteration / repetition** of prefix "anti-" intensifies, brings to a climax the power and lawlessness of the male:
- "antidote": several possibilities here — the wryly ironic one, that some women see a man as the solution to their problems, an antidote to the ills of the world and so rush into marriage at the earliest opportunity. The idea is a little out of date now, when young women put marriage and having a family on hold while they pursue their careers and sow their wild oats, the sole prerogative of men until recent years;
- "Anti-Christ" links with "Black Mass" in line 19, again made more sinister by use of capitals.
- "anarchy" also links with "Black Mass" and suggests that the male is the main cause of disorder, the cat among the pigeons, in the otherwise pleasant female dovecote.
- Lines 22–23, "threatening" emphasised, intensified by its position at the beginning of the line;
- "eggs" and "milk" in line 23 are basic female **symbols**;
- "well-rounded" — **pun**: literally, suitably curved — a male view of women? Also means well-constructed and complete, satisfactorily developed — the female view?
- "Self-contained" continues the idea in "well-rounded" — self-sufficient, but again, literally , has the idea of the egg containing the embryo woman (cf. the last line of Lochhead's *Mirror's Song*: "a woman giving birth to herself.").
- The underlying **irony** here suggests, however, that some women are responsible for their own fate; they are their own worst enemies.
- Line 23, "placidity" — contrast with "anarchy", line 21; links back to "mellow", line 18.

Verse 3, lines 24–31

- Line 24, "I ran": child's reaction to the bull;
- **personification**: pigtails "thumping" on her back like her heart thumping with fear.
- Line 25, "the big boys" have taken over from the bull; made more threatening by **alliteration**.
- Lines 26–27, boys anarchic like the bull: destroy beauty (butterflies) and indulge in wanton cruelty (frogs) — a bit of gender stereotyping here; but most females are more sensitive and unwilling to hurt animals. The **tone** in those lines is very matter-of-fact, suggesting that's what boys (and men) are like, that is their nature, and we just have to put up with them.
- Line 28, "thorned hedge and harried nest": literally, the boys raided the nests. **Lexical choice** in adjectives suggests the dangers which women face from men: "thorned" suggests sharp, physical pain; "harried" is interesting: a harrier hawk is a kind of hawk that preys on small animals, like certain types of men on defenceless women.
- Lines 29–31, she is afraid of breaking the eggs, which she has been sent to collect and of spilling the milk, which she is carrying in the jug, in her haste to reach a safe haven;
- **lexical choice**: "shattering", line 29, not just cracking but dashing to pieces;
- line 30, "small and shaking": the "and" isolates the two words giving each more emphasis, while the **alliteration** holds them together for the combined effect;
- but there is an underlying **irony** here: the poet seems to be sending up the "little women", of which she, herself, certainly is not one, in any sense of the phrase;
- "eggs", line 29 and "milk", line 31: on the symbolic level of meaning in those lines, she is aware of her own fragility in the face of the male threat.

Looking over the whole poem
- **Poetic form:** Free Verse is appropriate to the recall of a childhood memory.

- **Narrative structure**: three verse paragraphs:
  1. sets the scene; introduces the villain;
  2. a long parenthesis, introducing the potential victim symbolically;
  3. child's reaction to the villain and her escape to safety.

- **Dichotomy** between the remembered child's view and that of the remembering adult.

- Use of male and female **symbols**.

EVALUATION

- **Themes:**
- Transition from innocence to experience;
- the story — little girl afraid of large bull, in the same way that she fears the "big boys" who are rough and might hurt her; she seems to make the connection between the boys and the bull, as she runs from both.
- Sudden realisation that there is a difference between the sexes, and that the male sex is, on the whole, bigger, more powerful and will hurt her if she sticks around; hence the title.

- Gender stereotyping: should produce some good discussion in mixed groups!
- Is it possible to attribute certain characteristics to gender?
- What are the differences — are they merely physical?
- Does Liz Lochhead want us to believe that all men are aggressive, both physically and sexually threatening? She seems to suggest that this behaviour is inherent in the male, starting with small boys destroying and hurting creatures weaker than themselves, as if serving their apprenticeship for manhood, when they will be able to practise their base instincts on women who are weaker than they are. However, there is always an underlying irony in her descriptions of the female which, I think, indicates that she is just as critical of females who play "the weak little woman" as she is of the men who take advantage of them.

- The female condition:
- mainly based on size, which makes women vulnerable to the baser instincts of men.
- The high incidence of domestic violence suffered by women is proof that the problem certainly exists, but there are surprisingly high statistics of the reverse situation, violence by women against men, which receive much less publicity. The irony suggests, however, that some women allow themselves to become victims and that the solution to the problem is in their own hands.
- Women are often, or think they should be, held in high esteem because they bear children. How reasonable is that assumption? In those days of unprecedented, genetic development, the male may soon be redundant. Indeed, there may no longer be the need for two genders and mankind may evolve into a race of beings of a single gender.

- **Use of symbols:**
- How effective in conveying the themes?
- Part of gender stereotyping?
- Does it suggest that characteristics are inherently gender-based?

Using Your Notes for Revision: Checklist

UNDERSTANDING AND ANALYSIS *(Use these questions to revise important parts of the poem.)*

1. **Situation: "I remember once . . ." (line 1). Summarise the childhood memory recalled by the poet and explain the effect that the incident had on her.**
   - The poet remembers being taken, as a child, to see the bull once when she had been sent to the farm to collect eggs and milk. She is so frightened of the bull that she runs home.
   - She remembers the incident clearly as something of a rite of passage — when she suddenly realised that there was a distinct difference between male and female; and felt the threat of male aggression against women.

2. **Verse 1, the bull:**
   (a) **Note the way the poet builds up your expectations of the bull in lines 1–7.**
      - We know immediately that he must be fairly impressive as seeing him stands out clearly in her mind; he made such a strong impression on her.
      - "Bob" — the bull belied his name; far from being charming, she calls him a "monster".
      - The fact that someone held her hand indicates that the bull was dangerous, frightening.
   (b) **How does the poet let us see the bull through the girl's eyes in lines 8—14?**
      - Because she is looking into a dark shed, her eyes take some time to adjust;
      - her growing fear parallels her gradually improving vision, thus taking the reader with her.
   (c) **Revise the techniques / devices used by the poet to reveal the girl's reaction to the bull.**
      Details in Suggested Study Points, page 118
      - Poet reveals the child's perception of the bull through her senses:
      - first impression, a big, black object; aware of his smell — **synaesthesia** — "hot reek", line 9.
      - Poet uses **syntax** to reveal girl's reactions to the bull: non-sentence, caesurae — lines 8–9.
      - Size suggested by **lexical choice**: "immense, / his edges merging with the darkness".
      - His power / strength — shown by **synecdoche** and **alliteration**, lines 11–12;
      - line 12, **pun** on "tense" shows bull's strength and girl's feelings, connecting the two.
      - Line 13, "His eyes swivelled" — madness, lack of control;
      - his head, "great wedge . . . tossed";
      - line 14, his rage – intensified by **alliteration** / flaring nostrils;
      - two short sentences / **caesura** — girl's feelings reach climax — she is terrified.

3. **Verse 2, contrast:**
   (a) **Note the immediate contrast with verse 1. Which word signals the contrast?**
      - Starts with contrast in place: "in the yard outside", following on from description of bull in shed; line 15 begins with "And", making the link with verse 1, more subtle than "But".
   (b) **Note all of the contrasts set up in this verse.**
      - Reintroduces male / female contrast: bull / hens:
      - dainty movements of hens: "picked their way about", line 16; bull's "trampling", line 12.
      - Hens' perception of bull contrasts with the reality, intensified by linking "And":
      - "oblivious", line 16; bull's determined efforts to get out, straining on his chain, line 12;
      - "faint . . . festive tinkling", line 17, contrasts with "clanking", line 12.
      - Innocence of hens contrasts with evil of bull:
      - "Black Mass . . . Anti-Christ . . . anarchy": **pun**, capitals, **repetition** of prefix, wry irony.
      - Strength / force / aggression of bull; fragility of eggs and "placidity of milk", line 23.
   (c) **How does this verse fit into the structure of poem as a whole?**
      - This central verse is like a parenthesis between v. 1 and v. 3:
      - v. 1 ends with climax of child's feelings, v. 3 shows her reaction to the bull: "I ran . . .";
      - v. 2 does not move the narrative forward, reflects on contrast between male / female in terms of size, strength, aggression / passivity, evil / innocence;
      - point of view is entirely of the mature woman here.
      - V. 2 prepares reader for male / female contrast in v. 3, "big boys" / young girl.

4.   **Symbols:**
     (a)   **Poet's use of male and female symbols.**
     (b)   **Words / phrases she uses symbolically.**
             ● Introduces symbols in first two lines: bull / eggs and milk — basic symbols of male / female:
             - in verse 2, hens are female symbols; also eggs, "well rounded, self-contained" and milk;
             - bull is seen as aggressive, threatening the "placidity", fragility, vulnerability of the female, who appears to be unaware of the male danger.

5.   **Verse 3, the big boys:**
     (a)   **What does the poet accuse "the big boys" of doing in verse 3?**
             ● Pulling wings off butterflies; inflating frogs with straws; raiding birds' nests.
     (b)   **What does this behaviour tell us about those boys?**
             ● They destroy beauty, indulge in wanton cruelty.
     (c)   **How do those actions connect the boys with the bull?**
             ● They are just as anarchic, destructive, cruel, aggressive as the bull.

EVALUATION *(Use this question for exam practice.)*

6.   **How effectively, in your opinion, has the poet used symbolism to make a statement about the female condition,**
     ● Introduces symbols in first two lines: bull / eggs and milk — basic symbols of male / female.

     ● Title: transition from innocence to experience, refers to gender, sexuality;
     - poet remembers incident as turning point in her development — quote / explain / comment;
     - line 7, "someone held my hand" — quote / explain / comment;
     - description of bull concentrates on size and menacing aspects + girl's reaction to him.
     - She makes the connection between bull and "big boys", who are shown destroying / hurting — quote / explain / comment — (+ possibly comment on gender stereotyping).

     ● The female condition — unsuspecting victims, taken in by male charm:
     - lines 3–5 introduce contrast between appearance and reality — quote / explain / comment;
     - line 6, "threshold": quote / explain / comment;
     - v. 2 — contrast between hens and bull: if bull could get out he would trample over hens, break eggs and spill milk; bull's shed is like the veneer of civilisation with which a man covers up his natural aggressive tendencies; once the cover is down, violence and abuse are allowed out.

     ● But **irony** in this verse suggests some women are their own worst enemies; that they allow themselves to become victims; e.g., "festive tinkling", line 17; lines 22–23, "well-rounded, self-contained . . . placidity" — quote, etc. . . .
     ● V. 3, lines 28–31, "thorned hedge and harried nest" — quote / explain / comment;
     - fragility of "little woman" but underlying irony, especially in "small and shaking hand";

     ● Final comment on effectiveness of symbolism.

and to what extent do you agree with her ideas? (10 marks)
     ● Personal response but should deal closely with ideas in poem, justifying opinions; possibly suggest men have changed, girl power, zero tolerance, etc.; gender stereotyping.

H – well-developed discussion of symbolism and ideas, with good textual support + intelligent comment; Int. – clear understanding of symbols and ideas, with some textual support + some comment.

Suggested Study Points — *Box Room*

UNDERSTANDING

1. **The situation**
   - The person speaking (presumably the poet) arrives with her boyfriend at his mother's house.
   - They have come to tell his mother that their relationship is a permanent one.
   - She is shown into his old boyhood room. Mother makes it clear that the speaker's position is purely temporary, one in a long line of his past conquests, whom she has seen come and go.

2. **The themes**
   - Relationships: mother / son; prospective mother-in-law / daughter-in-law; male / female.
   - Childhood / adulthood.

ANALYSIS

§1: lines 1–3, The arrival . . .
- **Atmosphere** of discomfort / unease of situation — first meeting, stilted;
- three consecutive, short **non-sentences**; **caesurae**;
- the welcoming" — as if it is a performance, formality, not sincere.
- Lines 1–2, **enjambment** emphasises "space", indicates short time gap, reprieve . . . . "Then . . .";
- Line 2, **pun**: "she put me in my place" — literally showed her to her room; also showed her that she did not amount to much with her or her son;
- **cliché** — adds to the **tone** of **wry**, **reductive humour** which runs through whole poem; a common feature of Liz Lochhead's work;
- continued in the "afterthought" shown by **brackets**: ("Oh, with concern for my comfort.") One can easily imagine the "pan-loaf" accent in which those words would be said.

§2: lines 3–12, First chat . . .
- **Direct speech** brings mother to life in the poem; shows it is not just speaker's paranoia.
- Mother's hostile **attitude** to her guest is obvious; makes her claim to her son's loyalty clear: his room, when he comes "home" — he belongs to her;
- line 6, "Friend" — capital letter indicates **tone** — mother is letting her know that he has had other girlfriends and has brought them home too;
- lines 6–8, mother goes through the motions of being polite, hopes the bed will be comfortable, but her next remark, "He'll make do . . .", makes it clear that she feels the girl is putting her son out of his comfortable bed; "the put-u-up." sounds uncomfortable; poet could have written "couch" or "sofa" but "put-u-up" sounds less comfortable and continues the wry **humour** — connotations of "put up with you" — that the guest is the direct cause of her boy's discomfort.
- Lines 8–10: mother subtly informs her that her boyfriend has brought other girls home in the past.
- Line 10, "It'll all be fine I'm sure": **ambiguity** — ostensibly addressed to the guest about the sleeping arrangements, but also she is telling herself that this one will be like the others; she will not lose her boy.
- Line 11, **euphemism** — she's too prim and formal to mention the lavatory; not calculated to make the girl feel at ease in the situation.
- Line 12, the quotation suggests the **tone** of the guest's reaction to the chat — one can imagine her mimicking her hostess, eyes to heaven, etc.

§3: lines 12–18, Reflections on the situation.

- Lines 12–14, "My weekend case . . . and I" — **tone** of wry **humour**, suggests her hostess thinks as much of the one as she does of the other and what she thinks of the case is shown in the **ambiguous** words in brackets: "Lightweight" — good for a suitcase, not good for one's prospective daughter-in-law; "glossy" — suggests superficial polish, shallow underneath; " synthetic" — not the real thing; not good enough for her son; "Miracle" suggests "flash in the pan". Those are all examples of Liz Lochhead's **typically Scottish reductive humour** — we Scots are constantly sending ourselves up, inviting others to have a laugh at our expense, but underneath we know we are much worthier than we pretend to be; just as the guest refuses to be dismissed by her hostess, as the remaining lines of this first verse show.
- Lines 14–16, "her pathetic / shrine to your lost boyhood" — **tone** is dismissive; she knows she means more to him than his mother does; she doesn't have to cling on to him.
- Lines 15–16, "She must / Think . . . " — **tone** becomes sarcastic; mother thinks she can keep her son's love by preserving his childhood and constantly laying it before him.
- Line 18, balance between "for the weekend" and "my permanence" rounds off this first verse paragraph, restating the speaker's confidence in her position.

§4: lines 19–26, But her confidence has been shaken . . .

- Line 19, **repetition** of mother's words "Peace to unpack", no inverted commas this time but we make the connection easily enough: she cannot find peace, and her hostess's words are the reason for her unrest; their conversation has brought ideas into her head, unsettled her;
- "none" is emphasised by its position at the end of the line. Her confidence has plummeted.
- Line 20, "contained you" — was his world, as a child; lines 20–22, **brackets** show her thoughts about the room; the **tone** is somewhat rueful, as she realises that he was a different person then, whom she did not and never can know, but whom his mother did know, intimately.
- "Dun- / Coloured walls, one small window", featureless, dull; "frame / Your old horizons": compare "contained you", line 20 — **metaphor** — he looked through this window to the outside world; what he saw defined the limitations of his experience.
- Lines 22–26, she admits her fear; **personification**: "Persistent fear / Elbows me . . . " — fear is like her bedfellow, nudging her constantly; she cannot dismiss it; **pun** on "embedded deeply" — she is sinking into the soft bed; and the fear has taken a deep hold in her mind;
- "an outgrown bed" — he has physically grown out of his child's bed; and she hopes too that he has left his childhood ties behind him, that his creature comforts are those of an adult, not of the child he was and his mother thinks he still is.
- The **brackets**, lines 25–26, a "naughty", adult observation — that they have occasionally shared a single bed; what would his precious mother think of that if she knew! She is trying to fight back with the assertion that she knows him as he is now, better than his mother does.

§5: lines 27–33, His room, remnants of his boyhood . . .

- Line 27, she looks at the framed photographs on the walls, of him at different stages of his childhood: "long-discarded selves." "gilt-edged": each stage captured by the camera and frozen in time, treasured by mother. **Alliteration** intensifies the effect of her being surrounded by his childhood pictures and the false toothy grin children tend to produce for the camera.
- Line 28, **brackets** — again **tone** of wry **humour** — also in the **cliché** "fit into the picture" — under the humour, a serious sense of being excluded; this is not the person she knows as her boyfriend; she is not, nor ever can be, part of his history, what made him the man he now is.
- Lines 28–30: she looks at his bookshelves. **Alliteration** helps to establish the **tone** of "previous prizes"; the "p" sound gives the impression she is almost spitting the words out.
- The words are **ambiguous**, meaning school prizes, but also recalling his mother's words in line 9: is she just one in a long line of his "prizes", his conquests?
- "a selection / Of plots grown thin": as he has lost interest in the books of his boyhood, will he lose interest in her? A **tone** of resentment creeping in here.

- Lines 30–33, "Your egg collection": literally his collection of birds' eggs, but also his past girl-friends, "egg" being a basic female symbol, as in *Revelation*.
- Line 31, "Shatters me" — humour in **lexical choice** on two levels; "shatter" is appropriate to fragile eggs (cf. "shattering", line 29 "Revelation".); also informally meaning devastate; and, under both, a serious feeling of her vulnerability. Will she, too, be cast aside, forgotten?
- Lines 32–33, **brackets**: an almost feeble attempt to keep up the **humour**; talking about his method and principles when collecting birds' eggs, "one from each . . . never wrecked a nest", but on the symbolic level: he never two-timed girls, and never dated married women?
- "You said" — the **enjambment**, carrying those words over to the beginning of the next line, where they are stressed, suggests that she is beginning to doubt his word. **Tone** of growing despair.

§6: lines 33–36, total loss of confidence . . .
- Line 33, "Invited guest" — **rhyme** with end of previous line, seems to emphasise that she is no more than that, a guest, her status temporary. **Syntax** — the phrase is balanced against "abandoned object"; each noun preceded by a past participle, as if she too might soon be part of his past, "abandoned" like his other interests, his previous girlfriends; a very faint attempt at **humour** here.
- Lines 33–34, "my position / Is precarious": **enjambment** carries the **alliteration** over the line, the two devices combining to intensify the precariousness of her position. "closeted so" refers to the **title**; although it was his childhood bedroom it is presumably quite small but, more importantly, it contains all the things for which he no longer has any use, and she feels she may have moved into that category too. "it's dark" — **ambiguous**: it is literally dark, she is in bed; also she does not know what is ahead of her, how she stands with her boyfriend.
- Lines 34–35, "your past a premonition": **paradox** — but it does make perfect sense; having seen how he has abandoned his other interests she has a feeling that he might lose interest in her too. The paradox, along with the **alliteration**, gives the phrase impact.
- "I can't close my eyes to": **ambiguous** — she cannot sleep because of her thoughts; also she cannot ignore the possibility that her boyfriend is the kind of person who is fanatical about an interest one minute and drops it completely the next.
- Lines 35–36, all attempts at humour have gone; she admits her fears — "I shiver";
- "The electric blanket" — artificial heat; "the deceptive mildness of the night" — the apparent welcome she received from his mother, which was equally lacking in natural warmth.
- The tone of **despair** is absolute.

Looking over the whole poem
- **Poetic form** is complicated; a combination of irregular metre and rhyming couplets;
- appropriate to the sense of the poem, as the speaker tries to make sense of her circumstances but, in the end, is defeated by the apparent inevitability of the situation.
- The lines within the couplets being of different lengths has the effect of delaying the rhyme, in cases where the second line is longer than the first, which often adds to the humour; the inevitability of the rhyme — it's coming no matter how long the second line is! — adds the wry touch, which is such a common feature of Liz Lochhead's work, e.g., in lines 11–12; in the reverse situation, where the first line of the couplet is the longer, the rhyme comes early and has a surprise effect, sometimes humorous, e.g., lines 27–28, sometimes shocking, e.g., lines 33–34.

EVALUATION

- Discussion of relationships, how conveyed: covered in Analysis section.
- Childhood / adulthood: "The Child is father of the Man" (Wordsworth). Speaker deduces her boyfriend's true nature from the contents of his boyhood bedroom: reasonable or not?
- How will she feel in the morning?
- Humour — is it generic? Depends on individual's experience, background, e.g., "in" jokes?

Using Your Notes for Revision: Checklist

UNDERSTANDING AND ANALYSIS *(Use these questions to revise important parts of the poem.)*

1.   **Refresh your memory of the main characters in the poem,**
    • (1) Speaker is young woman; (2) boyfriend's mother.
    the occasion: Speaker is meeting boyfriend's mother for first time; she has come to stay for the weekend. They intend to tell his mother that their relationship is permanent.
    and how the characters relate to each other.
    • Mother is welcoming on the surface, smiles, shakes hands; polite to her guest but mentions other girls her son has brought home.
    • The young woman takes all this from her hostess politely, without retaliating, understanding that the older woman is jealous of her position with her son.

2.   **Arrival, first chat and guest's reaction to her hostess: lines 1 — 18.**
    (a)   **What is the atmosphere of the first meeting and how does the poet make this clear to you?**
        • Uneasy, uncomfortable, stilted: three short **non-sentences**, **caesurae**, **enjambment**.
    (b)   **How does the poet convey the mother's attitude to her guest?**
        • **Direct speech**; "home", line 4; "Friend" — **capital**, line 6; suggests other girls.
        - She politely hopes the guest will be comfortable but uses the opportunity to make clear that her son will be much less comfortable on the "put-u-up". Adding that it will be "All right / For a night or two", implying that the situation is temporary; he has brought other girls home.
    (c)   **Examine the tone of lines 12 – 18 and how it is conveyed to you.**
        • Line 12, exasperated — she has had to listen to veiled comments from her hostess: mimics her in her mind — quotation in line 12.
        - Line 14, confident: realises that mother is clinging to him, trying to retain the relationship she had with him when he was a child;
        - **lexical choice**: "pathetic shrine".
        - Line 15, sarcastic — thinks of mother trying to keep him as her child — "She must think . . . ".
        - First verse ends in tone of absolute confidence in her position:
        - **lexical choice**: "state my permanence"; balanced phrases.

3.   **Humour: verse 1. Note the various ways in which the humorous tone is created.**
        • Line 2, **pun**, **cliché** — wry, reductive humour; lines 12–14, description of weekend case; **brackets** + other examples detailed in Suggested Study Points, pages 123–124.

4.   **Tone: verse 2, lines 19–26**
    (a)   **How has the guest's tone changed at this point?**
        • Confident tone has weakened, she is uneasy;
        - time has elapsed (gap between two verses) and she is alone in bed.
    (b)   **Note the gradual descent from total confidence at end of verse 1 to fear in line 25.**
        • Line 19, **repetition** of hostess's words, "peace to unpack" + "none" stressed at end of line.
        - Lines 22–23, she admits to feeling uneasy, cannot sleep. Lines 23–25, she admits her fear.
        - But in lines 25–26, tone is defiant; final weak attempt to fight back? She knows him now in ways his mother does not know him and mother would disapprove if she knew.
    (c)   **Describe the box room of the title and revise the techniques / devices used to show the effects of this room on the guest.**
        • Lines 20–22, featureless, dingy, beige walls; small window, so not very bright; single bed.
        - She realises she does not know the boy who occupied this room, he was a different person then, but his mother knew him, intimately; she cannot find her boyfriend here; line 20, **metaphor**.
        - Brackets suggest she feels excluded from his childhood; he was a different person then.
        - Lines 23–24, fear has become her bedfellow — **personification, pun**.

5.   **Relics of childhood, lines 27–33. Note the techniques / devices used to show her growing doubts and feeling of vulnerability.**
   ● Pictures of boyfriend at various stages of childhood, in gilt frames;
   - line 27, **alliteration** — intensifies her feeling of being surrounded by pictures of a boy she did not know; suggestion of falseness of his grin; line 28, **brackets**, **cliché** — feels excluded.
   ● Bookshelves with many books, including school prizes: lines 29–30, **alliteration** helps to establish tone, p sound; **ambiguity** — tone becomes bitter, resentful.
   ● Collection of birds' eggs:
   - lines 30–33, eggs = female symbol; line 31, **lexical choice** — "shatters"; tone of despair growing.

6. **Tone: lines 33–36: Note the techniques / devices used to show her final descent into despair.**
   ● Line 33, faint attempt at humour — **rhyme**, **balanced phrases**; **enjambment**, **alliteration**.
   ● Lines 34–35, tone of resignation — **ambiguity**, **paradox**, **alliteration**.
   ● Lines 35–36, absolute despair — "shiver . . . electric blanket . . . deceptive mildness": **ambiguous**.

EVALUATION *(Use this question for exam practice.)*

7.   **Discuss the part played by humour in the poem, explaining the extent to which this feature helped you to understand the speaker's personality and the ideas expressed in the poem.**
                                                                                  (10 marks)
   ● Humour reveals speaker's personality — attractive; she appears bubbly, confident:
   - line 2, **pun** — quote / explain / comment; line 3, **brackets**: humorous posturing.
   ● Use of brackets throughout the poem, source of much of the humour; introduces an extra intimacy between speaker and reader, as if she is confiding in us and feels we shall understand her situation. Although her remarks are addressed to "You", her boyfriend, no suggestion that she would say those things to him; she is merely addressing him in her mind and enlisting the reader's support in the process.
   - Brackets are fairly unusual in poetry and, together with the **clichés**, suggest a genuineness in the ideas presented in the poem, concerning real people, like the reader perhaps.
   ● Reductive nature of humour gets reader on her side — we like someone who can laugh at herself a little — typically Scottish humour, one of our more attractive characteristics!
   - After chat with hostess, still confident, but more barbed: lines 12–14 — quote, etc.
   ● We admire her attempts to fight off the despair: line 17, "I laugh it off in self defence": she admits she is on the defensive but will not give in.
   - In the second section, time has elapsed and the humour becomes weaker but she goes on trying valiantly, e.g., line 28, **brackets**, **cliché** — quote / explain / comment.
   ● By exposing herself to us in this way, we can see the relationships mother / son, woman / man, potential mother-in-law / daughter-in-law operating in close up, understand the tensions between those parties, difficulty for mother giving up son to other woman, jealousy between them; realise that while mother knew the child intimately and the woman knows the man intimately, neither knows the whole person.
   - Speaker seems to think abandoned objects in his room indicate his true nature. She is overwhelmed by his childhood surrounding her and the fact that she can never be part of his past. We have the strong feeling that in the morning she will see that those things are part of his development into the person he now is and must be discarded; the adult version is the final and important one. She is obviously a strong personality and we are confident that her humour will be restored, with perhaps a little more understanding of his mother's position.
   H — well-developed discussion of humour and ideas, with good textual support + intelligent comment;
   Int. — clear understanding of humour and ideas, with some textual support + some comment.

Unseen Textual Analysis: Marking Scheme — *An Abortion*

Levels: Higher and Intermediate 2

All answers should be supported by close reference to the text.

1. **Explain, in detail, what happens in the poem and the part played in the incident by the poet.** **(2) U**
   - The poet sees a distressed cow in a field, goes out, witnesses the partial abortion of a calf.
   - The farm men come and yank the calf from the cow with a piece of string; poet watches.
   - The cow licks away at her calf all afternoon, trying to bring it to life, before being led away.

   H — full answer, showing the poet's involvement in the incident;
   Int.— main points + clear indication of poet's part in the incident.

2. **By close reference to *two* language features in lines 1–5, show how the poet becomes aware of the cow's distress.** **(2) A**
   - Line 2, "the something not right" — "something" not usually preceded by definite article, emphasises the vagueness of the poet's feeling at this point.
   - **Onomatopoeia** in "scrabbling", line 3, suggests the ineffectiveness of the cow's scraping at the ground; **repetition**: "scrabbling, scrabbling", line 3, suggests continued effort to rise,
   - **Syntax**: line 4, split infinitive graphically illustrates her inability to achieve a successful stance.
   - Three monosyllables line 5 suggests concentrated effort; **alliteration** illustrates the co-ordination which she cannot achieve. *Both levels – any two for 1 mark each.*

3. **Comment fully on any three of the following phrases / sentences, describing the beast's agony.** **(6) A**
   (a) *"her cow-tongue lolled then spiked the sky"*, lines 6–7.
      - Graphic physical description — not attractive; "lolled" — lateral liquid **sound** illustrates idea;
      - **lexical choice**: "spiked" — **contrast** with "lolled" — suggests sharp pain; **metaphor**: "spiked the sky" suggests intensity / extent of her pain, as if tongue reached sky in her agony. (2)
   (b) *"neck distended in a Guernica of distress"*, lines 8–9.
      - "neck distended" — stretched to its limit, swollen with the force of her bellow; sign of intense pain; **antonomasia** : "Guernica" — town in N. Spain, destroyed in 1937 by German bombers during Spanish Civil War; depicted in Picasso painting – suggests enormity of the pain. (2)
   (c) *"green foam flecked her muzzle and drizzled between the big bared brown teeth"*, lines 16–17.
      - "foam flecked": **alliteration** intensifies the cow's pain; "drizzled" — echo of "-zzle" from "muzzle" suggests teeth clenched with pain; "big bared brown": **alliteration** intensifies cow's pain, which causes her to grimace. Absence of commas suggests pain is constant, without pause.
   (d) *"Spasms, strong, primeval as the pulsing locomotion of some terrible underwater creature"*, lines 18–20.
      - Line 18, **alliteration + commas** — intensify spasmodic effect of the contractions. Lines 19–20, **simile**, contractions compared to movement of some monster ("terrible") from the deep; **lexical choice**: strong movement: "pulsing locomotion"; cow is at the mercy of the birth process; no control over it; must submit to the pain.

   H — full explanation of three examples + intelligent comment;
   Int. — clear understanding of three examples + some comment.

4.   **Look closely at lines 26–30.**
      Show how the language and syntax of those lines helps to establish the tone.   **(2) A**
      - **Language** is prosaic / simple: "membrane wrapped"; "hung out"; "wrong-looking bundle"; "rope-tail"; "steamrollering": blunt, almost crude word in this context, shocks the reader.
      - **Syntax** also prosaic: two long / complex sentences; "Then" at beginning of sentence; "under her": simple fact, baldly stated; emphasised at end of sentence (and separate line).
      - **Tone** is matter-of-fact; factual, resigned to the truth of the matter. Shocked — *(only half mark for H)*

      H — one example from each + tone, well explained and intelligent comment;
      Int. — one example from each + tone, clearly understood + some comment.

5.   (a)   **From your reading of lines 31–37, what is your impression of the two men from the farm?**   **(2) U**
            - Lines 32–33, they saunter out, replete with Sunday lunch; overalls to avoid messing good suits;
            - line 36, "curt" — short, rude to poet; "thank-you-very-much" — **hyphens** suggest the words were rattled out automatically, insincere; line 37, "dismissed me" — she was not wanted.

      H — two points fully explained, or more with less full but good general explanation + comment; Int. — two points clearly understood, or more with clear general understanding.

      (b)   **What can you deduce, from the language of those lines, about attitude to the cow?**   **(2) A**
            - **Synecdoche**: "the Sunday lunches" focuses the reader's mind on their appetites indulged, stomachs comfortably full, in contrast to cow's suffering in that area; together with "summoned", suggesting general lack of concern for the welfare of the pregnant cow.
            - **Lexical choice**: line 34, "knuckles" — hard, bruising part of hand, suggests inflicting pain;
            - line 35, "meant business": suggests dispassionate approach of men to the cow.

      H — two examples fully explained + comment; Int. — two examples clearly understood.

      (c)   **Referring closely to relevant areas from the whole poem, show how the men's attitude to the cow contrasts with that of the poet.**   **(4) A**
            - The poet understands and empathises with the animal's pain and distress:
            - line 10, **cliché / demotic** "got through to me all right" — suggests genuine concern; **contrast** with "summoned men". She shows her concern by leaving her work to investigate.
            - Line 25, **syntax**: short line, monosyllables, full stop — convey poet's shock;
            - line 28, **caesura** — idea of short time passing; poet holding breath to see what will happen.
            - Poet cannot go back to her work, watches what is happening outside:
            - line 38, "Shamed voyeur": feels she should have tried to help the cow; but more importantly that she is invading the cow's privacy by watching.
            - **Contrast** with men's treatment of the cow:
            - line 39, **onomatopoeia**: "quick hoick"- hard -ck sound suggests the painful nature of the action as well as the men's hard-heartedness, lack of sympathy;
            - lines 40–44, **syntax**: series of phrases, commas, present participles — all done quickly and without sympathy, confirmed by the fact that the men leave immediately the calf is removed; no attempt made to comfort the cow; laughing and joking;
            - line 43, **lexical choice**: "punchline" — cf. "knuckles"; suggests cruelty of men.
            - Men's indifference to cow's distress in this situation **contrasts** with poet's empathy, as she watches her licking the dead calf patiently all afternoon in a vain attempt to bring it to life. In the end, the men come and lead the cow away from the scene, like criminal.

      H — two main points of contrast, attitude and understanding, supported by textual references, fully explained + intelligent comment; Int. — two main points supported by textual references, clearly understood + some comment.

6.   **How successful, in your opinion, is Liz Lochhead in conveying her ideas concerning the female condition and experience in this poem,**
      - The poet, a woman, has an instinctive awareness that something is wrong:
      - lines 1–2, **lexical choice** — "inkling" — slight hint — shows female sensitivity / instinct.

- Poem deals with unique function of the female — viz. giving birth: cow is female symbol;
- line 13, "emblem-(bellow)" represents all female pain in childbirth; understood by female poet;
- line 18, "primeval" — women have suffered thus from the beginning of time;
- lines 22–23, "her groan was . . . no louder than a cough": women suffer in silence;
- line 42, "up again" — she bravely rises; like woman after childbirth, has to take care of child.
- Contrasting attitudes of female poet and male farm men highlight men's lack of understanding of female condition and experience: line 16, **pun:** "muzzle" — projecting jaws and nose of animal; figurative meaning — women are silenced, hide their pain, men do not want to know about it — sense that men have the sexual pleasure and women the pain of its outcome.
- Line 41, we feel sympathy and admiration for the cow "on her knees"- subordinate, submissive. (Dispassionate treatment of cow by men in verses 3 and 4, lines 31–43, dealt with in question 3; any points not used there may be offered here.)
- Cow's persistent licking in attempt to bring calf to life suggests the way women put the welfare of their children, and their responsibility for their safety, before everything else:
- lines 44–55, **syntax:** this whole verse is one long complex sentence, which mirrors the cow's patient, persistent attempts to lick her calf into life; intensified by line 44, **alliteration; rhyme / repetition:** "long tongue . . . strong tongue"; lines 49–50, cow's tongue is rough: can cope with thistles and "salt-lick" — a block of essential minerals, given to domestic animals as a dietary supplement, like "pumice stone"; line 51, "tenderly": delayed adverb allows the contrast between the rough tongue and the tenderness of her licking action; "over and over again" — constant, persistent.
- Line 52, cow feels responsible for "what has come out of her" — blunt, crude expression suggests stark reality of female's bond with her child. Lines 53–55, sentence construction reinforces the cow's persistence, willingness to go on trying for as long as it takes; line 56, gap between verses, time passed, cow still licking — **repetition** intensifies constancy.
- Final image of cow being led away like a criminal taken into custody by the police, suggests women's guilt; also suggests they are blamed by men, if anything goes wrong with birth.
- Line 58, "the men in blue" refers to blue overalls, line 32, but phrase commonly used to denote police force; confirmed in line 60. Line 59, "goes quietly": **cliché** lends **pathos** to the situation; the inference is that women are not in control, even of their most essential bodily function; they are at the mercy of men. Line 61, woman always blames herself for any defects in her children; strong sense of responsibility.

H — full treatment of cow as female symbol, men's attitudes, lack of understanding; good textual support + intelligent comment; Int. — clear understanding of symbolic aspect, some textual support + comment.

and to what extent do you agree with those ideas?   (10) E

- Personal response: may suggest Liz Lochhead is dealing in stereotypes, male and female;
- or that things have changed since this poem was written, with emergence of "the new man".
- Some readers may see this poem as a plea for understanding, from both men and women, of the way a woman feels having had an abortion, spontaneous or induced. Whatever the cause, the woman has lost a child and needs to be allowed to grieve, even though the foetus has not gone full term and she has never held the child.

Definite response to the ideas required : mark on merit   (Possible breakdown 7 / 3)

Level: Intermediate 1

1. **What does the poet witness in the field outside her house?**   (1) U
   - Cow trying to give birth (½) + falling back and squashing calf (½).

2. **Read over verse 1 again.**
   (a) **What is the first thing which makes the poet think something may be wrong?**   (1) U
      - Sees cow trying unsuccessfully (½) + to get to her feet (½).
   (b) **Write down one word from the first few lines which tells us that this was just a slight feeling which the poet had at this time.**   (1) A
      - "inkling", line 1.

(c) **Write down the sentence from further down the same verse which tells us the poet is now sure that something is wrong with the cow.** **(1) A**
- "That got through to me all right.", line 10.

(d) **What has the cow done to make the poet sure that she is in trouble?** **(1) U**
- Roar of distress.

3. **Look closely at the description of the cow in lines 16–23.**
(a) **Note *four* details of the cow's suffering mentioned in those lines.** **(2) U**
- Foaming at the mouth; teeth bared; spasms of pain; groan (½ mark for each).

(b) **Name or explain the poetic device used in line 18.** **(1) A**
- Alliteration / words start with b.

(c) **Write down another example of this device in lines 16–23.** **(1) A**
- Line 16, "foam flecked" / "Spasms strong", line 18.

(d) **Explain how this device helps you to understand the cow's suffering.** **(1) A**
- Attempt to explain alliteration intensifies the sense of the words so joined.

4. (a) **Write down the *simile* used in lines 18–20.** **(1) A**
- "primeval as the pulsing . . . creature."

(b) **What two things does the poet compare in those lines?** **(1) A**
- Contractions of cow in labour with movement of underwater creature.
  Difficult — ½ mark for less precise comparison.

(c) **What does this comparison tell us about the cow's suffering?** **(1) A**
- Suggests strong movement causing great pain / cow has no control over it.

5. (a) **What do the men from the farm do to help the cow?** **(1) U**
- They pull out calf with string.

(b) **How do the men treat the cow? (Give evidence to support your answer)** **(2) A**
- No compassion for the cow's suffering (1) + attempt to explain any two of following:
  line 35, "meant business"; line 39, "quick hoick"; line 43, "laughing", "punchline" (½ each)

(c) **Explain how their attitude is different from that of the poet.** **(2) A**
- Poet understands, men do not; poet empathises, men do not even sympathise; poet watches all afternoon, men do not come back until dusk.
  Any two for 1 mark each.

6. (a) **What does the cow do after the men have gone?** **(1) U**
- Licks calf patiently all afternoon.

(b) **Why does she do this?** **(1) U**
- Trying to bring it to life / natural instinct / feels responsible.
  Any one.

7. (a) **What happens to the cow at the end of the poem?** **(1) U**
- Men come back and lead cow away.

(b) **What kind of people are sometimes referred to as "the men in blue"?** **(1) U**
- Policemen.

(c) **Why does the poet use that phrase in line 58 to describe those men?** **(2) A**
- Must get idea of policemen arresting cow as if she were a criminal.
  Mark on merit.

8. (a) **What do you think poet is saying about what life is like for women in this poem?** **(2) E**
- Women suffer in silence; put children first; submit to men's will; are treated harshly by men / (male gynaecologists?).
  Any one, reasonably explained and linked to poem — mark on merit.

(b) **What do you think she is saying about men's attitudes to women?** **(2) E**
- They do not understand women's suffering; do not sympathise; treat harshly; use physical strength against women.
  Any one, reasonably explained and linked to poem — mark on merit.

(c) **To what extent do you agree with what she is saying here?** **(2) E**
- *Any definite personal response with some attempt to justify — mark on merit.*

Suggested Outline Plans for Critical Essays

1. **Often a poem is inspired by an incident in the poet's everyday life. Show how the poet uses her experience and, by skilful use of poetic techniques / devices, makes it important to a wider readership. (Revelation)**
    §1 Title, poet, brief account of incident at farm.
    §2 Poet's impression of bull **at the time**: introduction, description — quote / explain / comment.
    §3 Effect of bull on poet **at the time**: runs away, "big boys" — quote / explain / comment.
    §4 Symbols — bull / hens, eggs, milk: mature woman, looking back; irony + personal response.

2. **In a successful dramatic monologue, the speaker's "voice" is an important element. Show how the linguistic and poetic techniques / devices used by the poet are effective in revealing the speaker's personality. (Box Room)**
    §1 Title, poet, brief description of situation and main characters in poem.
    §2 Verse 1 — bubbly, confident, joking: Pun, brackets; exasperated: mimics hostess; but still able to laugh at herself: wry humour in brackets; becomes sarcastic — quote / explain / comment.
    §3 Verse 2, not so brash, confidence shaken but puts on a brave face: puns, clichés, brackets, ambiguities. Now alone in bed: admits fear but fights back — quote / explain / comment.
    §4 In the end, the remnants of his childhood make her doubt her boyfriend's ability to remain interested in her forever: despair creeps in — last two lines; + personal response to character.

3. **Choose a poem which either communicates very strong feelings or creates a mood of reflection and, by close analysis of the language of the poem, show how this has been achieved. (Revelation)**
    §1 Title, poet, brief account of what happened at farm when poet was a child.
    §2 Reflection: "I remember . . ."; constant juxtaposition in our minds between child / mature woman, child's impression of bull and effect on her — explain title — quote / explain / comment.
    §3 Mature woman, reflects on incident; male / female symbols — quote / explain / comment.
    §4 Irony; personal response to reflections — agree / disagree; how realistic? Quote line 20.

4. **Poems are often written as a result of reflecting on an intense emotional experience or on a significant event. Examine the techniques used by the poet to convey the significance of an experience or event, which gave rise to a poem. (Box Room)**
    §1 Title, poet, brief account of situation: importance of first meeting with future mother-in-law.
    §2 Uneasy atmosphere on arrival — syntax; sizing each other up; "friendly chat" in room, his as a child and still regarded as his by mother — lightly-veiled hostility to "other woman" in son's life — direct speech, pun, brackets show mother's character — quote / explain / comment.
    §3 Young woman realises there is part of his life which she can never share; but feels she knows him as an adult better than mother does: brackets, thought about single bed shared. Reflects on contents of room — accurate guide to his character? Title, puns, ambiguities . . .
    §4 Personal response: a timely warning? First doubts strengthen relationship?

5. **Liz Lochhead is a poet with a recognisable "voice". Referring closely to more than one of her poems, discuss the recognisable features of her poetry and show how the poetic techniques / devices which she employs help you to understand what she has to say.**
    (1. Revelation, 2. Box Room, 3. An Abortion: any two, or all three)
    §1 Titles, poet, general introduction of main features: female condition / experience.
    §2 and 3
        (1) Loss of childhood innocence, male threat to female vulnerability; (2) mother / daughter-in-law experience, mother / son relationship; (3) women's suffering / unstinting devotion to children / men's lack of understanding — devices covered above — quote / explain / comment.
    §4 Personal response — stereotyping / irony shows her disapproval of "own worst enemy" types.

SOME USEFUL DEFINITIONS

Address
A poem in the form of a speech addressed to some person, animal or object, present or not. [e.g., *To a Mouse*, page 7]

Allegory
A story in verse or prose, with a double meaning, which can be read and understood on two levels. [e.g., *To a Mouse,* page 9; *The Storm*, page 69]

Alliteration
The use of the same initial letter in two or more words in close proximity to create a particular effect, usually intensifying the sense of the words so connected. Sometimes the sound of the repeated initial letter adds to the effect. [e.g., *Assisi*, page 88]

Ambiguity
When a piece of language can be interpreted in more than one way; often used for humorous effect. [e.g., *Box Room*, page 123]

Analogy
An agreement or correspondence in certain respects between things which are otherwise different. [e.g., *The Horses*, page 48]

Anaphora
(pronounced ana`phora) A rhetorical device in which successive sentences or lines begin with the same word or phrase. [e.g., *Such a Parcel of Rogues in a Nation*, page 23]

Anthropomorphism
Conception or representation of a God as having the form, personality or attributes of man. [e.g., *Lo! a Child is Born*, page 34]

Antonomasia
A figure of speech in which an epithet or the name of an office or dignity is substituted for a proper name, e.g., "The Bard" for Shakespeare or Burns; and conversely, e.g., "a Casanova" for a womaniser; "a Hitler" for a tyrant. [e.g., in the second sense, *An Abortion*, page 128]

Apostrophe
A figure of speech in which a thing, a place, an abstract quality, an idea, a dead or absent person is addressed as if present and capable of understanding. [e.g.,*Trio*, page 109]

Assonance
Sometimes called "vocalic rhyme". Consists of the repetition of similar vowel sounds, usually close together, to create the effect of the sound of the particular vowel used, often with an harmonious effect. [e.g., *You Lived in Glasgow*, page 85]

Atmosphere
The mood and feeling, the intangible quality which appeals to sensory perception. [e.g., *Childhood* page 43]

Caesura
(plural caesurae) A break or pause in a line of poetry, often marked by punctuation. [e.g., *Visiting Hour*, page 94]

Cliché
An idiom or figure of speech (often a metaphor or simile) which has lost its impact through being over-used. [e.g., *Box Room*, page 123]

Conceit
Juxtaposition of images and comparisons between very dissimilar objects, usually for the purpose of disparaging the "better" of the two objects. [e.g., *Hotel Room, 12th Floor*, page 98]

Contrast
Bringing two objects together to show the difference. [e.g., *Welcome to a Bastart Wean*, page 14; *Assisi* page 90]

Dramatic monologue
A poem in which there is one imaginary speaker (see **Persona**) addressing an imaginary audience. [e.g., *Holy Willie's Prayer* page 20]

Enjambment	The continuation of the sense, without a pause, beyond the end of the line. [e.g., *Hamnavoe*, page 58; *Visiting Hour*, page 93]
Euphemism	The substitution of a mild and pleasant term for a harsh and blunt one, e.g., "to pass away" for "to die". [e.g., *The Old Women*, page 63]
Extended metaphor	A metaphor which is continued through appropriate lexical choice over several lines, or sometimes through the whole poem. [e.g., *Assisi* page 89]
Form (Literary)	The kind of work, the genre, e.g., dramatic monologue, sonnet . . .
Form (Poetic)	The shape and structure of the text, rhyme and metre, as opposed to the substance or what it is about.
Hypallage	(pronounced hypa` llajy) aka **transferred epithet** Is a figure of speech in which the epithet, usually an adjective, is transferred from the appropriate noun to modify another to which it does not really belong. [e.g., *Holy Willie's Prayer*, page 18]
Hyperbole	(hyper`boly) Exaggeration to emphasise the sense of the words; often used for satirical or humorous effect. [e.g., *Holy Willie's Prayer*, page 18; *The Starlings in George Square*, page 104]
Imagery	Figurative or descriptive language, often, but not necessarily, metaphorical to give heightened meaning, reveal feelings. [e.g., *Visiting Hour*, page 94]
Irony	Of situation, in which one seems to mock or to be mocked by Fate or the facts; [e.g., *Assisi*, page 92] or verbal irony, in which the meaning is contrary to the words, e.g., "That was clever!" when someone has done something stupid. [e.g., *Revelation*, page 119]
Juxtaposition	Bringing two ideas close together for literary effect, usually contrast. [e.g., *Assisi*, page 88; *Hamnavoe*, page 59]
Lexical choice	aka **word choice**: The actual words chosen by the poet to create a particular or striking effect. [e.g., *Old Woman* page 73]
Litotes	A figure of speech which contains an understatement; the purpose is to emphasise the sense and the effect is almost ironic, e.g., "not bad!" meaning "excellent!" [e.g., *The Horses*, page 48]
Metaphor	A figure of speech in which a thing is spoken of as being that which it only resembles in some figurative (not literal) sense. When dealing with a metaphor, you must: *(a)* explain the comparison being made, what is being compared to what; *(b)* consider the points of comparison, what the two things have in common; *(c)* consider how appropriate the comparison is to the sense; *(d)* explain the effect of the metaphor — the point being made by comparing those two things; and, in some cases, the connotations of the overall image being used. [e.g., *Visiting Hour*, page 94]
Metonymy	A figure of speech in which the name of an attribute or thing is substituted for the thing itself. [e.g., *Welcome to a Bastart Wean*, page 12; *Such a Parcel of Rogues in a Nation*, page 24]
Metre	The pattern of stressed and unstressed syllables in a regular verse form; Free Verse has no regular metrical pattern; it depends on natural speech rhythms.

Mood	Feelings of poet / narrator and / or the way the poet makes you feel when you read the poem. [e.g., *Old Woman*, page 74; *Visiting Hour* page 93]
Onomatopoeia	A figure of speech in which the sound of the word reflects the sense. [e.g., *The Starlings in George Square*, page 104]
Oxymoron	A figure of speech in which two words with opposite meanings are brought together to form a paradoxical phrase / statement. [e.g., *Visiting Hour*, page 95]
Paradox	An apparently self-contradictory statement. [e.g., *You Lived in Glasgow*, page 85; *Box Room*, page 125]
Pathetic Fallacy	A form of personification, in which an inanimate object is invested with human feelings, mirroring those of poet or speaker. [e.g., *Old Woman*, page 74]
Pun	A play on words which are alike or nearly alike in sound but different in meaning, often for comic effect but sometimes poignant. [e.g., *Childhood* page 44; *Box Room*, page 124]
Persona	An imaginary character speaking in a dramatic monologue. [e.g., *Holy Willie's Prayer*, page 20; *Iolaire*, page 82]
Personification	The attribution of human qualities to inanimate objects. [e.g., *Lo! a Child is Born*, page 33; *Box Room*, page 124]
Register:	Particular form of language appropriate to a given situation. [e.g., *Holy Willie's Prayer*, page 17; *The Horses*, page 48]
Repetition:	When a word or phrase is repeated to create a particular effect, usually to emphasise the idea contained in the words repeated. [e.g., *The Horses* page 49; *Lo! a Child is Born*, page 33]
Rhyme	Has two main functions: *(a)* aesthetic — it is pleasant to the ear, and an unexpected rhyme can provide a surprise, often humorous; *(b)* practical — it helps to organise the verse, intensifying the meaning, linking ideas by linking lines, concluding the sense.
Rhyme scheme	Is a method of denoting the pattern of rhymes in a stanza, usually represented by small-case letters, using *a* for line 1, *a* again for line 2 if it rhymes with line 1, otherwise *b*, and so on; e.g., in a six-line stanza, with lines 1 and 3 and lines 2 and 4 rhyming, followed by a rhyming couplet in lines 5 and 6, the rhyme scheme would be: *ababcc*.
Sarcasm	Language expressing scorn or contempt, often but not necessarily ironical; a jibe. [e.g., *Assisi* page 88; *Box Room*, page 124]
Satire	A literary form designed to discredit and ridicule men, institutions and ideas. It is at all times some form of attack, fuelled by the poet's indignation. [e.g., *Holy Willie's Prayer*, page 19; *The Starlings in George Square*, page 104]
Simile	A figure of speech in which one thing is explicitly said to be like another with which it shares some characteristics; usually preceded by "like" or "as". When dealing with a simile, follow the same steps as those suggested under **metaphor** (see above). [e.g., *Lo a Child is Born!*, page 34; *The Horses*, pages 49–50]
Stanza	A group of lines in a poem, forming a definite pattern of rhyme and metre throughout the poem. (Compare with **verse / verse paragraph**, see below.) [e.g., all of the Burns poems in chapter 1, *The Watergaw*, page 30]

Stream of Consciousness	aka **interior monologue**: A style of writing in which the poet appears to be writing as events are happening. [e.g., *Visiting Hour*, page 95]
Synecdoche	A figure of speech in which a part is used to refer to the whole. [e.g., *Visiting Hour*, page 93]
Symbolism	A symbol is an object, animate or inanimate, which represents something else, with which it has some connection. A literary symbol has the effect of combining an image with an idea. [e.g., *The Old Women*, page 64; *Revelation*, page 122]
Synaesthesia	Is the mixing of sensations; the concurrent appeal to more than one sense, e.g., "a heavy silence", "a hard voice", "a black look". [e.g., *Revelation*, page 118; *Visiting Hour*, page 95]
Syntax	The grammatical arrangement of words within their sentences. In poetry, the syntax is used to create a particular effect. [e.g., *Assisi*, page 89]
Tautology	Redundant words or ideas, e.g., "I myself personally . . .". Used for effect in poetry. [e.g., *Iolaire*, page 80]
Tone	The poet's or speaker's attitude to his subject, conveyed by the style of writing. Think of the tone of voice you would use if you were saying the words aloud. [e.g., *Holy Willie's Prayer*, page 17; *Old Woman*, page 73]
Verse	or **verse paragraph** is a group of lines which forms a unit in Free Verse, where there is no overall pattern of rhyme or metre. (Compare with **stanza**, see above.) [e.g., all of the poems in chapters 6, 7 and 8]
Zeugma	or **condensed sentence**, is a figure of speech, in which a verb or an adjective is applied to two nouns, though appropriate to only one of them; the verb is used figuratively in one case and literally in the other, e.g., "She threw a tantrum and a half brick." [e.g., *Hamnavoe*, page 59]

Printed by Bell & Bain Ltd., Glasgow, Scotland